PRAISE FOR *ADMISSIONS*

A MOST ANTICIPATED BOOK BY VOGUE.COM
• *PARADE* • ESQUIRE.COM • *TOWN & COUNTRY* • NYLON
• *NEW YORK POST* • LITERARY HUB •
BOOKRIOT • ELECTRIC LITERATURE • *GLAMOUR*
• *MARIE CLAIRE* • PUBLISHERS WEEKLY • BUSTLE • *FODOR'S
TRAVEL* • *BUSINESS INSIDER* • POPSUGAR
• INSIDEHOOK • SHEREADS

"Charming and surprising... The work of ADMISSIONS is laying down, with wit and care, the burden James assumed at fifteen, that she—or any Black student, or all Black students—would manage the failures of a racially illiterate community... The best depiction of elite whiteness I've read, nailing the belonging derived from institutional affiliation, which is therefore impersonal and false, but manifests value in spite of this. James writes to illuminate her experience as a Black student at Taft. She throws just as much light on the school's whiteness."   —*New York Times*

"The book is, not incidentally, an excellent memoir. James is unsparing and hilarious about her adolescent foibles, her outré fashion choices and insistence on telling everyone about her hobby of writing erotic fan fiction."   —*Los Angeles Times*

"[James] offers sharp-witted insight, incisive reflections, and an intense indictment of the cutthroat world of elite prep schools."
—*Parade*

"With humor, insight, and a near-superhuman depth of grace, James straddles an ever-shifting line as the school's first Black American legacy... The isolation that James captures, the uneasy and unspoken ceasefire she negotiates with whiteness at Taft, becomes an echo of the experiences of so many other students of color at the same schools that make up the world of the American elite. She takes up our repressed feelings and gives voice to the untold tales of neglect and disregard, of camaraderie and solidarity and survival, of those of us who were brought into spaces without anyone considering how we would fit."　　　　　—*The Cut*

"Thorough, necessary, and overdue...[ADMISSIONS] boldly nam[es] the confusion, fear, and trauma that can so often come with being the only person who looks like you in any given room."
　　　　　—Vogue.com

"James's memoir is a thoughtful story about coming of age and finding your place in the world; she's a funny, observant writer with a powerful, unforgettable story to tell."　　—*Town & Country*

"Frank and devastating in its candor, as well as incisive in its critique of elite academia, ADMISSIONS is a poignant coming-of-age memoir."　　　　　—Esquire.com

"An eye-opening examination of race, class, and privilege in America."　　　　　—*Publishers Weekly*

"What an extraordinary, razor-sharp book! Kendra James offers a gimlet-eyed insider's view of being an outsider, painting the complicated world of elite schooling with such vividness and dark humor. This is a crucial account for our moment—asking and answering the question of how power is held, shifted, and grasped after by even the youngest in our society. I raced through the pages of ADMISSIONS, hungry for James's voice and brilliant insights. The schooling she writes about may have been exclusive, but this book will electrify every reader."

—R. Eric Thomas, bestselling author *Here for It*

"Through frequent pop culture allusions and a dry sense of humor, Kendra James reveals a world largely unexamined—the life of an American Black girl at a prestigious boarding school. Readers will shake their heads at young Kendra's nerdy naïveté and frown at her classmates' bigotry and bullying. As Kendra discovers the fallout of her own parents' respectability politics and intraracial biases, she also learns more about her own identity and how she wants to navigate her life. Kendra James's honest reflections as she looks back on what it means to be Not Like the Others will leave readers thinking about their own experiences with privilege and marginalization. ADMISSIONS is a captivating memoir, highlighting the complicated notions of upward mobility, belonging, entitlement, and community. Kendra has written a true eye-opener."

—Nichole Perkins, author of
Sometimes I Trip on How Happy We Could Be

"In ADMISSIONS, [James] deconstructs the chokehold that whiteness and wealth have on private education. You'll laugh almost as much as you cringe." —*Glamour*

"James's social commentary and sparkling wit shine throughout this absorbing and insightful coming-of-age memoir." —*Booklist*

"James discusses how all too often the game is rigged, while infusing laugh-out-loud humor, poignant storytelling, and behind-the-scenes drama." —*Fodor's Travels*

"[A] unique and timely story." —*Kirkus Reviews*

"With wit and insight, ADMISSIONS explores the kind of upper-class education that most Americans have seen only in movies. James analyzes the racist attitudes she had to deal with, tells funny stories of her nerdy ways, and fondly recalls the days of AIM chats. People of color who survived mostly white schools are sure to sympathize with James's experiences, but anyone will enjoy her perceptive storytelling." —*Shelf Awareness*

"ADMISSIONS is a memoir of the highest caliber."
—Bitch Media

"ADMISSIONS is an open and honest social critique of race in the United States, as well as the coming-of-age story of a Black girl who is getting an education in a predominantly white boarding school." —*Book Reporter*

"James has crafted a book that is part Bildungsroman, part social indictment, and part scorching criticism of elite boarding schools. She meticulously skewers the behavior of her white classmates as alternately clueless and cruel and vividly conveys the captious claustrophobia that thrives in such institutions."
—*Waterbury Republican American*

ADMISSIONS

A MEMOIR OF SURVIVING
BOARDING SCHOOL

KENDRA JAMES

To Tahmir,

Thanks for coming out!

Kendra James

GCP
GRAND
CENTRAL

New York Boston

Copyright © 2022 by 1329 Prescott Street LLC
Reading Group Guide Copyright © 2022 by 1329 Prescott Street LLC and Hachette Book Group, Inc.
Cover design by Sarah Congdon. Cover copyright © 2022 by Hachette Book Group, Inc.

Hachette Book Group supports the right to free expression and the value of copyright. The purpose of copyright is to encourage writers and artists to produce the creative works that enrich our culture.

The scanning, uploading, and distribution of this book without permission is a theft of the author's intellectual property. If you would like permission to use material from the book (other than for review purposes), please contact permissions@hbgusa.com. Thank you for your support of the author's rights.

Grand Central Publishing
Hachette Book Group
1290 Avenue of the Americas, New York, NY 10104
grandcentralpublishing.com
twitter.com/grandcentralpub

Originally published in hardcover and ebook by Grand Central Publishing in January 2022.

First Trade Edition: January 2023

Grand Central Publishing is a division of Hachette Book Group, Inc. The Grand Central Publishing name and logo is a trademark of Hachette Book Group, Inc.

The publisher is not responsible for websites (or their content) that are not owned by the publisher.

The Hachette Speakers Bureau provides a wide range of authors for speaking events. To find out more, go to www.hachettespeakersbureau.com or call (866) 376-6591.

Interior map by Tim Paul.

Library of Congress Cataloging-in-Publication Data

Names: James, Kendra, author.

Title: Admissions : a memoir of surviving boarding school / Kendra James.

Description: First Edition. | New York : Grand Central Publishing, [2022] | Summary: "Kendra James began her professional life selling a lie. As an admissions officer specializing in diversity recruitment for select prep schools, her job was persuading students and families to embark on the same perilous journey, attending cutthroat and largely white schools similar to The Taft School, an elite institution in Connecticut where she had been the first African-American legacy student only a few years earlier. Forced to reflect on her own elite educational experience, she quickly became disillusioned by America's inequitable system. In ADMISSIONS, Kendra looks back at the three years she spent at Taft, from clashes with her lily-white roommate, to unlearning the respectability politics she'd been raised with, and a horrifying article in the student newspaper that accused Black and Latinx students of being responsible for segregation of campus. She contemplates the benefits of the education she got from Taft, which Kendra credits as playing a role in her career success, as well as the ways the school coddled her--perhaps, she now believes, too much. Through these stories, she deconstructs the lies and half-truths she herself would later tell as an admissions professional, in addition to the myths about boarding schools perpetuated by popular culture. With its combination of incisive social critique and uproarious depictions of elite nonsense, ADMISSIONS will resonate with anyone who has ever been The Only One in a room, dealt with racial microaggressions, or even just suffered from an extreme case of homesickness" -- Provided by publisher.

Identifiers: LCCN 2021033014 | ISBN 9781538753484 (Hardcover) | ISBN 9781538753491 (eBook)

Subjects: LCSH: School administrators--United States--Biography. | African American school administrators. | Private schools--Administration. | Minority students--Recruiting. | Racism in education--United States. | Elite (Social sciences)--Education--United States.
Classification: LCC LA2317.J35 A3 2022 | DDC 370.92 [B]--dc23
LC record available at https://lccn.loc.gov/2021033014

ISBNs: 9781538753507 (trade pbk.), 9781538753491 (ebook)

Printed in the United States of America

LSC-C

Printing 1, 2022

*For all the Black and brown girls
who never got a Crush can.*

Academic Facilities

5 Woolworth Faculty Room
8 Pinto Family Language Lab
15 The Arts and Humanities Center
24 Moorhead Academic Center
26 Mortara Family Academic Wing
31 Lady Ivy Kwok Wu Science/Mathematics Center
32 Hulbert Taft, Jr. Library
33 Nancy and Ben Belcher Learning Center
34 Laube Auditorium

Arts Facilities

4 Mark W. Potter Gallery
7 Choral Room
9 Bingham Auditorium
16 Woodward Theater
17 Video Lab
18 Photography Dark Rooms & Digital Design Lab

19 The Digital Recording Studio/Bristol Music Room
21 Pailey Dance Studio
22 Gail Wynne Sculpture and Ceramics Studio
25 Tremaine Art Studio

Athletic Facilities

39 Donaldson Family Pavilion and Tennis Courts
40 Donald F. McCullough '42 Athletic Center
41 Mays Rink
42 Logan Field House
43 Paul and Edith Cruikshank Athletic Center
44 Odden Hockey Arena
45 Girls' JV Soccer Field (fall), Boys' JV Lacrosse Field (spring)
46 Boys' JV Soccer Field (fall), Boys' Thirds Lacrosse Field (spring)
47 Taft's Course at Watertown Golf Club
48 Rockefeller Field
49 William Weaver Track

50 Parents' Association Field House
51 Football Practice Field
52 JV and Thirds Field Hockey Field, Girls' Thirds Lacrosse Field
53 Geoffrey C. Camp '91 Field (synthetic turf)
54 Snyder Field
55 Katie Jackson Morrison '92 Field
56 Lawrence H. Stone Baseball Pavilion/Rockwell Field
57 Girls' Thirds & Intro Soccer
58 Boys' Fourths Soccer Field
59 Softball Field

Residential Halls
3 Charles Phelps Taft Hall
11 John L. Vogelstein '52 Dormitory
12 Cruikshank House
13 Horace D. Taft Hall
28 McIntosh House
29 Congdon House

35 Upper School Girls Dormitory
37 Centennial Dormitory

Dining Facilities
20 The Donald A. Oscarson '47 Jigger Shop 27 Moorhead Wing

Other
1 Main Entrance
2 Main Circle
6 Lincoln Lobby
10 School Store
14 Admissions/Harley Roberts Room
23 Potter's Pond
30 Martin Health Center
36 Centennial Quadrangle
38 Wade House
P Parking

Map by Tim Paul

GLOSSARY

CLOSED WEEKEND: A weekend (usually during a campus event like Parents' Weekend or Hotchkiss Day, or final exams) in which students couldn't sign out to leave campus; the reason I didn't get to see *Hitch* on opening day.

FACULTY BRAT (FAC BRAT): A student whose parents teach at the school they attend.

FLIK: The company used by many independent schools to provide three square meals a day. It probably tasted better than I remember, as my palate was less refined than the sugar in the Nerds Ropes I used to eat by the dozens, but who's to say, really?

GRADES: Behavioral demerits that could be assigned by faculty for infractions ranging from skipping class or trying to hatch a goose egg under a desk lamp in your dorm room, to leaving a flat iron plugged in for hours after you've left for class or wearing the same skirt as your classmate while having a larger ass, thus somehow making it inappropriate.

HALL MONITORS: Student narcs selected by dorm faculty to help ensure that dormitory living runs smoothly.

HEAD MONITORS: Two seniors—one boy and one girl—voted in by the student body to lead the student government. These students tended to be less narc-y, as they were elected by their peers, not adults.

HONOR CODE: The Honor Code governs student life at Taft, putting in place standards and consequences specifically for theft and academic infractions. Assignments are signed with "I pledge my honor…" (short for "I pledge my honor that I have neither given nor received aid on this paper," which we were required to write on all larger term papers and exams). The theft clause allows Taft's campus to be a rather idyllic community, where backpacks and other personal effects are left lying around the school with a reckless abandon, a habit that students don't unlearn until they end up getting their wallet stolen from a condiments counter at a New York City Panera because they left it there while they got up to go to the bathroom. Honor Code violations are disciplined by the Honor Committee at Honor Court.

HOTCHKISS DAY: One day each year, usually in the fall, when Taft plays its rival, Hotchkiss, in as many sports as possible. Taft students spend the week leading up celebrating, which, in my day, culminated in a pep rally in which we would light the name of our own school on fire. I'm not sure why we were burning ourselves in effigy, especially since with two *T*s in the word Taft, every picture from one of those rallies looks like it's a Klan-hosted cross burning.

IN LOCO PARENTIS: Latin meaning "in place of the parents." If you're planning on sending your kid to a boarding school, make sure you're very comfortable with this phrase, because it's what you're gonna hear when you ask anything from why the nurse gave your kid Advil instead of Tylenol to why a dorm parent performed a full-on Steve Wilkos search of their dorm room because they thought they smelled something skunky.

THE JIG: Short for "the Jigger Shop." A small campus café where short-order line cooks slung bacon, egg, and cheeses, burgers, and fountain sodas in the afternoon when classes had finished.

LEGACY: A student whose parent or grandparent also attended and graduated from the same school. There is often, though not always, some sort of generational wealth involved.

LOWER MID: A boarding school freshman; the incoming year for most new students.

MIA LIST: The "missing in action" list is the list of students from that year's senior class who didn't make it to graduation, for whatever reason. It was printed in the back of the yearbook, and the class of 2006—whose senior shirts read, "I thought it was a good idea at the time!"—was rumored to have one of the longest in school history.

MID: A boarding school sophomore; a handful of new students are introduced to a class at the start of each mid year.

MORNING MEETING: A daily gathering in the auditorium in which a classmate, faculty member, or outside speaker gives a speech to the student body.

NON UT SIBI MINISTRETUR SED UT MINISTRET: Latin meaning "Not to be served, but to serve"; Taft's school motto.

OLD BOY/GIRL: An older student assigned to an incoming freshman or sophomore to show them the lay of the land.

POSTGRAD (PG): Contrary to what you might be thinking, this has nothing to do with graduate or doctoral work. There are many ways in which White Male Privilege manifests in the world, but one of my favorites is when a school lets a senior transfer in for a fifth (or sixth) year of high school (and a parent is willing to pay that extra year of tuition) so that they have another chance or two at getting recruited to play a sport professionally or at a D1 school. That said, the admissions professional within me asks that I note that a postgrad year also serves the purpose of simply strengthening an academic record for college admissions in general, and can help students acclimate to living away from home for the first time in a lower-pressure environment. But it also seemed to have a lot to do with hockey. Just saying.

PROSPIES: Prospective students who come to campus for either a tour or an overnight visit.

SCREW CREW: A punishment campus work detail assigned to students who racked up too many grades.

SIT-DOWN DINNER: A formal dining experience, once a week, where students and faculty are expected to dress up and seating is assigned; i.e., the only meal where The Black Table and The Asian Table don't exist.

TAALSA: The Taft African American Latino Student Alliance; basically a Black and nonwhite Latinx student affinity group.

TEN SCHOOL ADMISSIONS ORGANIZATION: A group of Northeast boarding schools (Choate Rosemary Hall, Deerfield Academy, the Hill School, Hotchkiss School, Lawrenceville School, Loomis Chaffee School, Phillips Academy Andover, Phillips Exeter Academy, St. Paul's School, and Taft School) that collaborate in terms of admissions outreach and standards.

UPPER MID: A boarding school junior; students rarely transfer into a class at the start of an upper-mid year, and the ones who do are usually demonic, running from something, or both.

UTC: United Cultures at Taft; similar to TAALSA, with more Asian students. White kids could join this one too, not that they were banging down the doors to do so.

PROLOGUE

FOR THREE YEARS after graduating college, my Saturday morning routine was set in stone. Instead of sleeping in, I would get up with a 7 a.m. alarm. I pulled on a pair of Kate Spade heels, squeezed into something professional and high-end-looking from my favorite floor at Lord & Taylor, and took the 6 train down to my designated Saturday morning haunt: a school theatre overflowing with parents on Manhattan's Upper East Side.

Each week from December to June, as many as 250 mothers, fathers, aunts, uncles, grandparents, and responsible almost-adult play-cousins of middle schoolers made their way to one of New York City's most prestigious and expensive schools by 9 a.m. They arrived to vie for admission to the Scholars Striving 4 Success ($S^3$4) program, which—after months of grueling extra academic work—would guarantee their child a spot in an independent school in New York City or a boarding school in New England. Schools built atop precise, sharp-sounding consonants, with single-name recognition, like Spence, Choate, Hackley, Exeter, or Collegiate.

Our program only accepted children of color, and this early in the morning they visibly slumped in their seats.

Their parents' eyes, on the other hand, grew wider with hope the longer the meeting went on. Some only brought their single young applicant, but many came with two or three children, because the child old enough to watch their younger siblings was the one old enough for our program.

They came to listen to us—all independent school admissions professionals—make them an offer that was a foreign concept to many, in a language that they might not even understand. There were never less than three distinct dialects spoken in that room at once: My Dominican boss would tackle the Spanish speakers, and I would torture Haitian parents with my very basic grasp of high school French and the patois I'd picked up from the bodega clerks and stoop sitters in my Harlem neighborhood, coupled with what was essentially a four-year-old's pronunciation. Thanks to a few high school and college friends, I could greet Korean speakers respectfully before staring blankly at the stream of language that followed. God help you if you spoke Bengali, or any other language that some Nick Jr. cartoon hadn't capitalized on yet. Those families relied on their children to do most of the translating. But they still came. Their commitment was palpable, and understandable.

We were selling what essentially amounted to seventy Get Out of Jail Free cards; one of the few golden tickets out of the New York City public school system, a ticket that most in the room believed to be the first step toward a better life for their kids. Even if their child was excelling in their current school, and even if that school was a good one, they believed that we would be able to give them something *better*. And instead of giving them insights on how to make the most of the public school system or working for an organization that would help improve it, our program opted for surgical student extraction. In our hands, the idea of the American

Dream was both a temptress and a cudgel. The schools we offered to their children in turn gifted them access to the highest echelon of society—the status that everyone outside of the wealthy 1 percent has been told they can bootstrap their way into through the bill of goods that comes with the American Dream. I peddled the illusion of ownership, delusions of grandeur, myths of American upward mobility, and the misconception that there is, indeed, a place where *everyone* can feel like they belong.

Everyone in the room was low income by some definition, whether they were truly surviving below the poverty line, or they existed within that warped sense of "broke" that comes with living in New York City for too long. The "New York Poor" peppered the auditorium each week alongside those who lived paycheck to paycheck or on none at all; people who were making over $250,000 a year, had no debt, and had only one kid, but because they couldn't keep up with their neighbors and didn't have an in-unit washer/dryer, they went around telling everyone they lived in abject squalor. This wasn't a meeting for those people, but it didn't stop them from trying. Everyone wants to give their child a leg up, and an upper-middle-class Black child often needs just as much of one as their white peer whose family receives government aid.

We weren't selling meeting attendees on the idea of being rich or New York Poor, but *wealthy*. Privileged. Well-rounded *and* well-off. Their children would finally be on a level playing field with the children of executives, movie stars, politicians, and Mike-down-the-street—that one inexplicably well-off neighbor whose great-great-great-grandfather happened to have grabbed a homestead and enslaved three people in Missouri at some especially opportune time in 1843 and they've just been wealthy ever since, because *America*.

"Your kid could be one of them! Well situated! Connected for life! Achieving the American promise that a child will *always* have the opportunity for an even better life than those who came before them," we told hopeful parents, once their children had been herded into another room to take the ridiculously outdated test they needed to pass in order to be considered for our program. Being granted access to upward mobility required, in this case, being able to neatly fill in a Scantron sheet, sit still during a three-hour exam, and solve math problems in a booklet copied via a machine that was just as likely to make a + look like a −.

In my nicest clothes, sometimes with the addition of my brightest string of pearls, I would stand in front of them looking every part the perfect graduate of a New England prep school. I smiled at them as I spoke, completing a package that said: *This is what your child could look like in ten years. This is what a Black woman with an independent school education and a college degree looks like. This is what she does on her Saturday mornings. This is the pleasing, unaccented American voice they'll learn. This is the kind of job they'll have.*

I gave the same practiced speech every week.

*So, here's the story I always start off with when I'm trying to explain why an independent school was right for me. The year before I transferred out to Taft, I did my freshman year at a public high school in New Jersey. I barely made it through the freshman Algebra 1 course; it was making me **and** my teacher miserable. Same with freshman-level biology!*

*Flash-forward to my sophomore year at Taft. I find out: Not only was I terrible at Algebra 1, but the Algebra 1 course at my public school was behind the same course at Taft. I still had to take it again just to catch up. It was just this constant struggle, once again, between me and my teacher. We both wanted me to get it, but it was quickly becoming apparent that I just **wouldn't**.*

But that's what's so great about independent schools, right? They're not beholden to state education requirements—that means no arbitrarily required classes, no mandated math and science minimums, and no standardized state exams on those subjects. So, because I was in a boarding school, there came a point where we could just all sit down and say, "Hey. This isn't working out. Let's try something else."

*In my case "something else" meant opting out of math classes after I'd done the bare minimum and putting me in more humanities classes. I never made it to physics in high school, but I took screenwriting and adolescent psychology. I can't balance an equation, but I can hang lights in a theatre and run a sound board. I began to figure out what it meant to really reflect in essays on my behaviors and personal interests, which has led to a fruitful writing career. I bet some of you out there have kids who think they're the next LeBron James or a budding CC Sabathia too, right? I never took statistics, but one Wednesday after lunch I finally landed my double salchow, because I could use one of my school's **two** full-sized ice rinks whenever I wanted.*

What would "something else" mean for your child? Think about all the ways an independent school might allow them to follow their own paths and succeed in ways that their current schools won't.

This isn't to say that your child won't be challenged. They will be. The standards at each of the schools we work with are incredibly high, and your child will be asked to meet goals that might seem out of reach now, at age ten. But these schools set the bar high so that your child can walk down the aisle after graduation knowing that the whole world is at their feet. Have you looked around this beautiful theatre? Did you take in the quality of classrooms while you were walking the halls? It's a short leap from a school like this one to a college like Columbia, Yale…or Harvard.

(Here, I always paused for the approving murmurs that simply *hinting* at the name "Harvard" brings out in a room full of parents.)

I know that this might feel like a very different environment for some of you and maybe you're worried that schools like this one might be isolating for your children. It is an adjustment! But it's a short one, and it's worth it. What you have to understand is that schools like this one want us there— Black, Latinx, Asian…everyone here. They're excited to have us, and your *kids won't be treated any differently for who they are or how much money you make as their parents. These schools are for **everyone**.*

One of the huge benefits of an independent school is the class sizes. For instance, I graduated in a class of just under one hundred students. By the time they're ready to graduate, your kid's teachers will know your child like the back of their own hand, and that means when it comes to college recommendation letters or references for summer internships you couldn't ask for a better resource. You won't find anyone more ready or willing to advocate for your child than a teacher at an independent school.

*And the other benefits? When you're in a class size that small, kids make so many friends, ones that will last for life and ones that will only benefit them later on as they're starting out professionally. Imagine going to school with Michael Bloomberg's kids! Your children will be in classrooms with the daughters of politicians, actors, bankers, and executives, and they're going to learn how to use those connections for their own advantage. For **your** advantage, even.*

I'm still excited every time I go back to Taft. It's a place I know I'm always welcome. I can walk onto the campus whenever I want and visit old teachers and friends and say hello and just soak in all the good memories of the place. My name is engraved into a brick on the ground there, along with the rest of my graduating class, and all the graduating classes before ours. It makes it feels like all of us—every student—owns a bit of the place. Taft was the first place that ever gave me a feeling of ownership about my surroundings, and I think that's so important when you're growing up a person of color in America.

I want that same feeling for your kids as well.

As an admissions counselor at Scholars Striving 4 Success I sold a lie for a living; at least, that's what it felt like. With my fake smile, pearls, and the rose-colored glasses I'd become accustomed to tinting my own time at Taft with, I lied to a roomful of people every time the word "racism" failed to arise in my speech. Every time the phrase "The Black Table in the dining hall" didn't come up. Every time I didn't mention the word "legacy." Every time I didn't let myself taste the bile I can still conjure to this day if I think too long and too hard of the name Emma Hunter.

Each year at Scholars Striving 4 Success we filled every one of the seventy slots in our program. Each year our waiting list grew ripe on its summer vine. We were very good at our jobs. I was one of the best.

MID

1.

I'M NOT GOING to pretend I know the full history behind the feud Ashley Davis and LaTasia "some people just like to watch the world burn" Ford spent our freshman year nurturing. However, I can say for certain that the straw that broke the camel's back was most certainly one day in late winter when LaTasia looked Ashley dead in the eye while they both stood at the condiments table in the small pizzeria near our high school, picked up a sticky New Jersey diner–style bottle of ketchup, and proceeded to maintain eye contact while she squirted it directly onto Ashley's white sneakers.

The ensuing fight made it all the way to the tabletop of the booth where friends and I were sitting, just trying to enjoy our lunch.

The table partially collapsed before all of us could get up, sending me and another friend tumbling to the ground. I landed on her chest, and the thick table edge landed on my leg, leaving my thigh black and blue and my synchronized skating coaches perturbed. It was a minor miracle that none of us were more badly injured.

I internalized that fight, letting it sit with me probably more than I should have—and not just because I had to beg my dad not to go down the street and confront Ashley's parents, who happened to be our neighbors. My parents had gently laid the groundwork throughout middle school, asking if our local public high school, Columbia, was *really* the school I wanted to commit this crucial four years of my life to, given that I did have other options. There would be more Ashleys and LaTasias there. More students like Darius, the kid I'd been paired with for our Egg Baby Project in the eighth grade, who'd promptly thrown our hard-boiled child against the white cinder-block classroom wall and told me, "You had an abortion." It wasn't that I was worried about being pulled into trouble (that sort of school disciplinary problem wasn't my ministry) so much as it was that it had been much easier for my friends and me to keep ourselves far away from this sort of conflict in middle school. The idea that high school marked the end of being a casual bystander taking in the free entertainment of other kids going at it was decidedly unappealing, and I didn't care to be around it for much longer. I iced my bruises and finished up my application to Taft School tout de suite.

A few months later, my mom brought my acceptance letter with her in the car when she came to check on me at the salon after school. Finding me sitting under the dryer, she handed me an envelope that was still sealed, but thick enough that we both knew what lay inside. I opened it while I waited and eagerly went through all the materials my new school had sent.

Pam, the woman who'd been perming my hair for years, walked over to check my progress and immediately asked what "all that" was in my lap loudly enough that the whole shop would be involved in whatever conversation ensued.

"I got into *boarding school.*" I gestured to the envelope in my lap and allowed myself a moment of smugness.

The palpable silence that immediately fell over the salon was not the reaction that I'd been expecting. The couple fighting on *Maury* even took the hint, as the woman ran backstage upon finding out that He Is Not the Father and the pandemonium on camera subsided.

I beamed at Pam.

She stared back at me. "Girl… what did you *do?*"

● ● ●

I would hear Pam's question repeated over and over again for the next four years from members of the uninitiated. People for whom "boarding school" conjured up images of oppositional defiant disorder, disciplinary issues, corporal punishment, and days regimented down to the millisecond. "Boarding school" made it sound like my parents had given up on getting me in line and were turning their parenting responsibilities over to God, the military, or both. So when school started in the fall, I was very glad to finally be arriving at Taft, if only because I was so tired of answering the never-ending versions of Pam's question that I'd encountered that summer.

Hell, I was even getting tired of the Hogwarts and Charles Xavier's School for Gifted Youngsters jokes (which a shocking number of people seemed to believe they had thought of for the very first time), even though those fictional places were at least closer approximations of what Taft was: a boarding school for very smart, and/or very athletically gifted, and very privileged children. A $35,000 high school education is not a normal thing, and one must be forgiven, I guess, for *not* assuming that a parent would spend that kind of money if their child was anything short of the next Chosen One themselves.

I started my sophomore year at Taft in late August. At the wheel of his Nissan Pathfinder, my dad was waved through the campus's iron gates by an older student from the welcoming committee. Some parents, those less familiar with the campus layout, would accidentally circle through the full driveway that rounded past the school's main entrance to its oldest building, bricks laid in 1914, where students were greeted by a bust of founder and forty-six-year head of school Horace Dutton Taft (yes, the bathtub president's brother).

Taft has only ever had five heads in its nearly 130-year history. The current head, William MacMullen, stood underneath a grouping of tents set up on the grass inside the roundabout, waving welcome at the caravans of cars and parents as they made their way through the narrow concrete drive. We waved back, having known Mr. Mac since the start of his tenure in 2001. He was the second head of school I'd known. I had been introduced to Lance Odden (head from 1972 to 2001) numerous times, and I would spend the next three years skating on the Olympic-sized rink named in his honor. Mr. Mac had attended the school himself, like my father who'd graduated in 1974.

"And there's my old room!" My dad pointed out the same landmarks every time we came to campus. He gestured to a set of windows above the creaky-comfy admissions waiting room, which, with its wood baseboards and formal furniture, would eventually become one of my favorite hangout spots.

My dorm that year was in a separate building. Congdon and McIntosh were both freestanding girls' dorms, set in a different roundabout behind the dining hall. Though the school hadn't welcomed young ladies until partway through my father's time there in 1971, the buildings had been standing on campus since the mid-1920s and were indistinguishable from the rest of campus.

Careful aesthetic management accomplished this. Whether it had been built in 1926 like Congdon, or completed in 2001 like the newer Odden Arena, each building matched the last, erected in classic red brick, topped with gray slate shingles. There was no hodge-podge here; no stone, painted wood flats, or, God forbid, *siding*—my mother's personal suburban enemy. The campus sat on three distinct levels of elevation—main campus, fields, and the gym—and sunlight bounced from building to building on each plane, as it reflected off the surface of Potter's Pond in the center of campus.

This uniformity made the sprawling campus feel slightly less intimidating—you knew you weren't going to take a wrong turn and end up in a forgotten turret. To my fantasy-oriented mind it looked like something out of an E. Nesbit or Edward Eager book. A campus that was quite literally timeless, where anything could happen.

They'd not even laid out an afternoon meal yet by the time we arrived, but we still had to jockey for a parking space. By the time I finally climbed out of the back seat I was ready to make moves.

"Now, you've never had to share a room before…" my mom started to say as I jumped out of the car.

And I still didn't; not for another night, at least. The students pulling into Taft that day were arriving early for a number of reasons. Fall varsity sports began practicing at least a week before the first day of classes, and with those students also came hall monitors and head mons, who arrived on campus in advance of everyone else to help prep their dorms for newcomers. Freshman students arrived early to simply learn how to *exist* at a boarding school, away from home for the first time at age fourteen. International students showed up early for their own orientation, which covered everything from campus rules to how to make collect calls, how to handle culture shock, and the answers to questions about the simply deranged ways Americans chose to do things (like, *why*, my Korean friend, Agnes, would ask many times, we refuse to include tax in the goddamn sticker price at the drugstore). I was there for the students of color orientation.

My roommate-to-be, Jenna Crane, was none of those things and wouldn't come to campus until the general move-in for new sophomores in another day or so, meaning I got the first pick of everything in our dorm room. My choice of bunk (bottom), dresser (closest to the back wall), and desk (up against the window that overlooked Potter's Pond in the center of campus) were quickly set.

We started unloading the car, my younger brother trotting along behind us, back and forth from the circular drive, up and down the flight of stairs to Congdon's front door. I'd never had to share a room before, no, but this corner dorm room was still bigger than my bedroom at home, which was—even as I moved away—covered in posters and prints of my favorite superheroes and characters, with an entire wall dedicated to *just* Orlando Bloom. The white walls of this new room were a tempting canvas.

My mom murmured gently, just before lunch and right after I removed a series of four battered journals from my backpack and carefully stacked them on my newly claimed desk, that perhaps it would be best to concentrate on unpacking necessities first. Things like clothing, school supplies, even my ice skates and softball equipment, should come before we focused on personalization.

We ate lunch together in the dining hall as a family, choosing an empty table after we filled our trays with my first-ever serving of FLIK food. It was not particularly delicious.

The greetings began immediately, boisterous calls of "*Andrew!*" as we were approached by waving mothers in white button-up blouses with broad triangular collars framing strands of statement pearls that just lightly skimmed their décolletage. Firm handshakes followed from dads in polo shirts and the short-sleeved version of That Year's One Nice Shirt from J.Crew (As Designated by the White Commuter Class), khaki cargo shorts, and leather loafers (sockless, of course) or a sensible pair of New Balances. As my father was recognized by other parents dropping their children off early too, our table began to fill, the exuberant greetings making way for more dining-hall-appropriate murmured conversation.

"George!" he would exclaim in return, as parents approached, their kids trailing around behind them. "Good to see you, sir!" He addressed everyone as "sir" on first greeting, whether they were an old friend or a brand-new acquaintance.

"It's been too long, Andrew," George Miller Sr. answered that afternoon. "This is George Jr.—a new sophomore!" It wouldn't be until years later that I realized that white folks rarely offered up "sir" in turn.

"Mine—Kendra, right here—is a new sophomore too. Kendra, this is George. We were friends back in the day. Haven't seen him since our twenty-fifth!"

Later on that fall, after George Jr. quit the soccer team, Mr. Lane would end up casting him as M. Thénardier in *Les Misérables*. He looked the part, with a blond Cesar cut and beady, watery blue eyes that were constantly on the move. His teeth were extremely white, but also long and rectangular, like little Lego pieces, giving him a very rodentesque appearance. Despite our fathers' shared history, I had a hard time remembering his name for the first few weeks of school because I referred to him explicitly as "Peter Pettigrew" in both real life and my journals. I didn't have much time to get to know him after that; George lasted less than a year at Taft.

Mrs. Jiordano, a member of the faculty, let out a yelp when she entered the dining hall and saw my dad. She joined with her curly-haired son, Frank, who had started Taft as a freshman. But, since he was a fac brat, arriving early wasn't really a *thing*; he lived there anyway. My admission to Taft displaced his former Morning Meeting seatmate, and we ended up sitting next to each other in Bingham Auditorium every day for the next three years, given our aligning last names. That afternoon at lunch was the longest conversation I would have with him until our graduation party.

As streams of parents and children entered, our table became a mini-reunion for the men, and the few women, of the classes of 1971 to 1977, while their spouses and children awkwardly dined and made small talk.

My parents are extremely divorced now. "That wasn't fun for me, Kendra," my mom confessed later, after I casually mentioned I'd seen on Facebook that my father had taken yet another girlfriend up to the campus. He likes showing it off, I think, feels that ownership I would capitalize on during parent meetings at S³4.

"Hmm?"

"Going up to Taft was not something I enjoyed before you started—when you were there, we had a *reason* to be there," she said. "It's something I tolerated for your father's sake. But oh, those people. I didn't have anything to say to his classmates, and they didn't have anything to say to me. Also, just wait until your fifteen- or twenty-year reunion—the men will all be alcoholics. Bright red. Bloated, like fish."

For all of my mother's equally expensive and fancy education, she wasn't *in* on the joke, you could say.

I, a new sophomore, belonged there more than she did. I had the necessary bona fides; because our parents had attended Taft, each student at the table was a legacy. Boarding schools' collective reputations as places you sent your unruly, poorly behaved, and often criminal children had nothing to do with why I was there. Taft was not a punishment, or even the reward with bragging rights I was choosing to see it as. It was simply inevitable.

My dad graduated from Taft after earning a spot at the school through the A Better Chance (ABC) program. Originally from the South Side of Chicago, he attended Taft and then went on to four years at Brown University. Meanwhile, my mother was born in the Bronx to a woman who would eventually have both a bachelor's from Fordham and a master's from Long Island University, and a leadership position in the local NAACP. My mom attended a mix of public and private schools before going to Smith College, where she graduated in 1977. Andrew and Lynn eventually met when they were both working in corporate banking in New York City; they moved first to Jersey City and then to Maplewood, New Jersey, where they had me.

Throughout my childhood, Andrew coached my softball and soccer teams; he was on every town board you could possibly imagine—planning, zoning, events, and more. In his spare time he built, by hand, two ponds (or "water features," as we call them in the suburbs) in our backyard, filled them with koi and other fish, frogs, and turtles, and then started the town's official "Pond Tour" and often spent summer Saturdays observing neighboring ponds and offering suggestions for better filtering solutions. Throughout my childhood he would run through interests; I learned how to bowl, change the water in a series of large complex home aquariums that I was responsible for minding while he was out of the country for work, strip and stain furniture, fly a stunt kite competitively, properly store a comic book, and slingshot the squirrels who ate our homegrown heirloom tomatoes, all because of his obsessions of the moment. I inherited that penchant for hyperfocused, short-period fixation; it haunts me every time I see a half-finished cross-stitch.

As a stay-at-home mom, Lynn had *time*. While my dad commuted to work in the city almost every day, Lynn never missed a parent-teacher conference, an impressive feat since she was also deeply involved in our community, whether it was running the town library for a time, organizing the church rummage sale for years, volunteering with the church homeless sheltering initiative, hand making me a series of first-day-of-school outfits (which I scorned, like any nineties child presented with handmade clothing), or shuttling me back and forth from the ice rink to school to the softball field. Our days together often started at five in the morning. She never complained, even after an older high school girl on my synchronized skating team had the audacity to show up for the carpool hungover and threw up in the back seat.

It's no accident that my parents were like this. They were products of their time, growing up in an era when they saw their parents' rights finally written fully into law for the first time (if not fully enforced). By the time they were of an age to attend school in Chicago and the Bronx, *Brown v. Board of Education* had been the law of the land for only half a decade. The civil rights movement ensured that they could potentially live that American dream and forge themselves better lives than their parents had been born into, and they had the same plan for me. Even with all the legislation that was supposed to level the playing field, they were overachievers, and they had to be in order to be Black in the America they grew up in and achieve what many middle-class white families simply saw as "normal."

Achieving that normality meant that I was used to situations like the dining hall that afternoon, being one of a few Black kids in a room. In Maplewood, this was what my softball teams looked like, my classrooms, my extracurriculars at the YMCA, and the three-hour Dungeons and Dragons class I took every summer weekday. I was the *only* Black girl on my synchronized skating team, and one of three who skated regularly at my rink.

It rarely stuck out to me, because while we were fewer, we were mighty, and I'd always *had* Black friends. My closest friends during my freshman year—as my mother often commented—made up one of the most peculiarly broad groups at Columbia. We looked like the diversity Maplewood Realtors bragged about in their open-house pamphlets.

Naively, I'd assumed that what my mother also often said would remain true at Taft. "You're so *good* at making friends, Kendra," she would remark from time to time, usually after she'd picked me up from someone's house. "It's quite remarkable; your group is constantly bringing new people in. You're all so welcoming." With our penchant for anime, *Harry Potter* and *Lord of the Rings* fan fiction—and, again, the fact that many of us made our parents pay for summer classes in which we simply sat in an empty classroom and played D&D all day while Mr. Davidson's old VHS recording of *The Star Wars Holiday Special*, complete with period original commercials, played quietly in the background—we weren't exactly *popular*, but we were a fun band of misfits.

Groups of misfits often do that, coming together and welcoming anyone else who doesn't quite fit in with the mainstream crowds. And this did remain true at Taft—just not in the way I thought it would.

I wasn't trying to be besties with George, Frank, or any of the other kids who sat down with us at that first meal, but I also assumed that by virtue of the fact that our parents had taken it upon themselves to introduce us, we would at least remain semi-friendly for the remainder of our time at Taft. But that was not to be the case either.

I made polite, quiet small talk with the table before making my excuses at a quarter to one. Every child at the table was white, except for me, and so I was the only one who had to attend the students of color orientation.

●　●　●

I didn't know it yet, but I was to be the first Black American legacy student to graduate from the Taft School. It would take a year or two before a bitter pride in that knowledge replaced the mortification I felt every time it was brought up like clockwork in front of an auditorium full of people during Black History Month.

Knowing this would not have changed the way I entered my orientation that afternoon.

My parents, bless them, started off as Respectability Politics Black People, which perhaps you have guessed as I was a legacy admit to a New England boarding school. My mother couldn't understand a rap lyric until approximately five and a half years into the Obama presidency. You could have played her a De La Soul track followed with anything by Outkast and she would have told you that they sounded exactly the same and that she couldn't understand a single word that those young men were "saying," while also hazarding a guess that everyone involved needed to pull up their pants.

While Lynn did often comment that I was quite good at making friends, the friends that I made were a reflection of the world my parents were trying to build for me.

Chances are if you're a New Yorker, you've lost a loved one to our manicured lawns and Hollywood-Rom-Com-for-Boomers town festivals like Maplewoodstock. But the *schools* are a huge part of the appeal. Six elementary schools feed into two middle schools, which then feed into Columbia High School, all shared between Maplewood and South Orange, the college town next door.

And they *are* good schools. Fights and all, I was mostly comfortable there, and had been in all top Level Four classes since entering the leveling system in the sixth grade.

The way it worked, you could be in Level Two, Three, or Four, or, once you got to high school, AP classes. I, personally, have no firsthand knowledge of what went on in Level Two or Three classrooms, because Lynn James simply wouldn't have allowed it. The way Lynn told it, those classrooms represented the very picture of anarchy, filled with Ashleys and LaTasias and other misbehaving students who had zero interest in learning and teachers who had even less interest in teaching them. I was told I would be bored by the level of work in those classes, tortured by lesson plans that catered to the lowest common denominator and nothing else, because teachers in those classes didn't teach so much as they just handed out a single photocopied worksheet at the beginning of the period before leaving to chain-smoke behind the gym. And when I had to sit in unleveled nonacademic classes—say, a health class with Darius, for instance—their warnings all seemed to be quite accurate.

I absolutely could have been a Level Three Algebra 1 student, but Columbia knew better, even before helicopter parenting became *en vogue*. No one wanted a visit from Lynn. I'm sure the call over the summer to make sure I *was* in Level Four was bad enough.

The levels you were placed in pretty much determined who your friends would be. It was easier to slip into a Level Four class if your parents could afford workbooks from the prep section in Barnes and Noble, standardized test prep courses, or private tutors, but my mom also understood that alongside socioeconomic status, the Maplewood leveling system was also driven more by the color of a student's skin than by their grades. It was harder for a Black or nonwhite Latinx student to move from Level Three to Level Four than it was for a white student to fall from Level Four to Level Three, and so the Level Three and Two classrooms were filled with students who, because they were no less intelligent than I was, were probably just bored out of their fucking minds. The deep racism and inequity in the system eventually caused the New Jersey ACLU to file a formal complaint against the school district.

But this is all hindsight. Race and implicit bias weren't talked about overtly. The messaging, as I understood it, instead boiled down to "You are here because you are smarter, and you must continue to be smarter to be here, or you will end up in classes with children who are not only less smart than you, but also *bad*." Many of those "bad" children happened to be Black and brown.

So while there were classrooms in Maplewood that were majority students of color, I had never been in one.

That day, the students of color orientation room at Taft was filled with kids who looked, more or less, like me. Where the dining hall was a steady buzz of muted conversations bolstered by the occasional shout of greeting, the orientation room was bubbling with excitement.

Groups had already formed. About twenty-five students sat with one another on top of desks or perched on the windowsills that lined the walls of this particular history classroom. Some seemed to already be in deep conversations, punctuated by laughter and the occasional clap. I froze in the doorway as the realization dawned on me: People knew each other already.

Someone tapped me on the shoulder. "Take a name tag, please!" The tag affixed to her chest read "Mrs. Gallagher." I recognized the name from my welcome packet; Mrs. Gallagher was to be my faculty advisor, and she was also the only grown Black woman I would see daily at Taft until my senior year. "Write your name down and find a seat."

As I wrote "Kendra" out in large capital letters, I started formulating a plan of my own. I wouldn't hesitate when I straightened up from the table. I would confidently and determinedly find a seat and join a conversation. Every kid in this room did *not* know the others; we were all new students and that was impossible, I told myself.

"If we could start quieting down, it's five after one," Mrs. Gallagher announced from behind me. "Everyone should start finding a seat. A seat, Miss Harris—c'mon, it's year *two* and you are here to answer *questions*..."

My eyes zeroed in on the far corner of the room, where two other girls sat next to each other. They weren't speaking to each other or anyone else, and there was an open chair. I gave my name tag one last affirming pat to my chest and made my way over.

"Hi!" I sat down in the free chair and turned to the first girl, tall and with box braids. She was wearing khaki Dickies, a white polo shirt, and red-and-white Jordans. She did not (nor would she ever) look particularly pleased to see me, but she nodded and grunted a hello.

"I'm Kendra," I tried again.

"Hi, I'm Francine," answered the second girl. In her, I saw hope; someone who looked as awkward in this room as I did, in her pleated skirt, unironically double-popped collar, and Chanel flats. Unlike my own outfit choice—dress-code-appropriate slacks from the Gap and an exceptionally shiny button-down shirt from the Limited Too—Francine seemed comfortable in what she was wearing. There hadn't been a mini-argument that morning about a *Pirates of the Caribbean* shirt from Hot Topic in *that* house.

But I think what I subconsciously zeroed in on was her hair, permed, but dull and dry. Another girl who had grown up in a house with a mother who didn't force her kid to wrap their hair properly, and who also probably couldn't braid beyond two perfunctory French braid pigtails. Frankly, the variety of hairstyles in the room overwhelmed me—from locs to intricate braids to perfectly shiny perms on the girls, and perfectly lined-up edges, fades, cornrows, and even a durag or two on the boys. I was especially shocked to see a durag present in such a formal setting; my mother hated them, my brother and father didn't use them, they'd been banned inside Columbia, and I had zero context for the fact that they actually served a *purpose*.

"Again," Mrs. Gallagher said, a bit more bass in her voice this time, "if we could find *seats*."

"It's nice to meet you," I whispered back to Francine. "What year are you?"

"I'm a fresh—lower mid," she said, correcting herself into Taft's parlance. It took time to get used to saying lower mid, mid, and upper mid, and absolutely no time to abandon upon graduation.

"I'm a new mid."

"Where are you living?"

"Congdon," I answered. "You?"

"Me too, second floor!"

"I'm on the first floor in the corner." I smiled, turning to the girl with the braids. "Are you in Congdon too?"

"Mac House," she answered after a moment.

"Sorry, I didn't catch your name," said Francine.

"Tamia. I'm a freshman." Tamia had not sipped the Taft Kool-Aid.

Mrs. Gallagher rapped her knuckles on the chalkboard. "All right, we're going to get started."

Everyone in the room respected Gail Gallagher, that much was clear immediately. As soon as it was *actually* time to start, the room quieted down, and everyone seemed to magically find one of those aforementioned seats within seconds.

"I'm Mrs. Gallagher," she announced. "I think I've met about ninety percent of you"—that explained a lot, I decided, as groups of students waved back at her—"but for those who I haven't, welcome to Taft! I am the director of multicultural affairs and admissions, and quite a few of you also have me as your advisor. If we've not scheduled a welcome meeting yet, you need to respond to my email right after this, all right? That kind of thing is your responsibility now. If you're having trouble getting your email or internet access set up, you need to visit the tech center, yes?"

This was where our orientation didn't at all vary from the meetings other new students were attending, or the Congdon welcome meeting we'd all have to go to once everyone had arrived.

Responsibility was a long-standing and overarching theme at Taft. It was baked into the very concept of boarding school. Sure, the phrase "in loco parentis" was used often, but as we were ultimately living away from home during our most formative years, we were also expected to display a level of maturity beyond that of our public school contemporaries.

"To start we're going to run through a day," Mrs. Gallagher said, picking up a piece of chalk. She wrote a series of times down on the board, starting at 7 a.m. and ending at 6 in the evening. "Your first responsibility on Monday is going to be getting to breakfast by 7:45. Lower mids and mids *must* check in with the faculty on breakfast duty and sign their names. Breakfast is a *required* meal, friends, along with sit-down dinner. We'll get to that."

"What if I'm not hungry?" asked one girl on the other side of the room. She was Puerto Rican, with a massive head of 3C curls.

"Then, Maura, you'll show up, sign your name, and learn your lesson when you don't have time to eat again until noon." Mrs. Gallagher rolled her eyes. "Depending on schedules, you'll likely have two classes after breakfast, before Morning Meeting. Your Morning Meeting seating assignment is in your welcome packet *and* on a slip of paper in your mailbox. If you think you're not going to remember your chair number, leave the slip in your box until Monday, then go collect it before Meeting."

"What's Morning Meeting?" asked a boy to my right.

His pronunciation threw me. The articulated "ing" was lost. Yet no one corrected him—almost as though the idea of speaking "Proper English" was a racist construct that meant nothing and didn't actually matter.

I started really honing in on everyone's voice then. As Mrs. Gallagher explained Morning Meeting to the freshman, Langston, and the rest of the room, anxiety about my flat nonaccent ratcheted up.

The idea of code switching was entirely foreign to me, and Francine had the same voice I did: flat, with just a hint of Valley Girl (but not too much), and fully formed suffixes that pleased the ears of white teachers.

What I would now consider my "podcast voice" was then just my speaking voice, and it was, I thought, one of the main points of separation between the Black kids who were in Level Four and the Black kids who weren't. Whereas I had no concept of what it meant to code switch, the kids in this orientation room were fluent. When gathered together, just us, they sounded like the kids I'd been subtly inoculated against for the majority of my life.

My parents wanted the best for me, but I think that often came at the cost of my broader social development, leading to a mindset that can happen for Black kids who grew up in "diverse" (white suburban) environments being told that they were more intelligent than those around them: "Well, other Black kids didn't like me because I was smart."

Maybe you've heard a variant of this complaint. "They didn't like me because I liked nerd shit." "They made fun of me because I got good grades." "They didn't like me because I was always reading." "I got teased for turning in my homework on time." "I don't fit in because I do well on tests and quizzes."

Maybe you've said it yourself. I trust that I'm not going to shock you here when I tell you that you were wrong and explain that you absolutely got teased because you were an asshole, not because you weren't dumb enough. I'm confident in saying this because, matters of race aside, we were all assholes in some way during adolescence. If you don't believe me, ask the adult closest to you at age thirteen. I'll wait.

I was still an asshole at fifteen, and unprepared to be greeted and (later) befriended by a large group of teenagers who represented a larger swath of the diaspora than I'd ever been asked to consider before. It is one of the few eye-opening experiences I am thankful to Taft for, though I suspect it was completely unintentional on the school's part. In the moment, though, I was terrified, sure that Francine would be my only friend at Taft. She looked as shell-shocked as I did.

At the front of the room Mrs. Gallagher was still speaking, now gesturing for students to join her in front of the chalkboard. The Miss Harris she'd yelled at before was among them, standing out as the only person in the room wearing pants that did not have a zipper. The ties on her basketball shorts were long enough that they bounced against her thighs as she moved.

"Has everyone connected with their Old Boy or Girl?" Mrs. Gallagher asked. "If you're not doing dinner with your parents tonight, definitely take the opportunity to eat with them. Pick their brains; they're an amazing resource."

I had not yet connected with my Old Girl. I do not remember my Old Girl's name either, as we spoke a grand total of two times. She was white and had brown hair and I think she was on the crew team. Let's call her Karen. She was not an amazing resource.

"So, I graduated from Taft in…well, let me not date myself like that," my advisor-to-be said with a chuckle as her student volunteers situated themselves. "And even then, Taft was a culture shock. I mean…I don't know about you, but this is an entirely different world than what I left back home."

There were murmurs of agreement, and I went out of my way to join in. Now, I sensed, was not the time to announce that I had been coming up to Taft for reunions and visits for a decade. Just prior to applying, I'd been here for the unveiling of that new skating rink and to watch my dad be voted in for a term to the school's board of trustees.

Mrs. Gallagher leaned back against the chalkboard. "None of that's really in the handbook, yeah?" The students who had joined her at the front all let out conspiratorial snickers as they nodded along.

"My middle school looks a lot like Taft," Francine whispered to my side. "Not that different."

"My high school was huge," I said. "But, yeah…different."

Time has changed this conversation, thankfully, "different" no longer standing for "whiter than you might be used to." We're allowed to be blunter now, as the Overton Window for Talking About Race in America has been moved enough to the left that white people are now more comfortable with the idea of people of color explicitly discussing race in spaces they consider their own. Thank God for *This Is Us*, I guess.

Jaded after months of dealing with microaggressions at my first school admissions job, I started whispering my own advice when I was alone on campus tours with Black parents. "I don't know what your background is—like where you live or what you do or anything. It doesn't matter," I would say to them. "A lot of the white kids at this school will have come from privilege, and whether or not you and your kid have a different lived experience or not, they will very likely assume that you do. You're gonna deal with everything from unintentional microaggressions to outright racism. And I'm saying that like…in general. That's going to be *every* school you apply to, not just here."

In some cases that speech was probably *too* blunt (the tristate area preschool application game is discouraging enough before you are assigned to southern New York's most maudlin admissions rep), but it contains the information I wish I had received, if only for the questions it would have prompted me to ask. Like, *What do you mean by assume?*

"So let's start our conversation—names, please, then we'll take questions from new students," Mrs. Gallagher prompted, pointing at her Von Trapp lineup of students at the front of the room. I had no idea what I was supposed to be asking.

Miss Harris went first. "I'm Yara. Mid. I'm from Prep 9."

A few cheers and whoops went up from other students in the room. I did not know what Prep 9 meant. Neither did Francine, it seemed, when I looked over at her.

"Charles, I'm a mid," said the next boy. He was tall and dark-skinned. "I'm from Newark."

"NJ SEEDS!" one girl yelled back. Charles sighed.

Thomas was the next to introduce himself, another Black mid—this time with cornrows, from Queens. He also shouted out Prep 9. When the next girl introduced herself (Becca, a senior from Yonkers), she added, somewhat reluctantly it sounded like, that she'd arrived at Taft via ABC.

That one I knew! So did a shorter girl with locs and a skinny face; she visibly bounced in her seat when the program was mentioned. Even Tamia looked up.

"What's ABC?" Francine whispered.

"A Better Chance," I said. "My dad came here with that one."

"Oh. They're all scholarship programs?"

"I guess, yep. That's why everyone knows each other, maybe?"

"Are you…"

"Nope. Are you?"

"No."

"I mean, I'm getting financial aid, though," I clarified.

"Oh," Francine said. Whether she was as well would remain a mystery.

When everyone had finished introducing themselves, Mrs. Gallagher spoke again. "All right—the floor is open. This is your chance to ask *anything* you might not feel comfortable asking your Old Girl or Boy," she said. "There are no dumb questions. And obviously, if you think of something later, my office door is always open. If anyone wants to walk back there with me after this, I can show you. It's right next to the mailroom. Questions?"

The room was hushed for a second, in that way that always happens at first when you ask a group of adolescents to speak up.

"I have a question." The small girl with the locs was the first to speak.

"Great. Introduce yourself first, please."

"I'm Tabitha—Tabi, please. I'm from Indianapolis and I'm a freshman," she announced. "My question is where do you go to get your hair done here?"

The room exploded with laughter; not because her question was a silly one, but because it turned the knob, slightly, on a release valve of awkward tension.

I laughed too, absorbing every ounce of awkwardness that other students were letting out. It wasn't that I didn't understand the importance of the question—I went to Pam's every six weeks like clockwork, as did my mom. I just didn't care enough to think to ask it.

Becca shrugged. "You just get nappy and then get it done when you go home for break. We're out of here in like five weeks."

"Some students don't travel home for every break," Mrs. Gallagher corrected gently. "Tabi, you said you're from Indiana?"

The girl nodded. "I'm going home for Thanksgiving, but not in October."

"You're in luck. My daughters, Jaz and Gina, love to do hair"— that got the attention of several of the girls in the room, before Mrs. Gallagher laughed and continued—"they're six and eight, and practice on a Barbie. But, in all seriousness, it *can* be a challenge. My suggestion is always that you coordinate with one or two other girls for appointments on the same day—*early* in the day, you know how it can be—and then let me know. Even if I can't drive you into Waterbury and wait, I can come pick you up, or vice versa."

Watertown's more metropolitan (in that it had buildings with more than six stories and was technically a city) neighbor, Waterbury, had a larger Black and Latinx population, meaning they had the Black salons that Watertown didn't. The majority of Taft students could walk down to the local barber on Main Street or hit the Supercuts just a bit farther down the road; easy and, most important, *walkable* from campus.

Black students usually had to hike to Waterbury via public bus, an expensive taxi, or Mrs. Gallagher's generosity. Though, she added, "At least one person will set up a salon in their dorm room by the time we get to second semester. Same with the boys— someone will bring a pair of clippers back after fall break before Halloween. We make do."

This wasn't Taft's fault, exactly. Watertown's demographics were what they were and did not warrant, I guess, a Black hair salon. And, it wasn't as though the school had a campus barber for white students while refusing to serve the Black ones. But at tens of thousands a year and an endowment that rested comfortably in the hundreds of millions, you would think that entire segments of your student body wouldn't be forced to simply "make do."

As students continued to call out their questions, I started hearing the same few cities mentioned repeatedly. The various boroughs of New York seemed to be the most represented; the city kids also seemed to come from whatever Prep 9 was, along with some from Oliver Scholars. NYC was followed closely by Newark and other large Jersey cities, which sent a lot of kids from NJ SEEDS. A question about her Jordans and the dress code revealed that Tamia was from Boston. Tabi was, of course, from Indianapolis, and when Francine finally raised her hand, I learned that she was from Athens, Georgia.

"Is joining TAALSA a requirement?" she asked.

"What's TAALSA?" Dante, one of the Prep 9 Brooklyn kids, shouted out.

"The Taft African American Latino Student Alliance," said Mrs. Gallagher. She looked bemused upon meeting Francine's eye again. "No, it's not *required*."

"But we meet every Wednesday night at seven after dinner!" someone shouted out before the conversation moved on.

I have always been bad at thinking up questions in the moment. I arrive at job interviews with at least five questions planned, and then spend the conversation praying that the hiring manager does not inadvertently answer them before they ask, "Do you have any questions?" leaving me to vamp incoherently and hope to God that they haven't noticed that I've sweated through my blouse.

When Mrs. Gallagher asked the same question, it felt as though she was staring straight at me, although I could have sworn that there were other new students in the room who also hadn't spoken up.

I would have questions, sure. But I hadn't even slept a night in my dorm room yet; questions about breakfast, finding my way around, Honor Code, athletic requirements, and the like would come with time.

Other questions—from the basic practicalities about where to go to get one's hair done, to the more philosophical ponderings about whether or not to join an affinity group—simply didn't occur to me yet. No one was saying the words "race," "privilege," "Black," "Latinx," or "white" aloud; I wasn't yet at the point where I thought I needed to ask *why* being not white at Taft in 2003 would be such a big deal.

My parents (my dad especially, I figured), wouldn't have sent me there if it were.

2.

OVER THE COURSE of my childhood I read hundreds of pages on the boarding school experience—and they hadn't even all been *Harry Potter*, though the friendship that Harry, Ron, and Hermione cemented during their first year studying the magical arts at Hogwarts wasn't too far off from what I was expecting from my own boarding school life. It seemed obvious to me that friendships made at boarding school would be the most intense, magical, meaningful, and, most important, solid friendships of my lifetime. Fourteen years of New Jersey friendships be damned.

Everything I'd read and heard about boarding school reinforced this. I had always preferred the boarding school setting of *Little Men* to the original *Little Women*. As a World War II–obsessed tween, I'd devoured *Spying on Miss Müller*, a YA novel about students at a British boarding school who suspected their teacher was a German spy and banded together to flush her out. Sarah Crewe's life in *A Little Princess* had its share of strife, but in the end she and her maid and confidante, Becky, emerge wealthy and friends for life. The girls at *St. Trinian's*, a mid-century British series of books and films that I discovered sometime in middle school, were constantly up to one wild scheme after another that always left them closer than ever before, even if someone suffered a very unfortunate archery accident to get there. I saw the same in my future, puncture wounds and all.

No matter where you went, as long as you were leaving home, you were in for something special—especially where friendship was concerned. My expectations were high, and I was not open for follow-up questions or revisions.

Here is what I failed to consider in my boarding school media diet:

1. Once every eight months, give or take, Harry, Ron, and Hermione found themselves staring down imminent death at the hands of a near immortal magical supervillain. Mutual trauma is a great, if not healthy, relationship adhesive.

2. The students in *Spying on Miss Müller* were trying to cope as they lived through several bombings amid the largest war the world had ever seen. That trauma caused a mass delusion that, understandably, had them convinced that their teacher was a German spy. Remember when George W. Bush's approval rating peaked at 92 percent after 9/11? Again, trauma unites us all, for a time.

3. Sarah Crewe and Becky grew close only after Sarah's father's death in the Boer War left her demoted from student to servant, living under Miss Minchin's tyranny right alongside Becky. The very moment money allowed, Sarah got the fuck out of there, and sure, the little princess brought Becky along too…as her servant. Still. This was not a friendship to aspire to.

4. Many of the friendships in *St. Trinian's* were cemented

after some act of violence, quickly turning the idea of an ideal boarding school friendship into an ideal *Goodfellas* friendship, and I had overestimated the level of actual cutthroat villainy I was willing to dabble in for new friends.

But these revelations would come only with time. When I arrived on Taft's campus that August, it was with the intention of meeting my new, lifelong best friend in that assigned Congdon double.

I slept in my dorm alone that night after our orientation to get a feel for it. My parents and brother retreated to the hotel, returning after breakfast the next morning so that they could be there when my roommate, Jenna Crane, arrived. Jenna's mother wanted to paint—paint a dorm room! Lynn's review of the ordeal once everything was said and done, bunk beds had been chosen, closet space had been divided up, and the question of whether or not the rug was *actually* clean had been answered, was simply, "That girl's mother certainly is a character."

Jenna was one of *those* Cranes. An Elizabeth Taylor–looking black-haired, violet-eyed, willowy distant descendant of one of the infinitely wealthy, tony families who'd benefited exorbitantly from America's early westward expansion. Schools like Taft attract those sorts. Jenna came from the sort of wealth that to this day allows her résumé to look like what you might expect from some sort of British royal—a lot of high-end education followed by a running list of year-long internships and "jobs" such as "board member" and "trustee." I do not trust anyone who has made it into their mid-thirties without the experience of reporting to a boss who can fuck up your livelihood with a single email should they choose to.

Jenna and I spoke over a landline prior to our arrival at Taft. We were both new mids, which was one of the reasons we were paired together. Hopefully, I'd assumed, we would be able to help each other navigate our new boarding school world. The pairing excited me. It was like a *Dear America* book: two greenhorn girls stepping off a boat and entering an unknown world, with only each other to lean on for support.

We had absolutely nothing in common. This was evident over the course of our first call when she started dropping phrases like "Hall & Oates," "Steely Dan," and activities that happened in places that ended in "on Hudson" while explaining her interests. The silence on the other end of the line when I started talking about writing fan fiction, ice-skating lessons, and watching baseball and anime (which I hated, but I had been convinced by my friends in New Jersey that being able to identify all of the men in *Gundam Wing* and *The Big O* was essential to any relationship, platonic or not) should've been telling.

My roommate religiously watches <u>Dawson's Creek</u>. *I watch* <u>Andromeda</u>, I lamented in my journal after our first call.

But, as a voracious consumer of boarding school literature, I had factored in time for us to exist as mortal enemies before finding a common bond over a difficult bit of Latin homework and becoming best friends for life. (Something to this effect seemed to happen in most stories about roommates as far as I was concerned, and all those *Harry Potter* spells were just bastardized Latin, after all.)

We didn't have any classes together that first semester, and alphabetically we sat miles apart from each other at Morning Meeting. I made note that these things, as well, might delay our bonds of sisterhood.

Yara Harris *was* in my first class at Taft, English with Mrs. Dalton. So was George Miller Jr. I walked into the bright classroom in the main building, three whitewashed walls with a fourth entirely of brick, aside from the two windows that let in light reflecting from the pond. Mrs. Dalton—who could have been anywhere between an exhausted twenty-eight and a Jane Fonda fifty, though the latter was more unlikely in this single-drugstore town still a few years out from twenty-step YouTube skin-care tutorials—welcomed us at the door with a smile and a two-page syllabus, inviting us to sit where we pleased at one of the desks set into a square formation.

In most humanities classes at Taft, students sat in some sort of rounded square or fully circular formation. Patterned loosely on the Harkness method, developed at Phillips Exeter and in turn based on the Socratic method of teaching, classes at Taft placed student participation in classroom discussion at a high priority. It was even judged on our report cards, playing heavily into the "effort" grade we received for each class alongside the regular grade we were given based solely on the quality of our academic work. Depending on the sort of parent you had, a 2.5 (a D+/C–) academic grade paired with a 6.0 (an A+) for effort could be seen as more successful than getting a 4.5 (B) with a 3.5 (C+/B–).

There were three or four other students already seated when I arrived. I chose a seat at one of the corners, where the seats to either side of mine were both still empty.

George seemed to recognize me when he arrived. He took the syllabus from Mrs. Dalton's hands, glanced around the room, and then made his way to one of the empty seats next to me.

"Is anyone sitting here?"

"No." I moved my backpack so that it was farther under my own feet to make room.

Yara barely took notice of the other students in class when she walked through the door. She grabbed her syllabus and made a beeline for me, sitting down without bothering to check whether the seat to my right was actually free.

There were no more than thirteen or fourteen students in the room when Mrs. Dalton finally closed the door and entered the classroom herself. As she wrote her name in perfect cursive on the chalkboard affixed to one of the white walls, it occurred to me to *look* at the syllabus she had handed us.

"My name is Mrs. Dalton. I'll be your English teacher this semester, and I might see some of you out for field hockey." I flipped through, looking for the first page of the syllabus. It was double-sided. "Welcome to mid English—North American Slave Narratives."

Yara snickered.

"I think I'm some of your first class ever at Taft," Mrs. Dalton said, smiling at a few students around the room. She nodded at a brown-haired girl with freckles, who I would learn was Olive Carson, from Seventy-Third and Park Avenue. Our teacher then glanced at either George or myself or maybe both of us; we nodded back in unison. "Welcome to all the new members of our community."

The chalk made a noise that was only *just* on the side of acceptable as she finished writing "North American Slave Narratives" on the board.

The syllabus had assignments laid out for each day until Christmas break, naming times and places for midterms and a large term paper as well. We would start the year with *Incidents in the Life of a Slave Girl* by Harriet Jacobs in full, and finish with the complete *Narrative of the Life of Frederick Douglass, an American Slave* by Douglass himself. Excerpts of others were sprinkled in as well. It is to Taft's credit that I'd heard of Solomon Northup years before Steve McQueen made the name famous again.

Mrs. Dalton continued talking as I took in the assignments on the page. "I expect to hear from each of you every class, whether it's sharing from your responses or participating in class discussions," she said. "There aren't that many of us here—I *will* be keeping track. Here, pass these around, please. Your first reading response will be due tomorrow. We're reading through page 22."

Next to me, Yara picked up her book, flipping it over in her hands. Her syllabus lay on her desk, untouched. She smirked again and added under her breath, "We will *definitely* be participating." Mrs. Dalton didn't hear her. George, who had, looked confused.

Yara and I were the only two Black students in Mrs. Dalton's English class. Two of the six total Black girls that we would graduate with, two of whom wouldn't even arrive until senior year. But those numbers weren't seared in my subconscious yet, and I did not understand that Yara had chosen the seat next to me that morning, not because she was yet extending a hand of friendship, but because she was choosing a partner in battle.

"I'd've sat next to you if we were doing *Oliver Twist* or Jane Austen or *Animal Farm* or *The* fucking *Dud Avocado*," she would say to me months later.

I had to look up *The* (fucking) *Dud Avocado*. But, by that point, I did not have to ask *why*.

● ● ●

I chose to sign up to manage Mrs. Dalton's thirds field hockey team in order to fulfill my activity requirement because Jenna chose to play thirds field hockey to fulfill hers, and I wasn't interested in playing hockey on any surface other than ice. I'd accounted for my Roommate Best Friend for Life plan to take some time to come to fruition, and I was willing to put in the effort, even if it took joining a sport and a team I was actively indifferent toward.

Had to explain to Olive, Madison, and Iris why the skirts they have to wear for field hockey and lacrosse are sexist. I don't know why they don't get it. If they practice in shorts they should be able to play in shorts instead of slutty skirts, I, a competitive figure skater who was constantly told she was not delicate and ladylike enough and had never once worn pants for a program, journaled after one practice.

But despite it all, I did *try* to bond with the girls on thirds. I participated in conversations on the bus to and from matches. I attempted to hang out with the other lower mids and mids on the team off the field, saying hello at lunch and in the hallways in between classes and trying to engage in their conversations about things I had little interest in. Ultimately, I was adrift with these field hockey girls and their extended universe.

"We should play a game," Mrs. Dalton said one afternoon on our drive from a match at Deerfield Academy. A trip back from Deerfield meant stopping at Wendy's on the way home. Every girl on the team had been waiting for this moment. My hands were slick with grease from a large order of fries. "Two lies and a truth?"

There were murmurs of approval, thick from Frosty-filled mouths.

"Kitty, why don't you start." Our coach–cum–English teacher gestured to the girl closest to her at the front of the bus. "We'll go backward in seat order."

The conceit of the game was simple—announce three "facts" about ourselves to the bus, and wait for the group to guess which of those facts was the truth. A veteran of church youth groups, I had a few standard answers and fast facts about myself prepared for games like this one. My three go-to truths at the time were:

1. I'd been on *Jeopardy!* at age ten. Yes, the *real Jeopardy!* with Alex Trebek, and *yes*, I did have pictures to prove it, and yes, I *did* lose quite impressively, but I still got to go to Universal Studios Islands of Adventure, so what of it?

2. My younger brother was adopted by my parents as a baby, and *no*, I was not just saying that because I wished it were true.

3. My very first memory in life is being on a beach down the shore, surrounded by very brown, very shiny, very muscular men in Speedos, while also being very upset because my mother—who famously hated beaches throughout my childhood—would not let me go in the water. I was on the older side of two, maybe three, and we were attending one of my father's many bodybuilding competitions, because being a corporate banker in the early nineties meant living through a revolving door of plots from Michael Bay movies.

Kitty revealed that she preferred 98 Degrees to N'Sync or the Backstreet Boys. The bus gasped.

I had plenty of time to craft my lies. As the manager (and resident weirdo, who no one wanted to talk to anyway), I sat near the back of the bus with the equipment, and there were only three other girls behind me—Madison, Kerri, and LoLo, offensive standouts on the field who were given the privilege of the long back-seat bench so that they could gossip privately and have a full view of their kingdom (the bus) in equal parts. By the time the game reached us, Mrs. Dalton had entirely lost interest in her own suggestion.

"One," I said, when the eyes of the bus turned to me. "I'm from New York City. Two, my brother is adopted. Three, I read *Harry Potter and the Order of the Phoenix* in eight hours."

"Well, I know she's *from* New York City," Jenna called out immediately.

We still had some roommate bonding to work on. That much was clear.

The other girls nodded in agreement, though I had not spoken more than a few sentences to half of them directly. "New York City is the truth," Madison agreed behind me. "Adopted brother and eight hours for *Harry Potter* are the lies."

I waited an extra second, to see if anyone would veer from the path Jenna had laid. It made sense to believe her; she was my roommate after all.

But. "I'm from New Jersey."

"*Jenna!*" several of the girls shouted in unison.

"I *thought* it was New York!" she offered meekly.

"So the lies were…?" Olive from English class asked.

"That one, and also that I read *O-O-T-P*"—I spelled out the book's initials as if I was typing an entry into my journal—"in eight hours. It only took six hours, *even* if you count the break I had to take for… *that* part." I'd cried for hours after Sirius Black fell backward through the veil.

It seems impossible, given what a phenomenon *Harry Potter* was at the time, that no one else on the thirds field hockey team had waited in line at a Barnes & Noble in order to read the fifth book at midnight on June 21 that past summer. But their blank stares implied that even if that weren't true, I was certainly the only person on this particular length of New England highway who had bawled over the death of a fictional character.

"It's supposed to be two lies and a truth, not two truths and a lie," Olive said.

I frowned. "Right, that's what I did."

"I think it can be played either way," said Jen, a quiet lower mid with wispy brown hair held back by pink sport tape fashioned into a headband in a way that only ever seemed to work for white girls.

"Your brother is *adopted*?" a lower mid named Janice blurted out.

"Yes," I confirmed. "The other two are the lies."

That gave everyone an obvious moment of pause.

"Where is he from?" Olive asked after a moment.

"Huh?"

"Your brother—he's adopted, from *where*?"

"East Orange, I think." I remembered the trips to the social worker's office and a building that was, perhaps, some sort of group home. I'd only been in kindergarten when my mother had a miscarriage, and so I was fuzzy on the exact details of the adoption she and my dad decided on as the next option. But I could clearly see us driving parallel to the NJ Transit train tracks that led east out of South Orange the first time we met him, the baby whose name I got to choose: Kyle.

"*Maybe* Newark?" I allowed. I couldn't remember *exactly* how far we'd driven that day in 1994. Far enough that my mom had pointed out the neighborhood where Dionne Warwick lived as she always liked to do, but close enough that I hadn't finished the Baby-Sitters Little Sister book I'd brought along for the car ride.

"Delaware?" another voice asked. I turned to see Kerri looking at me expectantly.

"New Jersey—where *I'm* from." Despite my pointed tone, Jenna did not have the decency to blush.

"Does he look like you?"

I did not hear the real question, because I didn't know to listen for it: *Is he Black?*

"He kind of looks like my dad, actually. It's weird! But I guess that's lucky, in a way? I look like my dad too, so we all definitely *look* related."

Madison confirmed. "Wow, that's cool. I didn't know you could adopt African American babies here. I mean, obviously I knew you could adopt African American babies *from* Africa, like my friend's parents. But I didn't know you could get them *here*, or that like, *you* would want to!"

"Me?"

"Your *parents*." Madison rolled her eyes, as if those two words were the most ridiculous part of this conversation.

These expensively educated children were, in that moment,

learning *brand-new* information. That Black people—or for that matter, any person of color—could, and often did, adopt Black children. It was just clicking that orphaned or fostered Black babies weren't just accessories for celebrities and nice white ladies from Utah who needed some color to spice up the extensive and expensive scrapbooking habit that they absolutely have 100 percent under control.

"I think Hugh Jackman's son is from here."

"Hugh Jackman is from *Australia*. LoLo, it's your turn!"

In retrospect, I should have just been impressed that Madison knew even *that* much.

Jenna only grew closer to her thirds teammates as the start of the school year barreled on, continuing to lay obstacles in the way of every plan I'd had for our roommate friendship for the ages.

Plopping down next to Jenna in the dining hall never felt *right*. I was her roommate, and she would introduce me as such if I didn't know someone at the table, but that was where the attempts to integrate ended.

It was obvious that Francine was having an entirely different experience at Taft, outwardly, at least. She was on her way to becoming The One—the Black girl each year who managed to cross over into the mainstream, white prep culture of the school by completely ignoring the rest of us. There was one in every class; occasionally two, if you added a white-passing Latina to the mix. They weren't always well-off either, though Francine certainly seemed to be. The boys had it easier in some respects. Athletics helped them walk the line between circles in a way it never quite seemed to do for the girls. Being good at sports was simply a Black male stereotype white people expected, and when Black boys fulfilled that stereotype it made the white people around them more comfortable; it was a supposed "norm" they could work with and eventually accept.

Upon realizing that we were the only two Black girls in our Algebra 1 class that semester (where I was also the only mid), Francine was perfectly nice, at least once she'd had a moment to get over the shock of my lack of quantitative ability. We stuck together that first week. The friendship seemed promising when we were one-on-one, and some of the other lower-mid girls in the class started inching their ways toward us too. Or, well, inching their way toward Francine, specifically, who in turn seemed pleased to have other girls to talk to. Girls who didn't alternate between dressing in purposefully clashing patterns (there was nothing against that in the dress code) and a Delia's catalog version of a goth.

To be fair, my interests were...*specific*. And I was reluctant to speak of anything else, even when others didn't understand. I wasn't prepared to not only explain what a LiveJournal was to most of the girls I tried to befriend alongside Francine, but also face their hesitant polite-but-what-the-fuck reactions to the fact that I was working on my Orlando Bloom romance novel, alongside a *Buffy / Harry Potter* crossover that, I proudly explained, had nearly two hundred reviews on FanFiction.net even though I hadn't even finished it yet. Maybe these preppy girls had similar interests, but if they did, they kept it to themselves.

My desire to keep my carefully cultivated aura of "weird" was probably at work here too, right alongside Taft's strong segregated foundations. I watched relatively mainstream shows like *Buffy the Vampire Slayer* and *Charmed* obsessively, but I took things to the next level, wearing multiple mood rings and pentacles and frequenting Angelfire Wicca sites for printout spell instructions that had me doing things like burying paperback romance novels underneath mature oak trees under the light of a quarter moon in order to find my one true love. Being an active participant in online fandom wasn't normalized like it is now. There was no Tumblr, Reddit, or Twitter. Talking to anyone about role-playing online or reading along at

Milliways Bar on LiveJournal elicited blank stares. (If you know, you know.) When Graham Norton read Orlando Bloom fan fiction out loud to Orlando Bloom himself on his show for the first time it was a shocking thing; a corner of the internet as strange and foreign as an 8chan message board is to someone who never leaves Buzzfeed.

But while I was an admitted weirdo and sometimes asshole, these moments of awkwardness weren't *entirely* my fault. The awkward silence from Jenna, Francine, and Olive, for instance, after I mentioned liking our dorm room because, even with the two of us sharing, it was still bigger than my room back in New Jersey stayed with me that year. So did the fact that Olive didn't believe me the first time I told her that my dad had graduated from Taft with George's dad. She was equally shocked to learn that he'd been a school trustee. I had to continue correcting girls on the field hockey team who never could get it straight that I wasn't from New York City and had not come to Taft through Prep 9, or an academic program of any kind. There was nothing wrong with having done so, but we weren't all the same.

I didn't know the word "microaggression" yet, so I didn't have the language for what each of these tiny cuts was, or more important, how they made me feel. As a sophomore, I wasn't even yet ready to acknowledge that they made me feel any kind of way at all. But I knew there was something different between the way the girls at Jenna's table treated me and the way the kids on the other side of the dining hall did.

● ● ●

Tamia had not forgotten Francine or me. She refused to call Francine by her name, referring to her instead exclusively as "The Oreo" when we all gathered for meals. It was the first time I'd ever heard the term hurled outside of a Very Special Episode.

Starting almost immediately in our first week of classes, the younger girl began teasing me openly and mercilessly. She had that ability so many bullies do to instantly home in on the things that would hurt the most. She ragged on my hair constantly, and somehow figured out that even more so than my acne, it was the dark staining on my teeth I was most self-conscious about. Part of this was her deserved response to my general demeanor. I had a pick-me attitude *and* a black pleather trench coat, lined in a shimmery purple sateen, from Limited Too, which I walked around telling people I'd bought to look more like Spike from *Buffy*. I was a much easier target than Francine.

Other kids at The Black Table in the dining hall took playful shots at me too, but also almost constantly at one another. It took me longer to grasp that part of this was just part of the currency that friendships were built on. Had I put in any effort whatsoever to socialize at family gatherings, instead of reading comics or handwriting fan fiction into a notebook while hiding in the quietest corner I could find, I might have been more able to adapt. (I was *that* cousin; my uncle recently told me rather bluntly that much of my extended family were "worried" about my social aptitude until about age seventeen.)

No one ever seemed to be upset; if anything, the constant digs seemed to leave them all feeling closer. That's how The Dozens works. I just didn't get it yet. Back home I would always *hear* the "Ooooooooooohs!" followed by raucous laughter coming from other tables in the cafeteria, but my friends were never part of it. At Taft, I would freeze in these moments when they turned on me, often trying to just welcome me into the game. But I was unable to come up with anything clever in response, especially if the insult came out of Tamia's mouth.

She focused on my clothing, just as much as anything else. In 2003, H&M was still producing clothing that wouldn't fall apart the moment it sensed the presence of a rinse cycle, and I had a few favorites that fit in with Taft's dress code but also didn't make me feel like a Lands' End–Abercrombie robot, like all the girls on the field hockey team with their short, three-tiered ruffle skirts and popped-collar polo shirts. One of my choice looks included a black, lacy midi skirt that was double lined and also tiered in a peasanty fashion but infinitely more goth. I would often pair it with a pair of all-black knee-length Chucks and a superhero tee, if I could get away with it. Shirts with logos or prominent images were against dress code—technically, so were those tiered Abercrombie skirts, but those with long backs tended to get away with more.

The entire look would be finished off with that aforementioned *winning* pleather trench coat.

I was wearing a version of this favorite outfit one day—still early enough in the year that we hadn't even been home for a long weekend or Thanksgiving break yet—when I hesitantly decided, once again, to try sitting at The Black Table in the dining hall. There was still *time* for Jenna and me, I told myself, but in the meantime I was going to have to find *someone*. I just wanted actual friends.

Taft's dining hall has since gone through a $20-plus-million renovation, but it was still quite nice when I ate there. Wood-paneled walls, stone floors, and three rows of long dining tables made up one room, along with a full food-service counter, behind which worked just as many Black and Latinx people as attended school with us, if not more. The second room in the dining hall had a freestanding salad bar, a mix of rectangular and circular tables, and a giant framed re-creation of Winslow Homer's 1872 oil painting *Snap the Whip* painted by Taft students in the 1940s.

That year's Black Table for younger students was located right at the front of the dining hall and next to the small, enclosed courtyard hallway that would lead you down into the second room. Depending on schedules, there were days when a second table needed to be commandeered as well. The older kids sat at a Black table in the back of the hall, a much cooler and more secluded location.

Me and my goth-adjacent stylings plopped down next to someone that day and said "hey," before I started to eat. The other freshmen and sophomores at the table were already wrapped up in conversation, which was fine with me. I could settle in, eat a few bites, and try to contribute when I was ready. Or, as was more likely, I'd be forced into saying *something* once Tamia went after one of her other favorite targets, my bright blue and monogrammed L.L.Bean backpack.

That day Tamia kicked my bag to the side (she *loved* to push, shove, kick, and otherwise move my things around unnecessarily whenever she approached—sort of like how you're supposed to frighten a bear by making yourself bigger if you encounter one in the wild; to her credit, it did work) and sat down in the seat next to mine.

Which insult did she pull out that day? The ones I remember best were the TV references, even though I didn't get them half the time, because I'd never seen an episode of, say, *A Different World* and did not know what a "broke Whitley" *was*. But I knew it had something to do with being bougie, because she called me that too, and "a Hillary" for good measure. The context clues were kind of impossible to ignore—when I understood them. And they hurt less to meditate on than anything I was truly self-conscious about. I could switch out my backpack (which, despite all my friends having them back home, was apparently one of those expensive social status symbols, akin to a Tamagotchi or an American Girl doll), but there wasn't anything I could do about my face.

Anyway. Tamia said *something* that afternoon that made my cheeks flush, and then proceeded to ignore me, which usually meant that the rest of the table eventually would too, as she dominated the conversation. Even if I'd had one, the chance to deliver a comeback passed too quickly.

Except that day, as I picked at my plate of food, one voice came to my defense.

"Hey, c'mon." When I looked up, Yara Harris was grinning at me. "Leave the Witch of Blackbird Pond alone."

3.

My best friend didn't turn out to be my WASPy roommate, but a Black girl from Staten Island named Yara. We had exactly three things in common to start.

1. We were both Black.
2. We both attended Taft.
3. We both loved the movie *Dogma*.

Our shared lived experience—the good, the bad, and the traumatic—of being Black at boarding school did a lot of the heavy lifting in our friendship, and that was more than enough.

Yara was cool, and I never found out why she came to my defense. She was the type of kid my mom wouldn't have let me hang out with at home. In fact, when we put in requests to room together each year following, she and Mrs. Gallagher decided that under no circumstances was that to happen. They had a "feeling," my mom would say for years on.

Was Yara's mom's house on Staten Island the first place I ever got absolutely hammered while underage? Was I with Yara and her older sister the next morning at the Roosevelt Field Mall Macy's when my first hangover headache hit me like a truck? When I returned the sleepover favor and Yara visited me in Maplewood, did she convince me to raid my dad's basement alcohol cabinet? Did we drink from a dusty bottle of gin that had an *A-Team* Mr. T sticker on it that had almost certainly lived through Wall Street in the 1980s with him? Yes, absolutely, without a doubt. But, had I stayed in Maplewood for high school, I would have done a lot more than that.

Frankly, my parents dodged a bullet when I chose Yara, a literal leap-day baby who blamed many of her proclivities on the fact that she was, technically, only four years old. Having started Taft as a freshman, Yara knew the lay of the land better than I did. She continued to sit next to me in Mrs. Dalton's English class and was always around to pass an eye roll or exchange a pained stare as we, as the only two Black students, somehow made it through an entire fall semester of reading slave narratives and biographies taught by the same white woman who allowed that adoption conversation to continue unchecked.

Yara was the one who told me to stop going to Scene, the late-night hangout spot on the Jigger Shop (more commonly known as the Jig; and, yes, certain white kids did *love* to slip up on that name) patio after evening study hall. "*We* go to the student union," she offered up as an invitation one night at dinner. The union room was next to the Jig, and it had couches, pool, foosball, and a TV that was almost always playing BET or, in a pinch, MTV. She made fun of me relentlessly the first time we took the public bus from the stop behind Taft, making our way to the mall in Waterbury, and I confessed that public transportation was not a part of my regular life back home; but then she gave me a thorough rundown of how to use it, which stops were sketchy, the riders who were regulars and who weren't, which bus I needed to be on in order to make it back to school in time for curfew, and which faculty to call if I missed *that* bus and needed a ride (Mrs. Gallagher *always*, but Mr. Huston, a favorite history teacher, was also fine in a pinch if you were ready for a Sunday morning study hall to accompany it).

"You're tall but you hate basketball, so they're probably going to try and get you to play hockey since you know how to skate and it'll look good in pictures if you're on the team," Yara advised upon seeing figure skates out in my room. "If you play on thirds, watch out for Rosie. She's a bitch."

No one had ever *needed* to ask Yara if they could interest her in touching a basketball, because she was probably already palming one when they met her. She was a varsity player who could hang and talk shit with the best of them, and she was Sanaa Lathan–in–*Love and Basketball* attractive. My wardrobe was strange, but it never hid the fact that I was traditionally feminine, whereas Yara stuck to dress-code-appropriate pants and collared shirts, but absolutely loved to be in a pair of basketball shorts and a T-shirt whenever possible.

With Yara also came Yara's friends, people I'd met but hadn't really gotten to know yet. There was Jason Santiago, an Asian Latino mid from Harlem who went exclusively by his last name and had arrived at Taft with Yara through the Prep 9 program along with Mike, another Black kid from Staten Island in our year. Sam Gutierrez was also Asian Latino, a mid from Edison who'd come through NJ SEEDS. They each had their own little bits of knowledge, pro tips, and tricks for Taft survival that they imparted to both me and Tabi, the freshman ABC kid from Indiana who eventually glommed onto our group through her slow-burning crush on Sam.

It was an outright relief to call them that—a *group*—and be able to count myself as part of their ranks. What's more, it was necessary, as my plans for a lifelong friendship with Jenna had stopped simply deteriorating and were now actively decomposing.

● ● ●

Between our mandatory evening study halls and my skating lessons, my nights were packed. To compensate, I woke up early. This wasn't anything new for me, and setting a six thirty alarm to get up, shower, and do something with my hair before mandatory breakfast sign-in wasn't a big deal. It was necessary, especially as my perm started growing out.

Jenna was not on the same schedule.

"She told me that just because I'm Black doesn't mean that I have to get up early to do my hair," I explained to Yara, Tabi, and Maura. Along with complaining about my alarm that morning, Jenna also had notes about the "gross smell" left in the room after I applied leave-ins and oils and ran the flatiron across my strands. That "gross smell" invited confidence, actually, reminding me of the shiny, hot-ironed curls Pam would press into my hair on Saturday mornings, the one time I'd look half as good as the other girls at school did on a random Wednesday. I could never get the styles to last until Monday, much less re-create them myself. "I don't know what she wants me to do. We *have* to go to breakfast, and I have to be clean."

"You should get locs," Tabi, who had locs, suggested. "But that's kinda racist, what she said."

In the early aughts, white people who were called "racist" could still sort of get away with reacting like a Black person who gets called a nigger while minding their own business in a Walgreens. Shock. Gasps. Tears. The faint call of "Worldstar!" in the distance before they squared up in defense. To be called "racist" felt like something you couldn't walk back from; some reactions would even have you thinking that to be called "racist" was worse than actually *being* a real-live racist walking the streets. We lived under a spell that had us convinced that racism *looked* a certain way. Racism was a word: "nigger." Racism was an action: lynching, a fire hose sprayed, a mob of people attacking peaceful protestors. Racism was a specific way of doing things: segregated water fountains, blackface, a cop literally planting drugs on a Black man after arresting him. Racists had a certain look: white hoods, missing teeth, a ruddy complexion, white tube socks, and *those* sunglasses. Racism was something that happened in a spectacular, *known* fashion.

Jenna invoking race in what needed to just be a discussion about an alarm clock compromise was not something I understood as racism at the time. Because I didn't yet understand that daily microaggressions wove together, layer after layer, to form the full tapestry of what racism looked like at Taft.

There were the obvious incidents, like on January 8, 2005, just before 2:35 p.m. when Justin O'Brian insisted in a history class that "the Indians" "lost" to European settlers a long time ago and needed to "get over it already unless they *really* want to know what it's like to lose." But then there were the Jennas of the world.

There are days when I am thankful that I began having these experiences in high school. I was already behind many of my Black classmates in that regard, and I shudder to think how insufferable I would have been had I arrived at college with my wow-everyday-racism-exists! cherry intact. Had these things been addressed at any point in our time at Taft, I might have realized that even a small comment like this was worth speaking to an adult about, even if there wasn't necessarily anything they could do about it. But there was no chance of that; there wasn't even language directly addressing racism in our student handbook.

My new group of friends were hardly as shocked by Jenna's actions as I was. And they could see her comment as what it was:

kinda racist. And, in at least some of their minds, racism deserved a comeuppance that the school was not going to deliver.

I won't blame just one of them for planting the seeds of revenge. I did not need any encouragement when it came to getting even. At fifteen I was already two or three years deep into my habit of saving select AIM conversations to floppy disks, printing them out, and alphabetizing them by username in a series of binders. Usually just to have particularly funny moments or bits of gossip on hand. Sometimes for just a bit more, like when I brought that binder to sleepaway camp, just to wreak havoc in the girls' cabins after one of our bunkmates said something mean about a good friend. I understood chaotic revenge.

Maura was skeptical when I explained my plan, which had, as all my plans did in those days, a blatant pop-culture throughline. "We can hex her out, like on *Charmed*," I said. "And like even if that doesn't work"—one had to hedge one's bets with hexes found on Wicca forums that began with a Geocities.com URL, after all—"it'll be like a placebo hex, because she'll *see* it and get freaked out."

Why it occurred to me to try to hex Jenna and not Tamia, I'm unsure. Perhaps I knew instinctively that hexing one of our own would not be looked upon kindly. Jenna was fair game, so long as I *really* knew what I was doing, Maura stipulated.

Like so many teen girls who were raised by the Devil's Triumvirate—*Buffy, Harry Potter*, and, of course, *Charmed*—I felt comfortable dabbling in Wicca (as though it weren't a real religion with actual practitioners who might have taken offense at my cavalier attitude). Especially when there was something I *wanted* that adults couldn't or wouldn't get for me, which is, of course, the reason you go through a witchcraft phase in the first place as an adolescent girl: seizing the illusion of control in situations where you otherwise have none.

This means that back then, even though I still would have been that first Black person to die in the horror movie, I was more likely to absently read aloud from a dusty tome marked *Book of the Dead* just to see what would happen than not.

Maura had a stronger sense of self-preservation than I did. She bounced while we were standing in the outdoor toys aisle of the run-down Watertown Kmart where I announced that we needed sidewalk chalk. "To draw runes on the walls," I explained.

"What are runes?" Tabi asked.

"They're like ancient symbols. You can combine them for protection and other stuff," I said, talking straight out of my ass. "It's part of how she travels back in time in *Outlander* too, I think. We just have to draw them on the walls, so we need to get white chalk. It'll be harder to see, but still like... *creepy* when she catches a glimpse, you know? And easier to wash off."

We walked back to school after stopping for Frappuccinos at Starbucks. I toted the bag of purchases—the chalk, a pack of tea-light candles, and a small ramekin bowl in which to burn a piece of paper with Jenna's name on it, obviously—while Yara and Tabi very patiently explained to me that the sign hawking early lay-away options for Christmas shopping we'd seen at the register on our way out was not, in fact, a holdover from a different decade. I can still see the bemusement on their faces saying *Who is this insane bougie bitch who can stage a scene from* The Craft *but has never been to a Kmart before?*

It was a Wednesday. Like many other boarding schools, we had classes on a version of the French system—six days a week with half days on Wednesdays and Saturdays so that there was ample time for sports in the afternoon. Stuck in my position of thirds field hockey manager, I was required to go to games on those afternoons but didn't always have to be at practices. After Jenna's comment I began stretching the definition of "mandatory," and since we'd left for our walkabout straight after lunch and practice didn't start until later in the afternoon, there would be plenty of time to do what needed to be done before Jenna came back to our room.

Yara and Tabi accompanied me back to the room and, still wary, both chose to sit on the bottom bunk and watch while I laid out my materials, glanced at the clock, and got to work.

I started at a window. "Have you ever heard of boo hags?" I asked.

"Kendra, you know I haven't," said Yara.

"I have this book of Black mythology my grandmother got me. It's not like Hera and Zeus and Ares—hey, do you watch *Xena* or *Hercules?*"

"*Kendra.*"

"Okay, well." I made a mental note to circle back to that later. "In this book there're these things called boo hags. They're kind of…they're like old-woman energy vampires. If you're not careful they'll sneak into your room at night, mount you—"

"Gross."

"—mount you, ride you around at night, and steal your energy while you do it. If you wake up tired for no reason it might be because a boo hag rode you—"

"GROSS."

"—the night before."

"You're *so* weird."

This wasn't an unusual conversation to overhear between Yara and me over the next three years as I tried (and failed) to drag her kicking and screaming into any of my stranger interests. When she cried in the movie theatre during Wash's death in *Serenity* a few years later, it genuinely felt like I'd won something.

"Just give me that chalk." When Tabi passed me the box, I continued, pointing at the window. "Anyway. I was just gonna say that I bet lining your windowsills with runes or something would help ward off boo hags."

Yara stared at me. "Are you *worried* about boo hags, Kendra?"

"Well, it doesn't hurt to be safe." I shrugged. "Two birds, one stone."

As a corner unit our room was large, even for a double. Our bunk beds sat in the back right corner, with one desk adjacent and facing a wall, and another against one of the two large windows. Instead of a perfect square we had six walls; an extra rectangle jutted out to overlook the courtyard and circular driveway that led into the dining hall. The walls were white, still, at this point, and I hadn't really decorated yet. Jenna hadn't either, both of us perhaps sensing that if we couldn't settle a dispute about an alarm clock, we definitely weren't ready to compromise on interior design.

On my desk, which overlooked the pond, my laptop was open. I clicked into Netscape and opened my bookmarks, scrolling until I found one of the many witchcraft message boards I frequented and landed on a post claiming to "translate" a variety of "Ancient Druid runes."

Carefully, I began copying the symbols from the screen to the white windowsill. The white chalk worked almost too well; I couldn't see what I was doing at all. But I kept going, scratching symbols into the paint until I guessed, more or less, that I'd covered each windowsill and the white wooden molding treatment that framed the windows too.

Tabi was the one who pointed out the obvious. "She's *really* not gonna see that."

"Yeah."

"So then what's the point?"

Tabi was right. If you knew what you were looking for and squinted you could maybe see that something had been added to the frames, but it was impossible to make out what. For all Jenna would know, it was just some oddly settled dust.

Dust was not going to fight racism for me, and while I wanted to believe that witchcraft would see me through, the setup I had planned was too subtle. Far more than Jenna's comment had been. Having Tabi correctly label what my roommate said as racism, I was now faced with this thing that had such a weight to it, and I needed to react appropriately. This was surely a situation that deserved escalation, and I knew how to do that. But what could I get away with?

My hands were grimy covered in chalk. I grabbed a bath towel from the back of a chair to wipe them off while I thought, and rubbed the cloth up and down my jeans too. The white streaks from where I'd wiped my hands before came off almost entirely. "*Oh.*"

"What?" Yara asked.

"More chalk, please?" I reached over, wiggling my fingers until she placed one of the white pieces in my hand. "What time is it?"

"Three," Tabi said. "How much longer? I want to get real food at the Jig before dinner."

Field hockey would be wrapping up soon. "Okay, okay, forget the spell. I have an idea."

"Like we knew the spell to begin with," Yara muttered.

I rolled my eyes and squatted down on our floor, eyeing the dark, short-ply carpet. "Gimme like…twenty minutes."

The closest thing to a supernatural occurrence that happened in my room that afternoon was the near-perfect circle I managed to draw freehand, from my knees, in white chalk on that carpet. It had a radius of about three feet, and unlike the runes on the windows, there was no missing it.

I bit my lip in focus as I started adding the lines that would connect to make a star, a pentacle drawn in chalk into the rug.

"*Nuh-uh.*"

"What?"

"Nah." Tabi got up from the bed and pointed at the rug. "That's some devil shit. I'm going to the Jig."

"The pentacle is where you draw the line?"

"I'll see y'all at dinner."

I managed a glimpse into the hallway when she opened and shut the door, noting that Congdon was still fairly quiet. Practices were ongoing, and the students who'd left for away games wouldn't be back for hours. But I still needed to move quickly. Now that I was in the middle of a definitive plan, the part of my brain that managed my more obsessive tendencies took hold. I was still as calm and focused as I ever was in seeking out revenge.

"Yara." I went from my knees to my butt so that I could reach out to her without falling over. "Could you please give me the candles?"

In some regards, Yara was fearless. Over the course of our friendship she would drink on campus before interschool dances. She would skip classes and seek aid on assignments that didn't tread the line of cheating so much as cross over it entirely and end up stuck in customs at the border. She smoked cigarettes while we waited for the bus back to school at the Waterbury Brass Mill Commons mall and often suggested stealing canoes from the backyards of residents whose properties butted up against the river we enjoyed exploring on foot.

Any trouble that I got into at school usually sprang from an insatiable thirst for revenge. There'd been the time in elementary when Tamra Bernard told everyone in Mr. McConnell's class that Leonardo DiCaprio was coming to her birthday party. *Titanic* had just come out, and anyone with sense knew she was lying. But when Tamra kept insisting, I marshaled my best friend and a few others to stand on a jungle gym at recess and sing "Tamra is a liar and we hate her!" at the top of our lungs repeatedly. I ended up with a two-day in-school suspension for "leading a gang," according to Principal Hart.

So while I wasn't going to be found drinking on campus, cutting classes, or doing anything else that would get me into trouble but wouldn't then benefit me in some way—even if that benefit was just the dopamine rush of vengeance—if I felt that someone had crossed me *at* school? Especially if that person had ruined my carefully laid plan to become BFFs for life with my roommate, thus invalidating everything *Harry Potter* had taught me? Well, then the gloves were off.

"Candles, please," I repeated.

The pack of six tea lights in lieu of the single large candle I'd been searching the aisles for was a blessing in disguise. I placed one candle at each point of the chalked star, and the sixth in the center, for added effect. Yara, the smoker, handed over her lighter and I lit them in order. "Okay."

"Now what?" Yara asked. "I thought you were going to do a 'spell.'" The air quotes were evident in her tone.

"You saw Tabi's and Maura's reactions," I said. "I don't need to do a spell. Jenna is going to think her roommate's a witch. That *is* the spell."

"You're *so* weird."

"I bet you"—I looked up, mentally calculating how much money I had—"a bacon, egg, and cheese at the Jig it works."

Yara was smart. "What qualifies as *works*?"

"I get a different roommate."

"Good luck with that." She snorted her laughter. "Fine. You're still weird."

The majority of our conversations over the next three years would sound like this one. Me, explaining some esoteric interest or laying out a plan to do something very dumb, very unnecessary, or both, but technically *not* against the rules; and Yara agreeing, but not before she reminded me that I was definitely one of the oddest people she'd met in our short lives.

She reclined in the bed while I got back down on my butt and arranged myself so that I was sitting cross-legged at the "top" of the pentacle, one candle sitting in front of me while the other five flickered dimly in the full light of the room. I did not turn off the lights; no need to put a hat on a hat.

And so that is how Jenna found us when she came back to the room. I set my back ramrod straight, staring unwaveringly at the center candle when I heard the doorknob jiggle; Yara didn't look up from the *Amazing Spider-Man* comic she'd picked up from my desk.

The future Karen stopped short upon walking into the room; a whirlwind of field hockey equipment, duffel bags, pink athletic-tape headbands, and muddy cleats that I had definitely asked on more than one occasion that she *not* wear into the room, seeing as we had to live there and all.

It took less than five seconds for Yara to start snickering. If there was any tension in the room, I couldn't feel it; I was in my element, finally, playacting at the supernatural goings-on I spent my nights writing and fantasizing about.

"What's going on?"

I did not look up. To get from the door to the clean clothing in her dresser, Jenna had to step across the lower half of the pentacle, and as she did a puzzle-piece-shaped chunk of mud fell from her cleats into the circle. I smiled, lowered my eyes, and murmured, "The spirits appreciate an offering of fresh earth."

Yara snorted.

Jenna snatched her shower caddy from the top of the dresser and bunched a handful of clean clothing underneath her arm. I lowered my eyes until she was just a dark shadow beyond my lids, and let out a deep breath.

There is no accurate way for me to re-create the exact litany of absolute "magick" nonsense that poured out of my mouth in that moment. Even if I could, I'm not sure that it wouldn't count as plagiarism, or that some nineties television writer wouldn't come after me for damages. This moment proved, as far as I was concerned, that Jenna and I had no chance at friendship. There was the racism, yes, but also the fact that she wasn't smart enough to recognize that I was serving her "witchcraft" I'd learned from Jenny Calendar on *Buffy*'s best season, J. K. Rowling's fucked Latin, and those episodes where Xena had to fight Alti, the Amazonian witch, in the spirit realm.

I babbled nonsense under my breath, quickly pivoting to Zatanna—the DC Comics witch who cast her spells by speaking sentences and words completely backward.

"*Oot tuo gnillaf strats riah ruoy epoh I dna.*" The *g* in "gnillaf" would be silent.

There were light footsteps and some shuffling coming from the direction of Jenna's dresser. The bedroom door slammed shut with *heft*. I opened my eyes and looked up. I had been so caught up in the fantasy and illusion of it all, I was surprised to see (when I looked at the bright-red numbers of our shared alarm clock, which had started all this to begin with) that no more than two or three minutes had actually passed. My Frappuccino was even still acceptably sippable.

"That was easy. Did she look scared or—" I stopped and frowned when I looked back at Yara. She was prone, completely laid back on my bed, a Spider-Man comic laid squarely over her face. The dark spot slowly bleeding through Spidey's chest on the cover told a better story than the issue inside.

Yara had laugh-cried onto the pages covering her face (an appreciated attempt to keep her muted snickering and highly expressive face to herself), thus rendering the thing unreadable. By the time our next vacation rolled around, Jenna was no longer my roommate. The comic book was a far worthier sacrifice than the dirt from Jenna's cleats.

I never did find out whether my *[Thunder and lightning. Enter three Witches]* technique was specifically to thank, or whether it was simply that from that day on, I also made it my mission to be the worst roommate possible. Probably the latter. I can be perfectly fine to live with, or I can take the Wi-Fi router with me when I go out of town on business; it's really up to you.

Charming my white contemporaries was no longer a priority, and so once Jenna moved out of our room, any pretense of our friendship (or any of its potential) was dropped. I did not ask after her, and no one, student or administrator, ever came right out and told me why she left either. There was no comment on what had happened between the three of us that afternoon after practice, no questions from the staff about Jenna's well-being.

After a final "You are *so* weird," said after we regaled Tabi and Maura with the story of Jenna's reaction in the student union later that afternoon, both eating bacon, egg, and cheeses that Yara paid for, my new best friend never mentioned it again either.

But from that moment on, we were inseparable.

4.

TAFT DID NOT assign me a new roommate after Jenna left. Ever. Like, for the next two years.

Our former double was a super single for the rest of my sophomore year, and the large amount of space piqued the curiosity of the other girls in the Congdon dorm—even the white ones. The walls remained unpainted, but with Jenna gone the essence of who I was—a weird little horny nerd from Jersey—began to make itself known.

We were home so often on long weekends and semester breaks that I was reluctant to remove any of the posters from my immaculately curated childhood bedroom. My signed *Lois and Clark: The New Adventures of Superman* poster that featured a young, open-shirted Dean Cain, a prized possession at the time, would remain at home along with the giant images of the early-aughts-era Green Lantern Corps, my *Star Trek* movie broadsheets and commemorative plates, and the full-wall collage of Orlando Bloom pictures, centered around a giant Legolas poster.

The latter was easy to replace. Soon after Jenna left, I found the life-sized cardboard cutout of Legolas that would live in my dorm room for the rest of the year. He stood, highly discounted, in the corner of the Waterbury mall's FYE, and—after she talked me out of buying the life-sized Xena cutout that spoke whenever you walked by it—Yara helped me navigate him onto the public bus back to campus without beaning the heads of our fellow passengers.

Legolas lived in the corner by the closet, though sometimes, when I was feeling cheeky, I'd place him in the window so that from the outside it looked like there was a grown man in the dorm. No shortage of concerned adults asked me who the blond man in my room was, and I was always pleased to tell them that it was a cardboard elf. The up-and-down look that followed (usually a teacher or administrator taking in my whole...*thing*) telegraphed their thoughts: *Well, ask a stupid question...*

Delores Pickford, a freckled freshman girl with limp brown hair and the disposition of a permanently startled field mouse who'd seen some shit in its day, also lived in Congdon and thought Orlando Bloom was cute too. She was from the Caribbean. Early on, in the small-talk phase of friendship, I asked her if she spent much time at the beach when she was home and told her that I'd loved going to the beachside Club Med in the Dominican Republic with my family. Delores told me that no, she did not. "The people who go to the local beaches that the resorts don't own are scary," she confessed as we sat in my room one day.

Tabi and Yara snickered together, exchanging knowing looks when I mentioned that I'd invited Delores over to my room to hang out one night after study hall.

Tabi barely looked up from her sandwich. "A white chick from the islands? Girl."

Yara just laughed. I was confused. "What?"

"My mom's people are from there," Yara said. "*Those* white people are the fucking last ones you can depend on."

Delores was definitely sheltered, at the very least. The next weekend, we all went to the movies in Waterbury. While I wasn't used to public transportation outside of the NJ Transit commuter trains, I was game to try most anything. My wide-eyed sense of adventure every time we left campus was likely highly strange to Yara and Tabi, who'd grown up using the MTA and CTA regularly. My insistence on grabbing a schedule and map from the front of the bus "just in case," while Tabi and Yara simply tucked into their minds the times and numbers of the three last buses we could take and still make it back to campus, probably bordered on embarrassing. But at least I was willing to try.

We could get Delores onto the bus, but she was a nervous wreck the entire ride. I watched her freeze when the bus entered downtown Waterbury for just one or two stops, clearly hoping that none of the "locals" sat next to her. The lack of seat belts prompted her to ask us if we could all possibly spring for and split a cab the next time we wanted to go to the mall, which in turn prompted Yara to ask me how rich I thought Delores *really* was; local cabs were expensive and every time we had to take one it meant sacrificing something else, even when we split the fare.

Once, Delores even sat outside the movie theatre for the full duration of *Underworld* because she was afraid her mother would find out she'd snuck into an R-rated film. She was afraid of everything, and so while she was just as privileged as many of the other kids at Taft, she was still something of a social misfit for her lack of worldly experience and desire to join in on the "fun."

As the school's largest group of social misfits, the Black kids at Taft were often deeply forgiving and accepting of those who didn't or couldn't fit in elsewhere. They'd done that for me (with the exception of Tamia) despite my attitude, and our table in the dining hall was a revolving door for other weirdos and misfits who couldn't find a home anywhere else. The only difference between

Black kids and white misfits was that the white students who sat with us rarely made our table a permanent home.

Delores wasn't perfect, but I stuck with her. In addition to sharing my Orlando Bloom fascination, she was able to talk about *Harry Potter* with gusto, and even knew what a LiveJournal was. And, when it came to decorating, it was nice to have an uptight friend who could spot a poster's dropped corner, even by a millimeter, from across a bedroom.

Helping me decorate and lust—mostly lust—meant that Delores spent a lot of time in my very large room, attracting renewed attention from those who had otherwise dismissed her as a socially awkward nerd than she might have otherwise.

The winter season (as determined by the gentle whirring of campus Zambonis emerging from hibernation, not the equinox) meant that I was able to fulfill the school's sporting requirement through my first love of skating, rather than riding the bench as the field hockey manager. Once I turned over my clipboard and drawstring bag stuffed full of scrimmage pinnies and field markers, my attempts at aggressive outreach into friendships with white students came to an end. I saw them in classes (how could I not?) and could be appropriately friendly, but I did not go out of my way to engage with them socially. And so when Francine began stopping by my room, bringing her passel of white girlfriends with her, it wasn't because I'd extended the invite. It definitely hadn't come from Delores either—she had to reintroduce herself to Francine, Olive, and another Congdon girl named Rachel all over again.

"We sat next to each other at sit-down dinner, last week," she halfheartedly pointed out to Olive, who wasn't entirely listening as she examined the new section of wall we'd been working on.

"Have they told you when you're getting a new roommate?" Olive asked. "Or asked you who you want it to be?"

"Nope."

"It's such a big space. And with the corner unit you only share one wall with another room." She was just fifteen, but she spoke like a seasoned New York City real estate agent. The sort of woman who would turn up forty years later, leathery and libated, on a reality show about renovating through a divorce.

Olive turned around from the desk and strode toward the bunk bed, letting her hand trail across the windowsills on her way. "I have an *A Walk to Remember* poster in my room. We could put it up right there, since you have Shane West stuff already. What *is* LXG, anyway?" She muttered the question before pointing to an empty spot above my dresser. "So when they start talking to you about a new roommate, you should mention me. We can put it up together. And dust." She held up her hand, covered in white chalk.

"Well, the room wouldn't be so big anymore if you moved in, Olive," Rachel chimed in. "Then where would we hang out?"

Not in my room, regardless; I knew that much. Besides, Rachel Buchanan had that covered, with the snack-filled after-study-hall get-togethers she hosted in her own dorm. Sessions filled with other girls who looked just like her with her skirts and popped collars and Vineyard Vines flipflops. She was also, according to Tabi, well-liked by teachers in the lower-mid classrooms.

"Mrs. Myers loves her," the younger girl said a few days later while lamenting about the Screw Crew she'd gotten for being late and improperly dressed to one too many breakfasts on mornings when the art teacher, Mrs. Myers, controlled the sign-in sheet. "And she *never* gives her dress-code grades because she's not...y'know."

"Black? Well, duh," Yara replied, lazily rolling her eyes. "Just wear pants. She can't get you for pants."

A few nights later, I was seated across from Rachel at sit-down, which was purely a coincidence, given the assigned seating. The point of this deeply boarding school tradition was ostensibly to encourage students and faculty to meet new people and strike up conversations that might otherwise be outside their comfort zones. For many Black and Latinx students, sit-down dinners were just another moment when our innate otherness in this institution was put fully and entirely on blast. Even as I started tentatively making more friends, my conversations at sit-downs rarely went beyond pleasantries and very basic yes-or-no answers.

I had no expectations when I gave Rachel a perfunctory smile as we sat down. Rachel grinned back before ducking her head for the evening prayer and proceeding to surprise me with her affability. She knew more people than I did at the table that night and introduced me multiple times as "Kendra—she has the room with a man in her window!" and I appreciated that. It was nice to hear descriptors applied to myself other than "Black" and "a mid."

The girl could in no way replace Yara, who had quickly become my boarding school ride-or-die, but because Rachel and Francine both lived in Congdon, it gave me a room to visit after evening study hall if I wasn't feeling up to walking over to Yara's room in Mac House or all the way to the student union. Delores never quite fit in, but I brought her along when I could because it gave me someone to talk to. But Delores didn't always enjoy those gatherings. Understandable, as I once heard Olive musing over Delores's near-translucent skin that refused to tan. "She looks *so* weird," she said. "For someone who claims that she's from the Caribbean."

I rarely did much talking. Rachel would occasionally address me directly, but when she wasn't focusing conversation my way, I had to fight to jump in. Still, though, I tried. I had never had trouble making friends or even socializing casually before, and the barriers between myself and the white students at Taft were still confusing, even as I could now acknowledge that they certainly existed.

But even when Francine, Olive (who never did get over the fact that I wouldn't formally ask the dean of student life to move her into my room), or any of the other freshmen or new sophomores who wandered in and out of Rachel's after-study sessions didn't put much stock into what I had to say, even when Rachel herself didn't allow a topic that I (or Delores) would bring up to flourish into a full-fledged conversation, I rationalized it by saying to myself, *If she didn't want me here, she'd kick me out.*

I wish that I'd not arrived on campus with respectability politics so absolutely ingrained in my way of moving through the world. To be fair, leaning full force into that upbringing probably would have made my time at Taft easier. Francine seemed to be having a great time, as far as I could tell. But if an adjacency to whiteness, behaviorally or otherwise, is the only way a Black child can thrive in your institution, then your institution has failed that child, no matter what the other benefits are.

My parents have evolved, and they just wanted the best for me—but "best" is a loaded term. The trappings it came with were designed within constraints of looking at the world that would take me years to unlearn. I realized over three years at Taft that there was a whole diaspora of Blackness I'd never been exposed to, and I did resent that over time. I wished that I'd *at least* been brought up with a specific understanding of code switching. Or, at minimum, to respect and *use* the unique vernaculars that Black people have cultivated across America, rather than being told that any hint of an "accent" or utilizing any sort of African American vernacular was simply wrong.

I would have wasted less time with people like Rachel and Francine, searching for a group of friends that mirrored the parentally sanctioned but hypersegregated Level Four classrooms back home, where friendships were dictated in part by an inherently racist education system.

I was seeking, subconsciously, the racism I was familiar with. Better the devil you know, after all.

● ● ●

"We should go to Brooks," Rachel announced from my doorframe one afternoon.

Watertown didn't have CVS, Walgreens, or Rite Aid, but we did have a Brooks, the regional New England drugstore chain, for all the basics. I bought many a maxipad at Brooks. Tampons too, after one afternoon, when Yara and I were peeing in stalls next to each other, a wrapped pad fell out of my bag, and she handed it back to me saying, "I use tampons because I don't like sitting in my own filth, but you do you."

It was spring in New England, meaning that it was freezing, but that at the same time you might see an incredibly stubborn crocus doing its best to ignore that. But Rachel's suggestion that day happened to correspond directly with my need for hygienic essentials and several packs of Nerds Ropes at 75¢ a pop.

"Sure." I saved the document I'd been working on and closed my laptop. "Now? I just have to change. Pants would probably be good."

"Yeah, it's cold," Rachel agreed. "Ten minutes?"

"Totally."

Bundled up, I walked upstairs to Rachel's second-floor room. There was no answer when I knocked, and cracking the door open confirmed that neither she nor her roommate was inside.

"She's in the dining hall!" another girl called out as I was headed back down the stairs. Her head just barely poked out from the room across the hall from Rachel's.

I gave a hurried thanks as I trotted back down the stairs and out of Congdon's front door. The two lower-school girls' dorms, mine and Mac House, both faced the back entrance to the dining hall, which made it even harder for freshmen and sophomores to excuse being late to mandatory meals like breakfast and sit-down.

Rachel was standing by the salad bar, which was usually filled with something light and easy between meals; bananas this time. Rachel was eating one when I walked in.

"Sorry, I thought you'd be up in your room. I went there first."

"I needed a snack," she said, waving before we fell into step together.

Rachel and I were not friendly-teasing-about-sitting-in-one's-own-menstrual-blood close, but our social interactions had begun to extend into moments like these in between classes and dinner when she might show up to ask if I wanted to do something.

Yara, Tabi, and I had very few common interests to start, but Yara made me laugh, and being friends with Tabi was like having a little sister. Neither of them would sit through an episode of *Star Trek* with me without loud complaints, but I was beginning to convince Yara that *Xena* was worth her time. Her fondness for the not-at-all-coded deep romantic love that Xena had for her sidekick, Gabrielle, made it fairly obvious from the jump that Yara was not straight. By virtue of some sort of unspoken agreement, we did not address her sexuality aloud or directly in this stuffy prep school environment until much later on, but the silent knowledge, first hinted at as we rewatched season one of *Roswell* together, was an important stone in the foundation of our friendship.

If Yara hadn't been at basketball practice that afternoon, I would have sought her out rather than take the trip to Brooks with Rachel. Yara knew how to work a teacher over, kneading them with her words until they agreed to do what she wanted. We'd have been making this journey in the back of Mrs. Gallagher's car.

Instead I trudged along next to Rachel, down the shady, steep Academy Hill from campus to Watertown proper, and the main drag lined with the necessities: Starbucks, Kmart, Blockbuster, an old bank turned fancy steak house where you could dine inside the vintage safe (for when your parents came to visit and they didn't want to drive to Applebee's or Ruby Tuesday at the mall for dinner), the local library, which kept me flush in paperback romances, a vintage single-screen second-run movie theatre (we never saw a movie here), and the local Brooks, where Yara, Tabi, and I were often peered at closely through the aisles by extremely attentive cashiers.

Inside, I grabbed a pack of Always on the way up to the counter and snickered remembering what Yara had said to me that one afternoon. Rachel and I didn't have inside jokes like that.

We made our purchases and left, almost immediately going our separate ways once we got back to campus—she back to her room, and me to mine.

● ● ●

The next afternoon, Yara, Tabi, Sam, Santiago, and I met up after class. It was warmer out than it had been the day before, the perfect time for another after-school adventure. But this would be different.

We'd never made it up as far as Leatherman's Cave, a series of rocky enclosures on a hiking trail off Route 6, where legend had it that starting in 1860 one man—clad only in patches of rough, weather-beaten leather—walked in a 360-mile circle from Watertown, through western New York, and back again. Our first attempt to get up there failed. Though we'd started out dutifully following a set of printed instructions, we got distracted by a farm stand and cornfield on the side of the road. Yara wanted to gather a bunch of corn to take back to campus but conceded when I pointed out that we did not have access to a microwave or even a hot plate, much less a fully functional stove. That didn't stop us from wandering through the cornfields, though, treating what was surely someone's property as our own private maze.

There are times now when I think consciously about the spaces I am to enter that day. How white will this space be? Will someone find it odd that I am here? Can I dress to augment the way people will receive me in this place? What signals of belonging can I place on my person to make myself more palatable to others who are here? These questions account for the number of Taft shirts and hoodies that I still own and wear on morning jogs or late-night runs through neighborhoods that I don't look as though I belong in; they are the reason that my car has both a Taft and an Oberlin College bumper sticker affixed to the rear windshield, in hopes that if I'm pulled over they'll temper an officer's initial reaction.

I don't remember the exact moment when these little steps—steps that, if anyone bothered to ask, they would find that many Black people in America also employ for their personal safety—clicked for me. I just know that as we traipsed through that cornfield, they most certainly had not. We were lucky that no one called the police, or worse.

When we set out that afternoon I had folded printouts from MapQuest in my pocket and knew that if we just followed the road, and then eventually took a right, and wandered through some woods, we'd find the trail.

"It's about three miles," I informed everyone.

"Sixty blocks, a minute a block, sixty minutes. Easy." Santiago quickly converted the distance into NYC-speak for everyone else.

This did not, however, account for the lack of sidewalk alongside the county road, the fact that we'd be walking up and down hills for most of the journey, or the notion that we would also have to walk back to campus from the caves. Or, frankly, the fact that we were all very easily distracted teenagers.

"Let's check out the graveyard first." I couldn't help but suggest the detour, so obvious and so close to campus.

"A real Kendra Suggestion, if I've ever heard one. Spontaneous, but also entirely predictable if you've spent more than an hour with her," said Yara. "You heard the Witch of Blackbird Pond—to the cemetery."

Tabi, not a Catholic, crossed herself. Sam, a Catholic, challenged Santiago, also a Catholic, to a race, and they dashed off across the baseball field ahead of us.

It was one of those days that made one understand why parents paid such a premium for their children to spend four years on this campus. The temperature sat somewhere in the fifties, but the sun was shining and reflecting perfectly off the pond in the middle of campus. Each redbrick building radiated a near-golden-hour glow, a rose-colored tint that would eventually shade every memory of Taft I shared with the parents of prospective independent school students later on in my career.

Santiago and Sam raced ahead of us, while Yara, Tabi, and I took it slow. We walked past the pond, through the lush grass where the baseball and softball diamonds' outfields met, to where the two boys had stopped to wait for us to catch up. None of us had cell phones, and no one was wearing a watch, but one glance back toward the main building told me that it was still early enough. The campus was still, and a few students playing catch on the Jig patio were the only signs of motion. No one rushed to or from anything; we had plenty of time before we were at risk of missing dinner.

The cemetery was just down the street from the bus stop to go to Waterbury, not a long walk at all.

"I should have brought a pencil to do etchings."

"The headstones aren't going anywhere." Yara rolled her eyes directly at me. "We'll come back."

We did go back. I eventually scanned, uploaded, and categorized all the pictures of our outings developed behind the counter at Brooks, and stashed them all in a shared folder called

"Minorities at Play..." with individual subfolders for locations around Waters-town-and-bury.

"...in Graveyards" became particularly prolific. Images of Tabi and Sam hanging upside down in trees. Me, Tabi, and Yara posed as a trio, finger guns up in the air as we did our best *Charlie's Angels* impression. One image captures Yara and Santiago hiding behind giant stone slabs the day we brought some cheap plastic water guns with us from Kmart. Another shows the expansion of our group, the five of us posing on different branches of one of the largest trees on the plot in a picture taken by Mike, another Prep 9 student from our year who began spending more and more time with us as the months passed.

Eventually I would have a spot, a place where I would occasionally bring my laptop, an apple, and three or four Nerds Ropes, and write *X-Men* fan fiction, leaning back against a headstone dated 1845, until the computer got too hot on my crossed legs or died entirely—my own rendering of the freedom and independence that Taft promised to instill in its graduates.

That afternoon, though, we simply explored for a bit, pointing out the smaller headstones engraved for those who had died shockingly young, and awarding points to those who found an eighteenth- or nineteenth-century headstone boasting that the person underneath their feet had lived past fifty.

Not wanting to miss dinner, but still wanting to see the caves, we left sooner than we might have otherwise. Our route out of the cemetery was through someone's backyard and down their driveway onto the residential Hawley Street—each step taken without a care in the world. As many times as I have played our graveyard excursions out in my mind, I can't begin to imagine how we would have reacted had someone called the police on us for trespassing. What would we have done if we'd accidentally tripped a home security alarm? We walked, somehow, with the confidence I spent years describing professionally, as though we owned the streets of Watertown, rather than as obvious visitors.

We had to backtrack a bit to get over to Route 6, and when we eventually made it, Santiago pointed out another distraction. "There's a river down there."

Santiago and I took the lead as we walked down to the riverbank, our cave excursion completely forgotten. We made a right where we should have made a left, and started following the brook back south through Watertown proper. The dirty water butted up against a row of large, unfenced backyards that met equally large homes.

"This would go faster if we had a canoe," Yara said. She wasn't wrong.

"Or a crew boat," I offered.

"It's called a racing shell," Santiago said with a smirk. "You didn't have a crew team in Jersey?"

"No, we were too busy being the best fencing high school in the state."

"Hey!" Yara clapped her hands together, and we all turned. She and Tabi stood next to each other, a few feet behind me and the boys. "Eyes on the prize. A canoe. Right there."

The two had found a boat in one of the backyards. It was flipped upside down in the lifeless winter grass, sitting next to a large wooden swing set. The yard itself showed hints of spring, a little green doing its darnedest to poke up here and there, though hard to see if you weren't explicitly looking for it.

Yara was not, and I had to clamp down on my Dad Instinct when her heel came down hard on a small bud attempting to claw its way up from the earth. "Help me lift this."

"We can't just take someone's canoe."

"We'll bring it back." The "duh" was implied. "Santiago, you grab that side."

"Yara, come on."

"There aren't any cars in the driveway; no one's home, and we'll have it back before they even realize it's gone," she said. "This is what happens when you leave shit lying around. You wouldn't ride your bike to Brooks and not lock it, right?"

Yara knew my answer. My twenty-one-speed red-gold Schwinn was a possession (one of many, if we're being honest) I was rather protective about. Anytime I rode my bike around Watertown, two locks came with me.

"I mean..." I trailed off. There was no "cool" answer here.

"Wait," Sam said. "There's no oars."

"There's no oars!" I echoed immediately.

Yara squatted down next to her end of the boat anyway. "We can find tree branches."

"This isn't the Oregon Trail, dumbass." Santiago rolled his eyes. "We're not on a pole boat."

"It's called a punt," I corrected as he passed me.

"Fuck off and get dysentery."

Unable to take the family's canoe, Yara instead grabbed a divot of grass up in her fist from the soggy ground. It flew past my head, toward Santiago's back, and by the time it hit him she was already sprinting forward, passing him to reach the bank first.

This sort of outing would become typical for us. If Taft did nothing else, it taught me, for better or worse, how to thoroughly explore and integrate myself within a new community. I learned that there was no need to be nervous about introducing yourself to someone new when picking up a local library card; I started to figure out what it meant to be a "regular" at a writing spot— it was only Starbucks, but they knew my name and order and that felt good. Whether we were wandering the streets adjacent to the city mall, randomly getting off the bus in the middle of Waterbury "just to see" what a beef patty tasted like from one corner store versus another, or walking through cemeteries and the backyards of Watertown homeowners, I enjoyed pushing the boundaries of the independence being at Taft afforded me.

We walked along the river that afternoon until it turned into the Heminway Pond, where sticking to the banks was no longer an option. Yara wouldn't let us hear the end of it when we realized that sans canoe our adventure was effectively over unless we were willing to swim for it. There was a little to explore in the pond's marshes, though as carefully as we stepped through them, all of our shoes were soaked through within minutes. This did not stop us from terrorizing a goose in order to take a large egg from its nest to raise as our own.

"Why do you get to keep it in your room?" Santiago asked me. "We can't go into Congdon."

"Because you'd build it a nest of dirty boxers," Tabi said.

"Because I have the biggest room," I said. "Come on, we have to go. It's about 5:30, almost dinnertime."

"How—"

Yara interrupted Santiago with a laugh. "Wait for it."

I pulled my Taft sweatshirt over my head, fluffed out the rough-fleece-lined hood, and held it open so that Yara could place the egg inside. Then, carefully, I wrapped the rest of the hoodie up around it until the package was small and secure in my arms, and warm enough (I thought) away from its nest.

"I'm not guessing. It's not exact, like to the minute. But it is about 5:30—that's where the sun is around this time. Sunset around sixish."

As we began walking back the way we came, Yara looked gleeful. "Ask her where she learned that."

I glared at Yara, though I didn't quite mean it. I was learning to take this type of ribbing and how to rib back too. Yara's teasing was inclusive, said on the brink of bubbling laughter, in the same tones she would use to make fun of the amount of gel Santiago used in his short spiky hair.

The rhythm of this particular conversation came easily.

"I used to do this thing at the Y with my dad—" I started.

"She loves to brag about how her dad was around for her childhood."

"Fuck you," I said, before turning back to the boys. "It was this thing for fathers and daughters in elementary school. You learn about the woods and nature and other stuff and go hiking a bunch, and you meet every week at someone's house."

"Oh, you did Girl Scouts," Santiago said.

"I tried Girl Scouts in middle school. It wasn't for me," I answered cryptically.

"The fuck does that mean?"

It meant that Evelyn Firestone and I didn't get along very well at all, and hadn't since a fight over who would be Scary Spice and who would be Sporty Spice in the fifth-grade talent show. But what really mattered here was that I was *right*, and we made it back to campus by 5:55, just five minutes before dinner started.

Still thoroughly damp, and close to uncomfortably cold now, as the temperatures dropped outside, I made a beeline for Congdon, followed by Yara and Tabi. My two friends sprawled out on my bed, and I, in my underwear, quickly transferred the goose egg to Jenna's empty desk, moving the light so it would shine directly down onto the sweatshirt nest.

Not one of us realized that an opaque sixty-watt lightbulb from Brooks wasn't going to cut it. But that didn't matter; we'd had an adventure.

● ● ●

Some days later, I was examining Crookshanks (the egg) when Rachel knocked on my door. She closed it behind her after she entered and crossed her arms.

"Why were you in my room last week?"

I turned. "During study hall?"

"No." She was frowning. "Jessica said you were in my room. I'm missing $20. Someone took it off my desk."

Jessica lived across the hallway from Rachel, and mention of her name was enough to jog an innocuous memory. "Oh, probably before we walked into town. I was looking for you."

"Why? I told you I'd be in the dining hall."

"No, you didn't."

"Yes, I did." Her frown turned into something darker, but I didn't give it the attention it deserved, nor did I know to. At that moment, imperfect Latin verbs and my inability to conjugate them when faced with one of Mr. Gorga's pop quizzes had the majority of my attention.

Rachel's attention was on me. "Well?"

"I'm sorry?" I offered halfheartedly.

"My uncle is a police officer, so I wanted to give you a chance to tell me, first, if you stole it." There were lines in Rachel's forehead when she turned on her heel and left the room.

5.

EARLY IN OUR sophomore year, two girls, one Black and one Latina (and visibly so), were expelled for an academic Honor Code violation, accused of copying off of each other and another student during a history exam. They were in my year, but there'd been little time for me to get to know them well.

Those who did were everything from misty-eyed to outright sobbing as we gathered out on the Mac House circle drive to say goodbye to Kelsey and Diana. It was a rushed farewell. The clock on their time on campus began ticking down as soon as Mr. Mac had signed off on their expulsion that morning. No longer students of Taft School, they had to pack quickly and get out before the end of the day.

"Kelsey's staying at a teacher's apartment tonight," Maura said later, once we'd gone back to my room. On the first floor of the building, it was the closest and largest retreat.

"Fuck this," Yara said. "Any other kid would have gotten a suspension, or a bunch of Sundays and Screw Crews."

"You think?" I asked.

Yara gave me a dark look. "We *know*. I watched Mr. Gatez send Jeremy to the Learning Center for a plagiarism 'rewrite' last fucking year. *Oh, you didn't* **mean** *to copy, you just didn't understand the assignment, right?"*

"And you know why she's staying at a teacher's place, right?" Still so new at Taft, Maura simply looked sad. She'd known Diana from Prep 9. "I heard in Mrs. Gallagher's office it's 'cause they didn't tell her parents she was getting expelled before they told her. She's not from around here. She can't get *home*. They wouldn't let her spend another night in the dorm while her parents figured it out; like her ticket and money and stuff. It's bad…it's really bad." Whether she'd heard correctly or not, the news clearly had her shaken.

Getting kicked out of Taft—or any independent school—is absolutely *not* the worst thing that can happen to a person. Since prep schools seem to rarely suspend or expel kids for doing something *actually* bad (St. Paul's in New Hampshire, for instance, allegedly covered up campus sexual assault incidents for *decades*; instead of facing charges from the state's attorney general, the school reached a settlement subjecting them to period of government oversight), all it means is that you probably did something that normal teenagers across America were doing every weekend, but forgot you were on a boarding school campus and not behind the local Wawa on a Saturday night (or in the master cabin on your parents' docked yacht—whatever happens to be the local Wawa of your heart). But when you enter a school that prides itself on providing everything that you could possibly need, that place quickly becomes your entire life, especially if you live there. We called it the Taft Bubble, and to be ejected from that unique ecosystem forcefully rather than ceremoniously matriculated was the equivalent of having your carotid pierced. White students always seemed to be given more opportunity to stanch the bleeding than the rest of us.

And so when Rachel continued to corner me about her $20 over the remainder of that week, invoking her uncle several times, I could see the writing on the wall and I was honestly terrified. At one point, she said she'd found my fingerprints on her things and implied that she was ready to send them off to have them identified.

Eventually, Rachel told someone, a campus adult, that I had stolen $20 from her room. That adult—probably one of our dorm parents—reported the incident to Mr. Tunstall, the dean who handled Honor Code violations.

"An Honor Code violation has been brought to our attention," he informed me after I sat down in front of his desk. "Did you take $20 from Rachel's room?"

The word "theft" was never used, nor was it ever said that I "stole" anything. He preferred the clunkier phrase "took something that did not belong to you." Over the next week I would hear adults conjugate that one verb multiple times over. I even started to do it myself.

"**Taking** something that does not belong to you goes against the school's social contract, held together by our Honor Code."

"She **took** it from a classmate's room."

"Well, that $20 didn't walk away by itself—it was **taken**." Like a group of hardened criminals had absconded with a checkbook belonging to Liam Neeson's daughter.

That afternoon I answered Mr. Tunstall, "No." I was already flop-sweating, understanding the consequences of an Honor Code violation thanks to Kelsey and Diana. "I told her that when she asked me."

He was silent for a moment. "Are you sure? If you're lying, Kendra, that would be a *second* Honor Code violation, and the consequences would be more severe." When I didn't immediately reply to his question, Mr. Tunstall continued, saying, "Rachel has mentioned that there's evidence."

"She told me that she was going to send fingerprints to her uncle at a police station." This was a silly thing to admit, in retrospect, but I couldn't help it as my heart began to race, as it dawned on me that it was likely Rachel had not been bluffing—not if she'd gone to the administration with claims of evidence. This had to be more than simply one girl telling another that she'd seen me looking for someone.

Mr. Tunstall nodded but did not ask the follow-up question that even my few years working with school-aged children would beg me to ask: *Wait—the police are involved? On my campus? And I, the person handling student discipline, don't know about it?*

It wasn't even until I was a junior or senior in college that I thought back and realized that someone—a student or an administrator—invoking the police in a high school dispute over $20 was *very* strange. I sat in a cultural anthropology class, thinking about this incident for the first time since it had happened as I debated whether to share the story during a class discussion about race and education, and the inequities that Black children, especially Black girls, faced when it came to punishment in educational settings. The internal acknowledgment of my own connection to the material pulled me under like a strong undertow, and I did not share with the class. Much like when I sat in Mr. Tunstall's office, I was too busy catching my breath.

"My dad is going to beat me," I said softly. The words, literally the first to come to mind, were not an attempt to manipulate, scare, or tarnish my father's good name; this was resignation, as I consciously decided not to fight. It seemed pointless.

I suspect my decision was visible in real time. The sweat soaking through my armpits, back, and crotch would have given it away. (I'm a crotch-sweater when I get nervous, a thing I've always figured it's just better to admit outright rather than have folks think I've wet myself.) I was quick to start blinking back tears, never someone to cry in front of others. My chest was tight, like it got sometimes after skating in a frigid rink. My pediatrician called this exercise-induced asthma, and I'd been prescribed an albuterol inhaler. But, like my EpiPen, I rarely carried it around like I was supposed to. I would have happily sucked it down then.

I knew my parents would believe the school and Rachel. First of all, I didn't really talk to them about *feelings*. Anything much beyond "I like this," "I don't like that," and "oh my God, I hate you, leave me alone!" went in my journal, where emotions could be laid bare and punctuated by something other than the slamming of my bedroom door. I don't think that's terribly uncommon for a teenager, especially when considering the often emotionally fraught relationships between teenage girls and their mothers. Second, I am perfectly comfortable admitting that there was a time when I thought very little of lifting $5 or $10 from my parents' wallets, or a handful of quarters from a basement change jar in order to afford the sugary Dunkin' Donuts and Starbucks confections I shared with friends on our walks home from middle school. (Never from stores, though; I took an organic fruit leather from a Whole Foods checkout line *once* in middle school, and got whooped within an inch of my life—*with* company in the house!) And it wasn't a big deal until it was a *big deal* and they noticed a few months in, at which point I would be punished—hence the beatings—and the cycle would begin anew. But I'd shed that cycle at some point in middle school to make way for the next fifteen years of resulting stress and the occasional surprise nightmare.

Mr. Tunstall did not respond to my statement, either not hearing me or simply not having the words. "You will have to attend Honor Court next week," he said. "And you'll need to apologize to Rachel, and return her belongings, of course."

I was tempted to ask for it to happen immediately. The approaching Saturday and Sunday were an open parents' weekend.

I would have happily gone to Honor Court that night, been told that I was expelled, and then simply packed my things and had my parents take me home in shame on Saturday morning. The police were involved, and while I usually had some scheme in mind to get out of trouble (or, at the very least, mitigate it), the options I often employed at home (general blackmail, running away and taking my younger brother *with* me, or threatening to tell an adult at school about the type of punishment I'd been given) weren't options here; nothing in my boarding school literary lessons had prepared me for this. Why prolong things?

I was nauseous when I left Mr. Tunstall's office, adrift and thoroughly at a loss for what to do, aside from focusing intently on the dread creeping up the back of my throat, tinged in bile and the sour bite of shame. The main hallway spun around me as I walked down and through to the dining hall to get back to my room in Congdon. I may have tried to stop in at Mrs. Gallagher's office, looking for the one adult on campus I figured was supposed to be in my corner no matter what, but I honestly recall very little of what happened between my meeting with Mr. Tunstall and the moment when my parents arrived that weekend, finding me sobbing and shaking and gasping for air in the midst of a full panic attack in the infirmary after both confessing and presenting Rachel with a $20 bill.

I don't know what their reaction should have been. I'm not sure that I would know even if I had children of my own. It is, among other things, hard to place myself in the headspace of a 2004 parent. If a school now told me that another student had threatened to send my child's fingerprints to the police (which I had assumed they'd told my parents, at the time) and that they were now using that evidence to consider punitive action, I would at the very least consider meeting with a lawyer.

"Well, at least you told the truth. Thank goodness for small favors.

God *damn it*, Kendra…" they both repeated in between many rounds of both straightforward and creatively phrased versions of "We're so disappointed." My parents were pissed, obviously. I had ruined this entire experience, tarnished their reputations, and potentially walked myself right out of First Black™ status.

"The truth" was already determined, had been since Rachel entered my room and declared that her uncle was a cop. I knew that my parents were primed to accept the same truth Taft did, and saying that I hadn't done anything was futile, I thought. Besides, they had my fingerprints from Rachel's room.

Someone made me leave the infirmary, eventually. Parents' weekend usually featured a number of sporting events, and subsequently at least a few injuries. Others needed that bed more than I did.

● ● ●

Taft did not make me wait long to attend Honor Court.

I must assume my friends knew something was up. I was quiet and withdrawn in classes and at dinner. My crotch and armpits were constantly soaked. If nothing else, Taft was a small place and news spread as quickly as oral gonorrhea, mutating just slightly each time it was passed from table to table in the dining hall.

I wore the most normcore clothes I had: an appropriately hemmed khaki skirt and a collared shirt from the Gap. I pulled a flatiron across the kitchen at the nape of my neck enough times to do permanent damage.

Honor Courts were at night, on one of the high tower floors near the day-student lounge. The small, circular brick room felt castle-like, and in that moment reminded me of the Tower of London. The "court" was made up of a jury of one's supposed peers and a few faculty members, and those accused were represented by their faculty advisor and a member of their class. Mrs. Gallagher was there, along with Lucy, another sophomore who would be acting as my student representative. She tried to be kind and reminded me to tell the truth once we got into the room, assuring me that if I did everything would be fine.

The court, along with those who spoke on students' behalf, would then be responsible for making a disciplinary suggestion. I do not remember if there were any other Black students or students of color on this panel. I hope there were.

One of the adults on the court was responsible for reading a statement explaining why we were all gathered there that evening, detailing Rachel's accusation of my $20 theft from her dorm room and noting that proof to that effect had been obtained. Plus, they added, another student, Jessica, had seen me at Rachel's room before the money had gone missing.

I was asked, then, for a more formal confession than what I had given Mr. Tunstall, and warned once again that due to the Honor Code, lying would compound whatever punishment I was already facing.

"She owed me $20," I said. "And since she wouldn't pay what she owed me, I just took it. But I know I shouldn't have, and I apologized to her this week. I'm very sorry; I really am."

After all, I understood the idea of revenge.

And so I was suspended rather than being expelled entirely, preserving my status at school and my ability to eventually get into college, all for the fair price of a bit of dignity and my long-term mental health.

6.

I HAVE NO doubt that Rachel's money was indeed stolen, taken, or borrowed, whatever your preferred verb is. In a completely unrelated incident, a girl in Mac House was caught stealing credit cards to make online purchases—these things *did* happen.

Still, there are a plethora of questions I never asked because these are questions I, a sixteen-year-old student, a minor, should not have been responsible for asking. Did Rachel's police officer uncle even exist? What was this uncle's name? What police department did this uncle work for? Had she really found my fingerprints? Had *he* found my fingerprints? Had she filed a police report? Should I be speaking on the matter without a lawyer present? Why was it considered okay for one student to threaten another with police involvement over a missing $20? If this uncle did exist, did he really think it was appropriate to get involved in his niece's nonviolent, one-off dispute with another teenager, and if so, why? Finally, if an adult did not have the answers to these questions readily available, then why on earth was the involvement of Cop Uncle going unquestioned while speaking with a minor?

Even after doing the therapeutic equivalent of swallowing a bottle of Drano, I still have trouble parsing the event, thinking about how easily I gave up and how very little I stood up for myself. It was, in that way, partially a problem of my own making because I *didn't* say anything—I can cop to that now (*hah*). But it is dehumanizing, even in a world where we have grown much more accustomed to discussing things like police abolition and shouting "ACAB" while marching down a freeway during LA rush hour, to admit that the police have been even marginally—*so* marginally in comparison—pitted against you like this.

More, it feels incredibly insignificant and embarrassing to have dwelled on, given the level of privilege I had, and continued to have following what happened. Like this should not be something that I've felt so emotionally blocked by for so long. It feels both superficial and shameful to have carried, for as long as I have, this incident that had little to no negative consequence on my life going forward and did not prevent me from accomplishing any of the things I wanted to do.

I can only assume that Rachel persisted so she could feel as though she'd receive the justice due to her—something had been taken from her. She had been wronged. She wanted it made right. She was a perfectly nice girl otherwise, so I *get* that and I afford her the same grace I afford myself, when I think back to some of the terrible things my holier-than-thou attitude led me to say and believe in my early days at Taft. Besides, if I didn't choose to assume she was just following what she thought was the best course of action at the time, then I wouldn't have ever stopped being angry.

But what I'm still enraged about is how the Honor Code was not applied equally; I find myself thinking about Diana and Kelsey too often for girls I barely knew. This probably comes as no surprise to any Black person who has ever gotten into trouble at a mostly white institution. It is arguably impossible to have a fairly functioning Honor Code—one that essentially operates on a two-strike policy—if even some of your staff are not aware of their own implicit biases and have the tools and practice to overcome them. In 2004 they did not. In 2020 it feels as though that toolkit is still in the process of being assembled, too uneven and too reactionary to approach being actually useful.

Much later on, when I started working at $S^3 4$, my face wrinkled each time I walked past the security desks that greeted people when they entered some of the fancy New York City schools we worked out of. They reminded me not of the welcoming, dark oak confines of the admissions reception room at Taft, but of the security desks at the NYPD precinct by my apartment in Harlem. I disliked that any school, especially another fancy prep school, would even want to evoke the idea of policing.

We would get complaints every so often, especially on weekdays when school was in session and the whiteness truly became over-whelming. Black and brown parents who would accuse security of profiling them as suspicious, when in reality they were simply there to pick up their children or learn more about the program. Their only crime was not looking like the parents the school's security staff, often Black and brown themselves, were used to seeing.

Around the same time, my mother began ratcheting up her com-plaints about the security desk in Columbia back in Maplewood. Kyle was there now and she hated that desk. She talked about it often, and I was prone to simply brushing her concerns aside, even going so far as to tell her that she was being "very dramatic" about the whole thing. To agree with her would have given away too much. She might have asked what caused my change of heart, allowing for the possibility that we might have had to speak about what I had gone through at Taft. I might have had to ask the questions that I wasn't ready to ask then, nearly a decade later. I might have also had to allow myself to be angry at both her and my father for not knowing to ask those questions themselves.

Guilt guided my hand too, just as steadily. Even as I was rolling my eyes at my mother's observations, I was telling myself that, all things considered, I'd come away from my own experience relatively unscathed. I hadn't even had the worst outcome you could have at Taft. Confessing and apologizing to Rachel had saved me from expulsion, but so did, I suspect, being a legacy and the child of a former trustee. I was privileged and lucky.

● ● ●

My father came to pick me up in his Pathfinder for my one-week suspension. I didn't bring much home with me—just my laptop and a stuffed L.L.Bean backpack. It was only a week after all; on the surface, the most inconvenienced person was my father, who would have to make this two-hour trip twice in six days.

After a requisite "I think it goes without saying that you are grounded," the drive was silent.

At home, I waited for more punishment to come; it never did. When I'm feeling generous, I wonder if it is because my parents also thought something about the whole situation was suspect. For the most part, though, I just assume it had more to do with my dad not wanting me to arrive back at Taft telling those fancy white people stories of belts and brushes. Instead, I was banished, with an abundance of parental disappointment, to my bedroom. This was fine for me; it's where I'd spent all of my pre-Taft time anyway. My room still held the desktop computer that I'd won on *Jeopardy!* I did schoolwork on my laptop and took out my frustrations on the desktop, writing short one-off fanfics that all coincidentally featured young girls working through situations similar to mine. But with mutant powers or magic to help.

In the immediate aftermath of my suspension, my journaling—putting tangible feelings down on the page—took a back seat to this more whimsical method of processing through the written word. But soon journaling and documenting my days would turn from the benign habit of a budding writer to a full-blown obsession. Instead of, for instance, just saving the AIM conversations that seemed important or contained a joke that made me laugh so hard I *Alex Mack*-ed my way from the desk chair to the floor, I saved *every* AIM conversation, even the ones that consisted of no more than two exchanged hellos. Eventually, I was able to install something that automated the process, and my computer began saving and archiving messages itself.

When I showed her my files as we were about to graduate, Yara said, as usual, that this was absolutely batshit weirdo behavior. So did my mom, when years later she stumbled across an old binder in my childhood bedroom that held conversations from as far back as the seventh and eighth grades, including some with my old French teacher (which, to be fair, also concerned her). But comprehensive documentation had become an extremely reassuring habit.

Mostly, what this obsessive compiling has done has made it easier for me to look back on how I've changed—forcing me to acknowledge things like the gross realities of what a Talented-Tenth-respectability-obsessed snob I was through my own words and observations. But at the time, it just made me feel safer, because I figured that if the entire world knew what I was up to, it would be a lot harder for anyone in the future to say I'd done something that I hadn't. Sometimes, I still whisper a reminder to myself that it is okay—even *better*—for moments to be ephemeral.

The rest of my week at home was fairly typical for a teenager on punishment. I told a select few friends I'd never met face-to-face, scattered across the world, what had happened—they would have noticed, anyway, when the internet didn't go off at 10 p.m.—and took some solace in the sympathies and retaliatory suggestions expressed between bouts of game plotting. I completed the schoolwork I was assigned. I sat silently at the dinner table each night. I didn't complain when my parents took advantage of the free childcare I was able to provide. I missed that week's episodes of *Charmed* and *Angel* due to a lack of TV privileges. I purposely broke my doorknob and pretended not to know what had happened when it was suddenly impossible for anyone to open my bedroom door and my dad had to climb a ladder and shimmy through my second-story window to fix it. Because underneath it all I was still pissed at them and this whole situation, and being forced to scale a ladder in one's late forties seemed like a manageable, appropriate amount of revenge. I was glad he wasn't hurt (mostly) but also disappointed they hadn't had to spend money on a locksmith.

Taft got its own small comeuppance as well.

"Kendra, what's this about an egg?" my mother asked the afternoon before I was set to go back to school. She was just hanging up the kitchen landline when I walked into the room. In the moment, I truly didn't know what she was talking about, and said as much.

She was clearly annoyed. "An egg, Kendra. Your dorm parent found a rotting egg in your room at school."

"Oh!" Recognition hit. "Crookshanks. Wait—Crookshanks is dead?"

"*Crookshanks?!*"

"The egg. She's a goose."

"There was a smell, Kendra," my mother said, her voice becoming tight. "A smell coming from your room! She said there was an egg sitting on a desk, basically cooking under a desk lamp!"

"Oh, yeah," I said. "We were trying to hatch it."

"You were—" she sputtered. "Who is 'we'?"

"Me, Yara, and Tabi. Maura's supposed to be watching it this week."

She took a breath. "When they removed it, it broke."

"Oh?"

"You need to get it together, Kendra," my mom said through gritted teeth. "Get it together up there. No more nonsense."

Later, I would find out that whoever had gone in to investigate the smell had found the egg sitting where I'd left it on Jenna's old desk. It was so old, fermented, and vile by that point that when they attempted to pick it up it had partially broken open in their hands, sending the smell of rotting egg and partially developed goose through the hall.

I was fine with this.

7.

FIVE YEARS BEFORE I started at Taft, Amadou Diallo was shot and killed by New York City police officers. Every night for weeks, I watched anchors report the story on the local NBC news. When I returned to the Diallo case in the wake of Mike Brown's horrific death in Ferguson and then again when Eric Garner's killers were acquitted, I was surprised at the amount and the accuracy of information I remembered. The number of bullets fired versus the number that actually hit the twenty-three-year-old Guinean immigrant. The $61 million his parents had eventually sued the city for, compared to the paltry $3 million they'd received for the death of their beloved son. Which borough Diallo had lived in, and even the last names of two of the officers involved—Boss and Carroll.

I was asked to appear on a panel in the days after yet another acquittal in a case of police brutality briefly made the news. At that point, I saw myself as more of a part-time entertainment journalist, not political. The best thing I'd written that past year had been a retrospective of the way race was handled through all six seasons (and two movies) of *Dr. Quinn, Medicine Woman*, and so I was hesitant to discuss anything as serious as police brutality.

At the time I was about four or five months into a new job, serving as an admissions officer for an independent day school just north of the Tappan Zee.

In my previous job at Scholars Striving 4 Success, we may not have always given a full picture of the truth, but every person there at least believed in the mission we were working toward of leveling the playing field in education for low-income students of color in New York City. We were almost all people of color ourselves; the majority were Black and Latinx. When the George Zimmerman trial started, one of us would often livestream testimony during our lunch breaks so that our small department could watch and discuss together.

My colleagues there were always supportive concerning my side hustle as a writer. After I penned an article about education and privilege that went viral, my boss practically shoved me out the door when a TV network called out of the blue and asked me to appear on air from their DC studios the next day.

My new position as an admissions officer did cross my mind when I turned down the panel invitation. But, as the internet's resident *Dr. Quinn* expert, I mostly just didn't feel like I was qualified to speak on the matter.

The Monday after the panel aired, I mentioned it to one of the school's English teachers.

"It's good you turned it down," she said in response. "A lot of parents would be concerned, you know—hearing any of their admissions staff speak about a case like that."

"Oh, I mean, I doubt I would have said anything wildly controversial or anything," I said. "Like, it was just to talk about the injustice done and sort of lay out a timeline of what's been going on this year. This fucking *year.*"

She nodded. "Exactly. The officer was acquitted."

"Right."

"So, then speaking publicly about it being unjust *is* controversial. You don't want to ruffle any feathers, and even if they do agree, what if a student sees you and asks their parents about it? That's forcing a conversation they may not have been planning to have."

Later, I would have pushed back at that statement. But when later came—at a different school and one that I loved—after Philando Castile was killed the summer before Trump was elected into office, the same question never presented itself, because race and social justice were on everyone's lips, even at that majority white, wealthy, New York City independent school.

Imagine not talking to your child about Breonna Taylor, George Floyd, or Jacob Blake, and leaving them that ignorant of national events, not to mention an entire history's worth of systematic racism.

But then, everything I knew as a kid about Amadou Diallo had been imparted to me by Sue Simmons, a twenty-two-year veteran of WNBC New York, not Andrew or Lynn James.

● ● ●

My mom sat me down to watch *Eyes on the Prize* at some point in kindergarten or first grade. Someone secured me a youth membership to the NAACP at birth. I received an Addy doll the very first Christmas she was available, having made my way through all six American Girl doll books cataloging her life from a child born into American chattel slavery to running away and becoming a free preteen in Philadelphia. At five years old, the scene in her first book where a plantation overseer forced her to eat the live grubs she failed to remove from the bottom of a tobacco plant scarred me.

The Maplewood library carried a series of children's biographies whose titles began *A Picture Book of...* by author David Adler and I would sit in the aisles and read them over and over again. I remember the hunk of iron thrown by an angry plantation owner that concussed a young Harriet Tubman, the illustrations of a young Frederick Douglass screaming in a closet as his aunt was whipped, Adolf Hitler turning his back on Jesse Owens because he didn't want to shake the hand of a Black man.

The history of racism in America had hardly been kept a secret from me, but growing up my biggest fear was the strange older woman who lived at the end of our street; I thought she was a witch. There is a balance Black parents are continuously working at, I think, trying to find the proper amount of awareness and hesitance to instill in their children. Enough to keep them safe, but not enough to prevent them from wanting to experience the world as fully as their white peers might. It evolves over time, family by family, but no one has the *right* answer.

In the future, I think my answer will involve repetitive frankness. This is partially because I am a part of an American generation groomed to announce everything from their engagement to an abnormally long period of menstruation in no more than 280 characters, or no less than a 2,500-word personal essay. We are not a filtered people, and I don't see myself repeating what I see as my parents' misstep of not deliberately discussing racism within the frame of current events.

Even without my father's direct connection to the Taft experience, I still had two parents who attended New England colleges in the 1970s. Navigating the world of white education as young people was a well-trod path for them, and like a Tusken Raider I followed in their footsteps precisely. But we did not talk about it.

I told my parents about how classes were going, often excited about one subject or another when I had a particularly compelling teacher. I'd tell them about our trips to the mall (and even the R-rated movies we went to see!) and the adventures we would have on our walks around Watertown.

Sometimes I'd drop a hint that something had gone awry, like when Kelsey and Diana had been kicked out. But my parents' reactions were never what I wanted, I suppose. Or, at least, they did not outwardly mirror the outrage, anger, and sadness of myself or my friends over losing friends in what we deemed to be a terribly unfair way. There were so few of us.

"Trust" is so loaded a word, especially when it comes to the bonds between parents and children. I still mostly trusted both of my parents then, but not when it came to broaching the subject of race, and I certainly did not know how to say even *that*. At Taft, I watched constantly as my friends did all the things my mother insisted were terrible. You could wear a durag and baggy jeans and listen to nothing but Ludacris *and* still be a brilliant student. You could have the straightest, shiniest permed hair, follow all the rules to the letter, pronounce your "ings" and "ers," and still end up being victimized by your mostly white institution of higher learning. Go figure.

Much like my future prospective students at S³4, Andrew and Lynn did not hear about how wary I was of Taft's white students after my sophomore year. They did not hear about how I felt invisible to the opposite sex at Taft, or about how interschool dances that bused in enough Black kids to *create* a dance both thrilled me and made me feel like even more of an outsider. I did not tell them about the numerous racist comments—innocent and not—I often heard from white girls in the locker rooms or on the field. I didn't even muster up the courage to express something as simple as that I hated having permed hair until the summer after my freshman year of college, because I did not think my mom would have approved.

I wish we had all been equipped to give each other more.

UPPER MID

1.

PLEASE UNDERSTAND HOW deeply pleasing it would be, for the sheer sake of narrative and my own ego, to say that my first year at Taft radicalized me. That I arrived home armed with a righteous anger and a real understanding of the word "racism" for the first time. That I spent the summer in my bedroom reading *The Autobiography of Malcolm X* instead of zooming through the latest in the Confessions of Georgia Nicolson series and trying desperately to see what everyone else was seeing in that damn *Eragon* book in between stacks of Susan Krinard paperbacks (she wrote the only werewolf romance novels worth reading at the time, as far as I was concerned).

I'm sure it would be more satisfying, even, to hear me say that instead of spending the summer vanishing entirely into the world of online role-playing after my summer job as a camp counselor at the local YMCA, I spent three months plotting the ways in which I would rain down vengeance upon Rachel, Mr. Tunstall, Mr. Mac, Taft, and the concept of boarding schools in general.

It would have been convenient had I arrived home and

demanded an immediate trip to Pam's, where I would cut off the perm that I would later decide symbolized all those respectability politics I had been brought up with. That I spent these three free months in a training montage, working toward becoming the most militant version of myself. I wore plenty of black already.

I did none of this that summer, instead continuing to mark the passage of time by journaling and writing extensively in online *X-Men* RPGs, collaborative world-building games where I would move multiple characters across a fictional world with friends across the real one. I spent most of my time writing long, angst-filled journal entries, not from my own point of view, but from those of the various mutant teen characters I played. Along with fan fiction, role-playing became another perfect escape from what had happened at Taft.

Some adult should have sat me down and forced me to process my feelings—whether they thought I was guilty or not, it had been an *event*. But since they didn't, I didn't either. And when I finally had to acknowledge the real world, it was as a glorified babysitter, chasing small children across our suburb's many parks and helping them master floating on their backs—or at the very least, keeping them from drowning—in the pools at the Maplewood Country Club for $10.50 an hour from the local YMCA.

I kissed a boy (a fellow counselor) and accepted nearly $400 in cash tips from the satisfied parents of campers at the end of August. We weren't supposed to take the cash that parents would slide us inside envelopes, thank-you cards, and even one empty cigarette carton, said the Y, but everyone did. Still conscious of Rachel's accusations, I squirreled the cash away in my room like Claudia Kishi hiding candy in a hollowed-out dictionary, so well done that I misplaced $60 until spring break next year.

Rachel's name would come to mind, yes, but not on purpose. Never aloud. Perhaps they simply assumed that I had learned my lesson, and thus, it never had to come up again. There was a point in my early twenties when, sure that it was impossible for the incident to have never been raised again, I had convinced myself that surely we *had* spoken about it—perhaps even had lengthy conversations or even sessions of family counseling that I had simply blocked out because *I* was the one still harboring ill will and resentment.

(This did not happen. As I learned during my parents' Very Stereotypically Nasty Suburban Divorce, therapy and counseling were not things my father naturally cottons to.)

Even now, years later living the life I dreamed of, I have to remind myself that it is *okay* to remember Taft as it *was*, not as I wanted it to be; I can be upset about parts of my experience. Like many Black people, the life I dreamed of was paid for with the American currency of a minor trauma.

Instead, we talked, in general terms, about having a "good year," because this, my junior year, was an "important" one. Underneath all the talk of "good" and "important," the message was clear: I needed to have a year that would draw attention away from my failure of sophomore spring. It was almost time to apply for college.

● ● ●

My parents brought me back to Taft right after Labor Day, early once again. But this time, instead of arriving to attend a mandatory orientation Q&A, I was there to help make one happen. These were the sorts of extracurriculars that would begin to help correct my record.

With my parents off socializing in the dining hall again, I walked back into the same wood-paneled room from the year before. I knew it now as my history classroom, a place where any student caught kicking off the flip-flops they weren't supposed to be wearing after Thanksgiving break risked a nimble teacher snatching them up and casually chucking them out the window into a snowbank while seamlessly continuing to lecture. But now, once again, it was the room that would hold almost every new Black and brown student on campus for the students of color orientation.

"What the fuck, where have you *been?*"

"*Yara!*"

The room was just as loud as it had been the year before, teeming with a diversity of voices and speech patterns that now made me feel at home.

Mrs. Gallagher mouthed, "Language!" at the back of Yara's head as we hugged, grabbing on for dear life. We lived maybe an hour from each other—two, if we relied solely on public transportation—but Yara and I hadn't hung out at all that summer. Sam and I lived even closer, but when he and Santiago walked into the room our group hug had to make room because I hadn't seen them either.

"Okay, but really, where the fuck have you been?" Yara repeated, once we all broke apart.

"What do you mean?"

"I thought you were gonna ask to switch to Centen."

"I thought *you* were gonna ask to switch to Voge!" I shot back, incredulous.

Yara and I had put in a request to room together, as every student did to indicate their desire for a roommate or a single on a form we turned in to our class deans. When my assignment had arrived in early August, it was clear that our request had been ignored. I logged onto AIM that day for my daily talk with Yara and was dismayed to find out that we hadn't even been placed in the same *building*.

My belongings were already strewn across a first-floor room

in Vogelstein, the newest dorm on campus at that point. It was gorgeous, red brick like the rest and on the opposite side of the pond from my room in Congdon. The rooms there weren't so lived in, and the tile in the bathrooms was still bright white. Most important, instead of having a traditional roommate situation, Voge roommates live in "suites"—two rooms separated by a door that each pair could choose to leave open or closed at their discretion. Voge (pronounced like the magazine) was the campus hotel, *and* it was closer to the Jig.

Upon realizing how far away from each other we'd be (Centennial, known as Centen, was at the base of the hill that led up to the gym—practically light-years away), I had suggested that Yara try to switch into Voge. It was nicer, and thus the obvious choice. But clearly, our wires had crossed.

I rolled my eyes. "Why would I switch *out* of Voge?"

"That's insane," Sam agreed. "That's like moving out of the boys' senior dorm."

That dorm had the distinction of being the only freestanding boys' dorm on campus—and for good reason. Rumor had it that seniors got up to and away with absolute murder there as it was far too easy to sneak out of. Unsurprisingly, it has since become a girls' dorm.

"Who's living next to you?" Yara asked.

"I think I saw Margot—you know, the one whose parents are ambassadors or diplomats or something?" I said. "But it's definitely a suite next to me, and I don't know who her roomie is."

"Margot? Like, Margot Lewis? Diplomats?"

"That's what I thought I heard last year. Margot from Milan? Or Munich, right?"

"She's from New York; we did Prep together." Santiago smirked. "I can't believe you fell for that," he added, before glancing over at the door where other students were streaming into the classroom. I recognized some of them as other juniors and sophomores who had returned to answer questions, and others as wide-eyed, nervous-looking newbies. Santiago waved at a fellow junior. "Yo, Mike!"

"Do we know where Tabi is?" I asked as the room started to settle.

"Congdon, maybe?" Yara said.

"Mac House," Sam answered, too confidently.

"I meant like, is she here yet?"

"Tomorrow," Sam jumped in again. "She's not doing orientation; her flight gets in tonight."

Mike looked over at him. "Are you her dorm mom or something?"

Sam just shrugged as Mrs. Gallagher began the first of no less than fifteen attempts to get the room quiet and under control.

There were plenty of new faces, and I tried to memorize their name tags so when they inevitably found themselves sitting with us in the dining hall later, I would be able to greet them like a friend. I had come to understand the inevitability of social segregation. I even appreciated it, perhaps. We were loyal; we kept each other safe. And those who weren't or couldn't simply didn't have to be on my radar anymore—I did not lament Francine's absence from this room, but I certainly clocked it. Tamia wasn't there either; at some point she vanished from the school entirely.

That year's orientation was nearly identical to the one the year before, except this time I understood the inside jokes. Knew when to laugh or snicker when one poor freshman with a head full of braids asked where she could go to get them taken out and redone. Caught on to the careful use of "they" or "other students" when talking about our white contemporaries. Read between the lines from my own firsthand experience that when Mrs. Gallagher spoke about "differences" between us and those "other students" she meant "racism."

In the interest of having that mythical "good year," I'd signed up early for Taft's Admissions Council—a fancy name for the group of students who gave campus tours to prospies and their parents.

"Anyone who signed up for a tour can follow Kendra and Thalia," Mrs. Gallagher announced once we were done taking questions.

Thalia was a senior from—yes, you guessed it—Prep 9. Before the three students who had requested tours joined us, we quickly decided that I would take one girl, Esther, while Thalia took the others. They all played volleyball and would have that to talk about. Esther and I were both from New Jersey.

"Cherry Hill," Esther confirmed when I asked.

"Oh cool, I'm from Maplewood!" I wondered, briefly, if she'd come from NJ SEEDS like Sam, but I didn't want to assume. Others did the same to me, and even if the reality of the numbers *did* make it a perfectly reasonable assumption, I still found it annoying. After a year at Taft I understood, a little bit at least, why my dad kept talking about the importance of a "diversity of recruitment" as a basis for the school's diversity work as a whole.

We turned left, walking down the glossy stone hall to Lincoln Lobby, a hub of activity at Taft that connected the auditorium, the upper boys' dorms, classrooms, and Voge. It was named for a bust of the president, which sat atop a short set of stairs, and it was lined with grand wood-carved meeting rooms filled with gorgeous, early-century fireplaces that I was not old enough to appreciate at the time, endless built-in bookshelves, plush rugs underfoot that muffled, just slightly, the noise of the original wooden floors beneath them. I am shocked teenagers were ever allowed to gather in these spaces for student coffeehouses or dances.

There was an art room too, Potter's Gallery, the same namesake of the pond outside, where through the glass doors you could always see what was on display. Sometimes simply student art, other times a visiting photographer, or a group of monks setting up shop to create a sand mandala for a week or two.

Past Potter's we made another left and took a shortcut to enter the Harley Roberts Room, the admissions welcoming space where the petite Mrs. Frances and her 1970s Mary Tyler Moore haircut ruled with a gentle touch. Her domain was always open as an escape if the day became overwhelming, and she would welcome you with snacks and a plush window seat, until you made the mistake of putting a sneaker on her upholstery. Those of us who respected her rules were able to hang out and drink the best selection of tea on campus undisturbed, sometimes in front of a roaring fire. Being the extremely normal sixteen-year-old that I was, tea selection was very important to me.

After picking up Esther's parents we stepped back out into a busier hallway than we'd left. FLIK staffers were suggesting to families—as aggressively as any nonfaculty campus workers could ever suggest anything to Taft families—that they vacate the dining hall, and so the halls were full of students, parents, and siblings making their way back to the dormitories.

Every office lining the hall belonged to an administrator. I pointed out the assistant headmaster's office, and the door just beyond his where the college counselors' lounge would have been hidden, had every door not been splayed wide open and welcoming.

"You have comics in already!" Ms. Hardy, the mailroom head, waved and shouted as we walked by the front mail booth. "And something from Australia—nice vacation, eh?"

"Pen pal!" I called back, knowing that the idea of students sending handwritten letters would delight the older woman. "I'll come get everything before dinner!"

We pushed on, passing two deans' offices, Mr. Huston and Mrs. Beard, one of my softball coaches from the spring before. She was talking to a group of parents and students I didn't recognize, but when she saw me, she made a point of poking her head around them and waving an enthusiastic hello.

Mr. Mac waved too, from his secretary's office, a large space, almost as ornate as the admissions room. So did Mrs. Myers, our sole art teacher, whom we passed as she was making her way up the stairs to the massive lofted art classroom that sat above the dining hall.

"You said this was just your second year?" Esther's father commented after Mrs. Myers turned and continued up the stairs, greeting another student and their much younger sister on the way.

"Yeah, but it's a really small school and everyone kind of just knows everyone," I said, leading us into the dining hall.

I was hardly the only student receiving these effusive greetings. When we walked into the dining hall the same scenes were happening en masse, but I had been *suspended* the year before. Aside from a routine fifteen-to-twenty-minute "Welcome back to campus, here is what it means now that you've had an Honor Code violation, and I'm sure, given all the lessons learned, we won't have any problems going forward" chat with Mr. Mac, there had been no follow-up about the Rachel incident, but I wasn't allowing myself to be tricked. I expected it to come up again. I thought at least Mrs. Gallagher would certainly pull me aside to encourage me to have a "better year" this time around, but that did not seem to be the case.

If Taft liked to tout the belief that serving out a punishment for one's supposed crime fully redeemed you in the eyes of a community and restored all your rights and privileges therein— thus making the concept of Honor Court more effective, in some ways, than the entire American criminal justice system, I *guess?*— who was I to challenge that, as it played out before my eyes?

"I've also been up to campus a lot, since I was a kid," I offered Esther's parents, for lack of any other explanation. "My dad went here."

I showed the school off to the new family (keeping the color commentary to myself) before returning them to the Harley Roberts Room and then retreating back to Voge, where I hoped to hang out with Yara more before dinner.

● ● ●

If Chip and Joanna Gaines had been redesigning high school dormitories in the early aughts, they might have given you something like Voge; there was not much charm or character to the interiors of the rooms. Behind the brick exterior that matched every other building on campus, there was a series of stark white dorms. Singles and doubles-that-weren't-quite lined gray slate hallways with wood-paneled walls. The common areas had fireplaces we would certainly be suspended for trying to use, and high ceilings vaulted with visible wooden beams that gave an almost church-like feeling. Honestly, a little shiplap would have spiced the place up.

Voge was a space that encouraged quietness, if only because the acoustics were *too* good. A giggle over an inside joke or a gasp as you enjoyed a VHS recording of last night's episode of *Lost* could travel forever. Even from behind walls and closed doors, I always knew when the girls next door were home, and I'm sure they could have said the same for me, especially when Yara was over.

"I missed you, dumbass," she said when she arrived, slamming my door shut behind her. The noise echoed through the hall.

I was at the base of my twin XL bed, sitting on my knees as I carefully affixed my bulletin board to the wall. "We IM'd each other like every day."

"I meant since you left to give tours." She laughed. "I thought I was gonna help you hang stuff while we watched *Dogma.*"

My friend never decorated her own space quite like I did. That summer, I'd carefully preserved magazine covers and photoshoot spreads, printed new images from the internet, and dutifully bought the *Wizard* magazine poster issue so that, in addition to the *Some Like It Hot, Lost Boys,* and *Princess Bride* posters I'd picked up from my local comic book store, my room's walls would have a solid grid-shaped foundation to grow on right away.

Yara would sometimes tear a picture of Michelle Rodriguez out of an *Entertainment Weekly* and slap it on her wall with some Sticky Tack without first cutting away the jagged edges. Still, I appreciated the help.

"Do we even have time now?"

"Does it matter if we finish it, on this, our hundredth viewing?" she asked. We had an hour or so before dinner.

I nodded. "Sure, lemme find it." I loved to act as though my growing DVD collection wasn't perfectly organized. I was delighted to seem "surprised" when I pulled out a movie I thought might be impressive. There would come a point during my time at Taft—around spring of our junior year—where it was somewhat known that I was the person you might go to in order to watch a film like *Y Tu Mamá También* or *Tigerland* or some esoteric K-pop concert film. I trawled eBay as regularly as the Used DVD bin at Blockbuster, so that I would *always* be the first person to have a copy of something like *Love Actually, Camp,* or *Dirty Dancing: Havana Nights,* even if it meant scrounging up a Region 2 DVD drive (and I had one of those too).

"It's Kim, by the way," Yara said as we got comfortable. She stacked some pillows against the wall to lean on, pointedly ignoring the one covered with a *Lord of the Rings* pillowcase I'd found at a Spencer's.

"What's Kim?"

"Margot's roommate, next door."

"Oh. She's nice. I had art with her last year." I popped open a bag of Australian licorice from the mailroom, mango-flavored, and took a few pieces before handing it over to Yara. "Lights on or off?"

"This is fine," she said after a few chews.

I'm not sure what it was about *Dogma*, for us. I can't even remember how we found the film, though I doubt it was Yara's doing since she cared only for basketball; movies where Michelle Rodriguez hurt people with her fists, a gun, or a large motor vehicle moving at great speed; *Sister Act 2*; and Lauryn Hill's single studio album and masterpiece, *The Miseducation of Lauryn Hill*.

Yet, the comedy about two fallen angels trying to find their way back into heaven worked so well on both of us that by the time we graduated we were almost exclusively referring to each other as Bartleby and Loki. I was Bartleby, the Ben Affleck–looking angel still bitter about his expulsion from heaven by God herself and looking for any way to get revenge. Yara was Loki, Matt Damon, the angel who'd gotten too drunk a few eons ago and impulsively resigned from his job as the Angel of Death. Their punishment for insubordination was being banished from heaven to spend eternity in Wisconsin. Taft, we liked to say (in the pretentiously profound way that only a teenager can), was our Wisconsin.

The two angels fed off each other in a sick, circular fashion that the professional I should have been talking to after my sophomore year probably would have had a field day with. In retrospect, the reasoning for my fixation on Bartleby was quite obvious. I held on to grudges the way I held on to journal entries, AIM messages, and emails.

Yara is Loki, I would write in an English assignment later that year. We'd been asked to put together memoir proposals, setting up three distinct ways of telling our life stories to that point. *She's smart (but slow on the uptake with some things, like I am on others; a "simple creature" as he's called in the movie), impulsive, more up front about things, and sort of just trying to get through life without having to expend too much energy. I, on the other hand, am Bartleby, smart, manipulative (not always in a good way), always having to [rein] the other one in, unless I get power hungry. Then she has to rein me in. Both characters have a [flair] for the dramatic, which I see in both Yara and [me] daily.*

"Snape is not hot," Yara muttered, head in her hands about thirty minutes into things.

"You're correct," I said. "Snape is not hot. *Alan Rickman* is."

"He doesn't have a dick in this movie."

"Who needs one of those, really?"

"Literally all you read are books about dicks and where to put them." She was referring to my collection of historical supernatural and urban fantasy romance novels.

"There're less dicks involved than you think when it comes to sleeping with vampires…more of a teeth situation," I said. "Also hot: Ben Affleck."

"Again, dickless."

"Yeah, but *wings!*"

Yara made a face. "Yeah, but bestiality."

"Sleeping with an angel wouldn't be bestiality. It'd be *spirituality.*"

Because Yara was a good friend, she laughed at my terrible joke and really sold it. She fell sideways, where the remaining pillows against my headboard caught her. It seemed like an eternity before she realized that her cheek was resting against a wrinkled polyester Legolas. "Gross. Even *smells* like sin."

"It's not like I'm like"—I had to brace myself to say the word—"masturbating on it. It cost me a few weeks' allowance."

She smirked. "Allowance? Mark it down—day one and she's bragging already."

"I hate you."

"You don't." Yara pulled herself back up straight, looking away from the small screen for a moment. "Can you believe we have to do this for another year?"

"Watch *Dogma?*" I asked, laughing slightly. But when Yara shot me a look, I nodded quickly. "No, no…I know. We're back in Wisconsin."

On the laptop, Bartleby and Loki had finally *escaped* their prison, making a pit stop in a fast-food company's corporate headquarters on their way to a church in New Jersey. This scene, in which Loki got his smiting mojo back by killing a boardroom full of white and wealthy sinners, was a favorite of ours. We could each recite Ben Affleck's monologue from memory, performed as he named and shamed each sin, and did, every time we watched.

"'Your continued existence is a mockery of morality,'" I quoted. "'Like you, Mr. Burton. Last year you cheated on your wife of seventeen years eight times.'"

"'You even had sex with her best friend while you were supposed to be home watching the kids,'" Yara finished the line perfectly, even clucking her tongue along in disappointment before she laughed. "Fuck Mooby. We could take out the entire school board. Smite them all."

"I mean, that *might* be a little extreme," I said, grinning. "My dad was on that board once."

My friend raised an eyebrow. "Would it be, though?"

Her words were an invitation for a conversation to which I was not yet ready to RSVP, but also her way of letting me know that she *knew*, perhaps, that something fishy had gone down the year before. I could talk to Yara about it, if I wanted, elaborate and give her the full story. But that was the thing—if Taft didn't want to talk about it, then I certainly didn't.

2.

IT WAS HARD to be a horny teen at Taft in 2004. I'm willing to accept that it was probably hard to be a teen anywhere in 2004—who were low-rise jeans *for*, actually?—especially a horny one, but I lived, worked, and socialized at Taft; it was the center of my universe by design.

Based on the timeline laid out by every high school movie and TV show I'd ever watched, I was due for romance, having finally arrived at my junior year. Figuring out how to navigate through Taft's social circles for friendship had taken the majority of my energy the year before, but now with friends figured out and an okay academic baseline in place for everything besides math and Latin, I could focus on being horny just a little more. Here I was, after two nights of restful sleep in my new Voge single, ready not only to catch up, but to conquer.

On the first day of classes, our dining hall table was full of the new faces I'd noted at orientation, including the wide-eyed freshman with a look of dread who was repeating, "The internet went *off* at ten last night. *Ten*," while two other new girls nodded along solemnly. His name was Malcolm, and he was *also* from Newark and NJ SEEDS.

After being officially welcomed back to school by Mr. Mac in Morning Meeting (still sitting next to but never speaking to Frank Jiordano, who had become a bit less lanky over the summer), I walked with Mike to our upper-mid English class with Mr. Martinez, where, I hoped, we would not be spending another year on North American slave narratives.

The classroom's dry-erase smartboard read, in precise, all-caps marker, "Nature, Self-Reliance, and Individualism—Essays and Poems."

This was worse. I hated poetry. But Mr. Martinez had something going for him that Mrs. Dalton had not. Mr. Martinez was hot, and on that merit alone, I was willing to give him at least a week's worth of attention.

Mr. Martinez was a former soldier. A Daniel Radcliffe–sized pocket square of a human with a good face, which you could see clearly because of his spiky crew cut; he'd retained more muscle in his post-military career than is probably advisable for any person who intends to teach high schoolers with raging hormones, even a morally good one. That muscle was maintained in part by coaching one of the lacrosse teams, but also via the doorframe pull-up bar he had installed in his on-campus apartment. We would occasionally have class at his place, and when Johnny Sanderson (who we all *knew* intended to join the army when we graduated, and *yes*, it did make him hotter) challenged Mr. Martinez to a pull-up contest I *did* see God. Laura Parker almost fainted.

That first day we gathered would be the final time that Mike and I sat next to each other. For whatever reason that year, we in Mr. Martinez's class began sitting separated by gender. Mike on one side of the classroom and me, with the likes of Laura, Olive, and Madison, on the other. Competition.

If comparing myself to the other Black girls last year had been hard, positioning myself against the blond Stepford wife aesthetic of a girl like Laura Parker was simply opening the door to disappointment.

But I did it, every day. Mr. Martinez's classroom just happened to be a perfect storm of hormones. Even without our teacher, there was still a line of five or six other boys who (now that I was forced to notice) were also not terrible to look at. Even *Mike* had gotten cuter that summer. But glancing over at Mike, one of my only options, just reminded me that I wouldn't even be considered one of hottest Black girls in our *grade*, and there were only four of us.

The laws and bylaws of dating on campus weren't inscribed into stone or anything, but they were made clear simply by looking around at who was dating and *not* dating whom.

With *very* few exceptions, Black and Latinx girls at Taft dated other Black and Latinx students at Taft. I was not hot or free-wheeling ("loose," the older women in my life might say) enough to be one of those exceptions. Therefore, my options as a straight Black girl in this hypersegregated environment were as follows:

1. Straight Black boys.
2. Straight Latinx boys who did not pass for white.
3. Anyone I met in the comments of a LiveJournal post.

Had he been a student, I probably would have had a better chance with Mr. Martinez, who was Filipino (and my only teacher of color that year, which was already one more than I'd had the year before), and my internal competition with Laura would never have existed. He would have been invisible to her.

● ● ●

Dating is not a requirement of high school, but it is something teens are expected, for better or worse, to at least *want* to try. And should you want to, of your own volition, try as a teen, it's fine to go for it. *Great* even! When else—how else—are you supposed to start detangling the knotty concept of desire and all that comes with it?

(Best not to end up a single loser with a Legolas Greenleaf pillow that you *definitely did not use to masturbate*!)

Trying to date at Taft sucked, to put it simply, but most frustrating of all was that while I hadn't completely reconciled with the way race played into what was going on, I knew that it wasn't just *me*. Although there were quite a few factors working against me.

I knew that I didn't have the best face. It was covered in acne and the scars it left behind. My teeth were (still are) stained due to a combination of some medicine my mother had taken while I was still in utero and having had braces in the third grade, before I was ready for the responsibility of putting *that* much extra effort into cleaning my teeth. The majority of the makeup at my disposal had been purchased for skating competitions, chosen by the white parents of my synchronized skating team, on which I was the only Black member. I insisted on trying to wear it anyway, not understanding that there were an infinite number of red lipsticks out there, and that if I looked, I'd probably find one that didn't leave me looking like the Joker.

I didn't have the best style. I styled myself like Lucy Lawless's cameo as Punk Rock Girl in *Spider-Man*. Spike and a pre-season-six Willow from *Buffy the Vampire Slayer* also heavily influenced the garments I'd idly run my fingers over during our weekend excursions to the Waterbury mall's Hot Topic. When I requested a pair of Dr. Martens for Christmas in 2004, my parents obliged and presented me with a pair of maroon steel-toed lace-up boots instead of the standard pair of soft, easy-breezy Pascals that every millennial now owns. They took twenty minutes to get on, and each step felt like trying to climb out of a sarlacc pit. My feet, already gnarled, hewed messes that had broken in pairs of tough leather figure skates, couldn't break those boots in, and you could see it in how I walked. And yet, I insisted and persisted in wearing them anyway.

I didn't have the best hair. My mother had been out of her depth when it came to styling my hair, and so I was also out of my depth. That she didn't know how to braid beyond two perfunctory French braid pigtails, and couldn't cornrow, twist, or anything else, wasn't as obvious back home (at least not to *me*, I'm sure the other Black girls talked), but as soon as I left, I saw the deficiencies of my standard every-four-to-six-week perm in stark clarity. Tabi had locs, and other girls went back and forth between silky-straight perms, protective braids and twists, and intricate dorm-room cornrow designs. I tried to lessen the effects of my terrible style by throwing a box of Manic Panic on it. Patches of my hair turned a Ronald McDonald–esque red before fading in the sun to a hayseed burnt orange.

I didn't have the best body. I was tall and skinny, at least. I'd finally reached an age where my height, five-eight, and shoe size, 10–11, were unremarkable—not that this stopped people from assuming that they could interest me in touching a basketball. (No, thank you.) As I saw it at the time, these were my only advantages, and truly only in the summer and fall. Skating thickened my thighs in the winter, as did Mr. Vance's obsession with having his softball teams do the sort of calisthenics (a word he genuinely used) that, while they *did* make us look like we were reenacting a very horny, very homoerotic number from *Gentlemen Prefer Blondes*, were also stealthily bulking. Variations of the phrase "My shoulders are linebacker-y" traipse unchecked through my journals. Spaghetti straps and halter tops were not for me, but they were the style of the day. Thin strings winding around here and there did me no favors, since "Hulking out" was not the look I was going for.

I was, to my mind, skinny, yes; tall, yes; but ultimately unfuckable.

But despite all these things, I also knew that the lack of face sucking and crush reciprocation I was experiencing *wasn't* just on me and all my perceived flaws. After all, I'd kissed Quentin that summer. Sure, it had been just once and fleeting in a corner of the town country club while our charges flailed around in the kiddie pool outside, but it had *happened*.

In middle school, Diego and I had full-on made out ("With tongue," I'd emphasize the next day, just to drive Sasha Medvedeva crazy) while *Princess Mononoke* played in the background as we sat in my parents' basement. It was not the world's most satisfying kiss. Tongues thrust here and there with little direction or true confidence. Our teeth touched, and we couldn't figure out where to put our hands. It was not Diego's first kiss (according to him, a fourteen-year-old boy, so take that with a shaker of salt and a Lipitor) and he did not try to follow up with an actual date.

This was fine, as I would have plenty of time to date boys who, like Diego, owned katanas purchased from that one store in the back corner of every mall that sells a strange menagerie of Japanese blades, Guy Fieri shirts, manga, and Kickstarter-funded puzzle games and makes you wonder, *Why?* and *How?* In fact, the next person I kissed, slept with, and then proceeded to date on and off within a *week* of starting college was also that boy. I had a type.

Kissing boys was not hard in college. It was not hard after college. It wasn't hard in the second grade when I chased Justin Akino around the playground until he agreed to kiss me during a game of pretend *Power Rangers*. It wasn't even hard during ninth grade when, confidence bolstered by my one kiss with Diego the year before, I kissed two boys at the movie theatre at Essex Green. ("Netflix and chill" has always been my most successful mode of seduction, even when it was "DVD and fumble through a vague idea of what kissing meant, based solely on whatever a hot adult had done on the WB that week.")

But it was so, *so* hard at Taft. Arguably, I could have made myself more available, but the facts were that I was not overly interested in any of the options presented to me. It was one thing to note that Mike had gotten cuter over the summer. But that didn't mean I wanted to kiss him; we were *friends*.

Crushes so unrealistic as to make themselves unattainable were better, frankly, and less disappointing. I had as much of a chance of hooking up with an elf from *Lord of the Rings* as I did of kissing someone at Taft. I knew I couldn't have Mr. Martinez. And—despite snickers around our dining hall table to the contrary—I knew Laura couldn't have him either. None of them could (or *should*, at least), no matter how petite, clear-skinned, and perfectly put together they were. In that, at least, we were equal.

● ● ●

With the start of a new school year and new students joining The Black Table at meals, our group outings to the Brass Mill mall in Waterbury grew in numbers.

A school year's worth of riding the public bus had turned me into an expert, and I sat on the long back-seat bench now with all of Yara's confidence; muddy Dr. Martens resting on the seat, meeting her Vans in the middle as we leaned against opposite windows. That Saturday in the mid-fall, Santiago had the next row to himself, while Tabi and Sam took up the two seats across from him, making out and refusing to come up for air.

Sam didn't seem to *like* Tabi all that much. Their constant fighting was infuriating and had only *started* once they'd made their relationship "official" sometime in October. This sort of implosion wasn't a particularly unusual phenomenon—how long would you last in a relationship chosen from a dating pool you could count on one hand?

Their kissing had a distinct slurping quality to it. Yara waved at Esther, sitting next to a stranger in front of Tabi and Sam, and pointed at the seat next to Santiago.

"Move," she told Santiago. "Young ears shouldn't have to listen to that."

"They're disgusting," Santiago agreed. "We still have to decide what we're seeing."

"They don't get a vote. You wanna touch that?" Yara gestured at Tabi and Sam.

I nodded, agreeing. "I want to see *Ray*."

My friend shook her head. "If Wanda's not in *Ray*, then I don't want to see *Ray*." She meant Wanda Wayne, Jamie Foxx's character from *In Living Color*.

"I think he's gonna be nominated for an Oscar, though," I said.

"Pass," said Santiago.

"*Saw*?" offered Esther.

"That looks *really* gross," I pointed out.

"You'll like it. The Dread Pirate Roberts is in it." Yara quickly made a face, as though she'd tasted something deeply unpleasant. Cary Elwes had also been in *The Princess Bride*, a movie I'd forced her to sit through thinking that its combination of fairy-tale romance, pirates, and the Chicago Cubs would have the same effect on her that it'd had on me since the age of five. It had not. "I cannot believe I knew that."

"Are we really *that* against *Ray*—" I stopped as I took in the looks on my friends' faces. "Okay, *Saw*."

"*Saw*!" Sam echoed enthusiastically, before immediately re-attaching his face to Tabi's.

I spent most of *Saw* with my face buried in Sam's left shoulder, and so by the time we left the theatre, Tabi and I were in a fight that I didn't actually know we were in simply because I had not been interested in watching the object of my childhood fantasies saw off his own foot. The numbers game being the way it was at Taft, any encroachment onto your relationship could be seen as a threat.

Yara found the whole thing hilarious. "Like you'd be into Sam!" She couldn't stop laughing as we wandered through Spencer's later, mostly bemoaning the fact that Taft had banned having lava lamps in the dorms.

"That new PG keeps trying to talk to you, though," she said after a moment.

"Who?"

"You know who I'm talking about. William Abdi."

I wrinkled my nose at the name. I did indeed know who William was. "He's gonna be almost twenty when he graduates. I'm sixteen."

"Going on seventeen. And you literally told me the other day that Legolas is five-fucking-thousand years old."

"Two thousand nine hundred and thirty-one in the movies," I corrected as I flipped through a display of typical dorm-room posters. "'Five hundred times have the red leaves fallen in Mirkwood' in the books."

"I don't know what that means." Yara rolled her eyes. "So?"

"So?"

"You should give him your screen name so you guys can talk."

"Why would I want to do that?"

"Because he *likes you*, Bart. And he's not an imaginary friend in the computer!" she said, punching my arm lightly. "It's a miracle I'm even telling you this, you know. I would never want a man to come between us.

"Don't worry." I snorted, thinking about the "old" Kenyan postgrad, with his sharp, angular face and low fade. "He won't."

"He likes all that boring baseball shit you like too. I'll never have to watch a three-hour game again. We both win." She shrugged. "You could do worse."

"You're really selling him, great job," I said, voice dry.

I had about as much interest in William Abdi as I had in Santiago or Sam, and at two months or so into the school year, I barely knew him. Anyway, the Black senior girls had first dibs on a Black PG—and they could have him, as far as I was concerned.

Taft never directly addressed the campus segregation, platonic or otherwise, that was obvious to the rest of us. The ways Black and nonwhite students on the one hand and white students on the other separated themselves felt as though it should have been obvious to anyone who visited for even just a day but was not spoken about unless there was an *incident*. And even then, it was hard to hold the school's attention on said incident for more than a month or so. If that.

It wasn't that Taft didn't know there was a problem. Positions like "director of multicultural admissions," "diversity coordinator," "head of multicultural affairs," and others didn't just start springing up in the early aughts by coincidence. Taft and other schools were aware not only of the lack of color on their campuses, but also of the nonexistent relationship between the student groups. It's just that instead of really drilling down and doing the work necessary to examine the ways in which race, privilege, and class interacted at these elite institutions, they just agreed to things like interschool dances.

● ● ●

If one wanted to cause a riot during a Morning Meeting, all one had to do was say the words "headmaster's holiday." Mr. Mac had the power to cancel classes at the drop of a hat, and when he did (now, oftentimes with the help of a celebrity like the Rock, Will Smith, or Robert Pattinson, teleconferenced in by director and alum Peter Berg), Bingham Auditorium and Lincoln Lobby, just outside, would not know peace for at least the hour that followed as students celebrated their upcoming free day.

The words "interschool dance" were not quite as riot inciting, but only because there were fewer of us to cause said riot.

Every month or so, a school within the Ten School Admissions Organization would host an interschool dance—"minority dances," as our official student handbook called them. At around six on a Saturday night, a bus would pull up and a line made up of Black and brown students and, rarely, one very brave white girl who was mad at Daddy and determined to *show him what rebellion looked like!* would climb on board to be driven to another school, where the Black and Latinx kids from every other boarding school would also arrive for a dance. But when the interschool dance was held on our own campus and they didn't have to leave the comfort of a home-court advantage, our white contemporaries called it "the best dance of the year."

We simply called it "an actual dance, finally, thank God."

Taft had dances. We had Winter Formal every year at a nearby Hilton Garden Inn. We didn't do prom or homecoming, but there were a series of themed dances and parties in one of the large meeting rooms with the ornate woodwork, creaky floorboards, and cavernous fireplaces. We had '80s Night, Disco Night ('80s Night with thirty minutes of the Bee Gees around 9 p.m.), Hawaiian Night ('80s Night with leis and *Miami Vice*–inspired outfits for the boys), Crazy Dress Night ('80s Night with feather boas), Roaring Twenties Night ('80s Night with a brief pause for the Cha-Cha-Charleston Slide, "Get it kids?!"), and plenty of others. Kids at Taft would give their right arms for any excuse to wear a scrunchie and a pair of fucking leg warmers.

The rigidity of Taft's social circles did not change much at these events. Occasionally, you'd see a freshman who didn't yet know any better attempt to bridge the divide, but more often students of color would pop in for thirty minutes or so, stay for the few danceable songs that would play (Usher was a safe crossover, and he'd had a *great* 2004), and then retreat to our rooms or the student union.

The first time during my tenure that Taft was chosen to host an interschool dance, I did not plan on going. I tended to need time to myself to decompress on Saturday nights after a busy week. If they were showing a movie in the auditorium I could be found there, and if someone wanted to watch a movie with me (quietly) in my room, I was more than happy to oblige. Otherwise, I spent a lot of time alone, writing. Saturday nights were also the one day a week when the internet *didn't* go off at 10 p.m. The people I role-played with were scattered across time zones; my best friend in our *X-Men* game lived in Australia, and my co-moderator was studying abroad at St. Andrews. Saturday afternoons, stretching into the early Sunday morning twilight, were the best times for giant group campaigns or even intimate two-person scenes that required time and thoughtful written responses.

I used my Saturday nights to "see" my friends outside of Taft, and because our school was not alone in its recruitment pools, my classmates were able to use the off-campus interschool dances to really see theirs. Other boarding schools also did a significant portion of their students of color recruitment through programs like Prep for Prep, NJ SEEDS, and ABC. So for a lot of my friends, going to an interschool dance meant not only the luxury of choice in dance partners, but also seeing people they'd been close to since middle school. I'd had some experience with these gatherings the previous spring, when track-and-field meets would bring up to a dozen schools to campus on a Saturday afternoon. Yara,

Sam, Santiago, and others would introduce me here and there, but mostly I sat to the side and smiled and nodded while they caught up with their program buddies.

But this dance, it occurred to me, might be the one chance I had to dance with somebody, and so my interest in attending keened.

Less sentimentally, but just as important, the DJs hired for interschool dances were more likely to come from an actual radio station. Even a regional, wannabe Hot 97 DJ was better than the discount wedding DJs Taft hired for other dances. These inter-school dance DJs came correct with song catalogs that included Usher *and* Petey Pablo. They weren't scared of the *Speakerboxxx* side of *Speakerboxxx/The Love Below*. You'd get to hear the unedited version of "Tipsy," followed by "The Whisper Song" so that you never actually had to stop grinding—which you could *do* because there were more than ten Black kids in the room and finally you had options.

The dancing—the amount of dancing, specifically, and, I guess, the quality of it—is what prompted our white classmates to pre-emptively refer to this upcoming interschool dance as the "best one" in the week leading up to it.

Yara followed me back from dinner the night of the dance to change. We both decided to go with jeans and collared T-shirts from the Gap; I hadn't shaved my legs, and Yara didn't "do skirts." I flipped the bottom edges of my hair with a curling iron and had a rare, brief moment of enjoying what I saw in the mirror. I was still not cool, stylish, or traditionally good-looking in the way Taft's popular girls were (and plenty of that was on me; over the summer I had added a choker to the menagerie of necklaces I couldn't or wouldn't remove, this one a hemp cobra-stitched chain with a large paw-print bead in the center that symbolized my love for Sirius Black), but in this moment I had made a little something out of nothing.

"I told Margot that we would walk down with them," Yara said.

The two girls who lived next door had well-developed urban sensibilities (Margot being from Bed-Stuy, and Kim coming from Kyoto via half a dozen other places—her mother was in pharmaceuticals), so they weren't great adventure buddies. When Kim and Margot went to the mall they were going *to the mall*, not "eventually to the mall, but first a Jamaican patty tour of the greater Waterbury area."

But the three of us were in Mrs. Myers's general art class together, and between talking through still life paintings and gossiping while Margot developed her photographs in the campus darkroom, we'd started making inroads. I never asked Margot about where she was *actually* from and Yara didn't betray her either. We all respected one another too much.

Yara returned with both girls and we took pictures on film before the short walk down the halls of Voge to Lincoln Lobby, where a small crowd of Black and Latinx students waited impatiently outside the trembling double wooden doors that opened to one of our usual dance venues, vibrating from both the bass tremor of the DJ setting up and testing his equipment, and the tail end of whichever *Fast and the Furious* movie they were showing that night in Bingham.

There had never been this many Black and Latinx students on campus before. At least not down in the main buildings, not during my time there. Visits like this one were more common up the hill, by the fields and courts.

The year before, a scene like this one would have sent me into a tailspin of nerves. Even now, the confidence I'd found when looking in the mirror earlier was not stalwart. I still compared myself to those around me. Better hair, of course; several of the visiting girls had even laid their baby hairs for the occasion. Everyone had earrings in, which I never bothered to do; I was, in fact, at the time, actively hoping the holes in my ears would hurry up and close. And shorts, some girls were wearing shorts; why hadn't I thought of that? (It was November in New England, that's why.)

At least my self-consciousness was now filtered purely through the lens of physical beauty (a problem that would leave a normal amount of psychological scarring) rather than a worry about being perceived as "Black enough" (a problem that no adult at Taft was equipped to deal with).

"I'm actually a little tired." Abandoned almost immediately by Margot for friends from Bed-Stuy, Kim made her excuses before we'd even entered the room.

"We should just go inside," Yara said as Kim turned back toward Voge.

The auditorium doors were now propped open, allowing students to stream out of the Saturday night movie. Mike and Santiago were easy to spot in the crowd, and I was surprised to see them walking with Delores and her new boyfriend, Lucas. But when we waved the four of them over, we only got two.

"That's gonna be a 'no' for them." Mike smirked.

"Shocking," Yara said dryly. "What, does she think her mom'll find out she listened to music with curse words?"

"I told them we'd see them at the Jig later, maybe," said Santiago.

Mike rolled his eyes. "I thought they were 'too tired'?"

I gave Delores and Lucas a short wave as they passed us by, along with the rest of the students leaving Bingham. All their faces looked similar: a heightened curiosity paired with something too complex to be called *just* fear as they took in the scene in the lobby.

White kids watched interschool dances the same way white tourists in Harlem used to watch in fascination as I did wild things like leave my apartment, curse out the self-checkout machine at Duane Reade, or struggle with bags of groceries while passing them by as they stood in line for Sunday morning services, or while walking five abreast on a city sidewalk as they openly gawked at women running errands in their bonnets. It reminded me of a book from grade school, *Running Out of Time*, where no one knew they were living in a historical reenactment that normal people were paying admission to observe. This was the zoo and we were the zebras.

Mike was the one who threw open the doors to the room, revealing a dance that looked like what I assumed most normal high school dances looked like. The DJ had a Sean Paul B side going and everyone was moving.

Those with partners had assumed their positions: girls bent over at the waist or seated in a semipermanent deep squat that would have made Taft's varsity softball coach proud, and boys standing dutifully, hands placed on either hip to help brace their partner as she ground her ass against him. Girls without partners danced with each other, unbothered, showing their friends which eight-counts they'd picked up from *106 & Park* that week. And it wasn't like they were without partners for long. For once.

I saw this for what it was. So did Yara, Mike, Santiago, and the rest of our friends we found on the dance floor as Sean Paul transitioned into Lil Wayne. "Go D.J." wouldn't be my first choice of song to make a baby to, but Tabi and Sam were giving it their all.

Where we saw a more-fun-than-usual school dance, our classmates—judging by the awe-filled looks on their faces as they popped their heads in and out of the double doors—saw the dance break from the "Yeah!" video, fully executed to perfection.

Or, to choose a reference more of them would have understood: Where we saw a dance where (finally) the majority of people participating simply had rhythm, they saw Usher calling everyone to join in on that choreographed Fat Boy Slim prom number from *She's All That*.

They seemed intimidated. Maybe that was wishful thinking; eventually some of them would break in—mostly the boys. Those interschool dances were the single time outside a school musical that I saw a white boy publicly place his hands on a Black girl in any manner even vaguely signaling attraction. It was also the only time we didn't have to fight for attention that we were never going to get anyway.

William Abdi tapped my shoulder to ask whether or not I wanted to dance, rather than just sidling up behind me out of nowhere and announcing his presence with a semi pressed into my backside like most of the other boys there. In the right mood, I would have seen this as chivalrous, but starved of the "real" high school dance experience as I was, it was just a disappointment.

Still, I allowed myself to be separated from my circle and started in on an awkward shuffle with William. I could dance, in that I could easily repeat moves others were doing on the dance floor. William could barely match that.

"Can I have your screen name?" He posed the question as Nelly's request that we all flap our wings began to fade away, replaced by Beyoncé, Kelly, and Michelle's demands for a soldier.

"Why?" I asked.

"I asked Yara for it. She said she didn't know, because you only give it out to people who are not from America," he said, grinning. "I am not from America."

William was paraphrasing, surely. I could hear what Yara had really said quite clearly, knowing she shouldn't give him my AIM without my permission, and confident that she would have wanted to sound nonchalant while doing it. Something along the lines of, *It's not even worth having—she barely answers my AIMs 'cause she's so busy talking to people in Bumblefuck, Australia, and Scotland. I don't know, man, Bart's fucking weird!*

Like any self-respecting too-online teenager of the early aughts,

I had multiple screen names. The one I gave him after flipping through my mental rolodex—OrliBloomedMe583—was a backup throwaway that I used when I didn't want certain members of the games I played in to know I was online.

"You don't need to write it down?" I asked, after repeating it again as requested.

"No—it's very simple," he said. "I'll message you during study hall. Maybe we can hang out at Scene."

Thank God, I thought. He would most certainly forget in the hour of dancing left, not to mention the hangouts and Jig debriefs afterward. His suggestion of hanging out at Scene—something I'd not tried to do since becoming close with Yara—anchored my already tanking interest.

When the music began to transition again, Diddy's pleas to find a girl from one of the *Barbershop* soundtracks, I allowed myself to be swallowed back up by another circle of girls—a tactic which, unbeknownst to me at the time, would become extremely important when it came to escaping unwanted male attention during my clubbing twenties. Taft helped its students hone all sorts of lifelong skills.

● ● ●

I did not like William Abdi. There was no one particular reason, at first; it was just my right as a sixteen-year-old girl who wanted nothing more than to fuck an elf and did not find that to be too big of an ask.

But in all seriousness, with zero real relationships tucked under my belt, I didn't yet know how to separate personality and physical attraction. There was no point, I figured, in getting to know someone for the purpose of a romantic entanglement if you didn't look at them and instinctively know that you wanted to kiss. I was also still hung up on his age (nineteen, now, after his birthday). Had I been in any way interested in him, I might have viewed this as an aphrodisiac of sorts (I had raised myself on historical romance novels, and trysts between spies posing as tutors who cannot help but fall in love with their young charges, after all). But I was not, and so in my mind he became "sketchy"—the exact word I used to describe him to Yara and Margot, each time he persistently IM'd me during study hall.

The messages began promptly, the first study hall after the weekend of the interschool dance:

> **TheRinger250:** hey. it's william.

When I didn't respond immediately, the "heys" kept coming, and my away messages acted as consistent buffers.

> **TheRinger250:** how r u?

> **Auto response from OrliBloomedMe583:** Skating with the bitches. Back later.

> **TheRinger250:** watch this i am talking to a phantom

> **Auto response from OrliBloomedMe583:** Biking to the graveyard. Comics, and RPing.

> **TheRinger250:** knew it

TheRinger250: kendra, holla back when you're back from skating

Auto response from OrliBloomedMe583: If you knew me, you'd know that on Wednesdays I'm skating.

TheRinger250: u back?

Auto response from OrliBloomedMe583: If you knew me, you'd know that on Wednesdays I'm skating.

TheRinger250: wad up!

It went on like this for weeks, and Yara found it hilarious when I described how often he tried to contact me, or how unsettled the few conversations I *had* had with him on the messenger made me feel. One afternoon after skating, I jabbed my finger at my laptop screen when a flashing icon interrupted our 734th viewing of *Dogma*.

"It's not you!" I said, nearly shouting. "It's not any of my RP friends, 'cause time zones! It's fucking *William*."

"It could also be any of your *other* friends," Yara said. "Real ones! If you have those."

I leaned over Yara's legs to pull the computer into my lap. "Nope. Look," I pointed to the window, where it was indeed William's screen name in the orange blinking window. "It's him. I don't know why he's not taking the hint. I do not *like him*."

"Have you told him that?"

"No, but like, you'd think he'd get the fucking message," I said. "He's *sketchy*. I don't want to give him a reason to get sketchier."

"He's not sketchy," she said. "He's just not *American*."

I shook my head. "Watch this." I quickly changed my AIM

status from "away" to "online" and pulled up the window to read the messages William had sent me.

TheRinger250: yo!

Auto response from OrliBloomedMe583: Bother us during Dogma upon risk of smiting. You have been warned.

TheRinger250: come on now

TheRinger250: kendra!!

TheRinger250: kendra...

"You see this shit?" I said, pointing at the screen.

"Yeah—he wants you to answer, dumbass." She grinned, and quoted easily from our collective childhoods, "'I'm wearin' you down, baby. I'm wearin' you *down*.'"

I glared at Yara while typing my response.

OrliBloomedMe583: ?

TheRinger250: how u doin' gal...dis is william

OrliBloomedMe583: yup I know, hey

TheRinger250: you had skating?

OrliBloomedMe583: yeah

TheRinger250: how did it go?

OrliBloomedMe583: it wasnt one of my lessons. just practice and some pretty shitty axel drills.

TheRinger250: i heard . . .

TheRinger250: what you told margot :-)

"What did you tell Margot?" Yara asked.

TheRinger250: are you still there?

"I don't *know*," I said, still typing. "Watch."

OrliBloomedMe583: huh?

TheRinger250: about me liking you

TheRinger250: i have a feeling that you're not the only one reading this so I'd rather talk to you face to face

OrliBloomedMe583: no, I'm seriously alone

"You're not alone."
"I know, but is that any of *his* business? Also, keep watching."

TheRinger250: can i call you?

OrliBloomedMe583: not right now, im gonna have to shower before dinner.

TheRinger250: can i ask you something?

OrliBloomedMe583: yeah?

TheRinger250: who is that i see reading from your computer?

At that, Yara jumped straight up, planting her feet firmly on the ground as she shouted, "Oh *hell* no. *FUCK.*"

I pursed my lips and pointed at the screen. "See? He pulls this shit when I'm *actually* alone too. He'll do it when I'm in the library; he'll do it if I'm up at the gym. That's how I know he can't really see in here—but this is what he *does.*"

"Block his ass!"

"I did, but then he *definitely* said something to Mrs. Gallagher, because she told me I wasn't being friendly enough to him." It was 2004, and the idea of a boy pursuing a reluctant girl who was quite obviously not interested was still often seen as the makings of a potential meet-cute, rather than what it was: budding harassment. I certainly found it "sketchy," but the idea of reporting it to an adult fell firmly into the category of overkill. An AIM message didn't seem worthy of a Sunday morning study hall, especially not for a fellow Black student.

"Oh my God." Yara dropped back down next to me and peered down at the laptop again. "You *would* attract a psychopath. Very you, very Kendra."

OrliBloomedMe583: wow, stalker much?

TheRinger250: tell her to get a life

TheRinger250: whoever is there tell them that they should stop being nosy and back off. they should leave us alone to talk in private...

TheRinger250: you reading this!!! leave noW!!!! leave kendra's room...

TheRinger250: stop telling her what to write

TheRinger250: i hear you

TheRinger250: did you say "freaking out"?

OrliBloomedMe583: see now I think you really weren't joking and this conversation needs to end. Now.

TheRinger250: are you alone?

TheRinger250: huh?

TheRinger250: well are you?

Yara, who generally knew better than to ever actually *touch* my laptop, reached forward with all the swiftness her varsity basketball training could provide and slammed the thing shut, our screening of *Dogma* now entirely forgotten.

"So, do *you* wanna tell William that I don't like him?" I said, glaring at Yara with the weight of an I-told-you-so in my tone.

"Fuck no. I—"

There was a light knock on my door and Yara and I both froze, remaining preternaturally still as our eyes met. I slowly raised a finger to my lips, begging for silence as the knock sounded again. My heart was pounding, even though in the back of my mind I *knew* that William couldn't have made it from his dorm to Voge in such a short span of time.

"*Fuck*," Yara hissed under her breath. I pressed my finger to my lips once more.

The knock sounded again, harder this time. There was a beat and still neither Yara nor I moved.

"Kendra?" Margot's voice, her sharply affected New York City housewife accent, floated into the room.

Yara and I both absolutely deflated, taking simultaneous gulping breaths of air.

"Margot? Hey—it's open!"

My next-door neighbor walked into the room, clad in a white terry-cloth robe and a towel wrapped around her wet dirty-blond hair. She looked perturbed. "Oh, Yara, so it's *you*."

"What're you talking about?" she asked.

"That PG William," Margot said, frowning. "He sent me and Kim these *weird* IMs while I was in the shower. Like, talking about how he knows we're both in your room with you, Kendra. But he must be talking about you."

"*Jesus fucking Christ*," Yara and I cursed simultaneously.

"What is going *on*?"

"Kendra has a stalker," said Yara.

"Basically," I agreed.

Margot crossed her arms and huffed. "Great! So we all get to deal with *this* for the rest of the year."

She was not wrong. William seemed to know what he was doing. He never approached me inappropriately in person, but the IMs never stopped. When I didn't reply (and I very rarely ever did) he would bounce increasingly deranged messages off my automatic replies before moving on to trying to get in touch with the people I was closest to and trying to get them to contact me *for* him.

Eventually, it got to the point where I simply had to stop using that screen name. I created another throwaway account at some point that spring. I also decided that perhaps Taft—this world where I was effectively the tiniest fish in the largest pond—was not a place where I needed to be dating at all. It was a grim realization, but I didn't want to be forced into liking someone any more than I wanted someone to be forced into liking me, all for lack of choice. I wanted to be tenderly held and wantonly desired. Not stalked.

I doubled down, then, in placing all my sexual eggs in two baskets: celebrities and fictional characters. Fucking an elf, it seemed, would be my only option after all.

William graduated that May. When I was in college a few years later, I signed back on to my OrliBloomedMe583 account, looking for the screen name of a gaming friend I'd wanted to get back in touch with. It didn't occur to me that William would still be a problem. I'd barely thought of him since my own graduation.

The swiftness with which he messaged me was genuinely impressive.

TheRinger250: yo

TheRinger250: hi

TheRinger250: orli bloomed have u bloomed?

TheRinger250: hello

TheRinger250: lol

TheRinger250: hi kendra

I blocked him immediately.

3.

I PLAYED VARSITY softball my sophomore and junior years at Taft because there weren't enough girls interested to field JV and thirds teams. In addition to wearing a full face of makeup to every game, our pitcher also fast-pitched every single inning. This probably accounted, in part, for our 1–11 record; we weren't great. After the adjustment of my sophomore year, though, I'd finally become comfortable with the level of play in the boarding and day school circuit, and was seeing some good personal improvement as a leftie at the plate.

"You're *fast*," Mr. Vance, our calisthenics-obsessed coach, said after a Wednesday afternoon practice early in the season. We hadn't even had tryouts, much less played our first game yet. "You're *so* fast—wait, why are you limping?"

I was, a little bit. Running sliding drills, I'd scraped my thigh against a second-base corner, leaving a welted bruise peeking out from underneath my shorts.

After I'd explained this, our coach did one of the little things that made Taft such a unique school experience. The next day at practice I was presented with a crisp and unopened plastic package containing a pair of under-short baseball sliders—basically a pair of padded boxers that'd keep you from tearing up your leg on a forced run into second or third. My parents could've afforded to purchase them, and absolutely would have, had I mentioned needing them. I'd been playing for years, and this wasn't my first pair of sliders. But my mom and dad were paying for a concierge-service high school experience so that they didn't *have* to think about things like this.

Because these were just padded shorts, when you got down to brass tacks—those washable period panties, but for the baseball diamond—they really showed off the ass. The effect of the pads on my butt and hips didn't go unnoticed when I looked in a mirror, especially as Mr. Vance ramped up the squats.

I played right and left field, so no matter what, I was generally warming up in a circle with the same group of girls, our other alternating fielder, Marielle, and Veronica, who always played center. They were both seniors. Normally, we made awkward small talk as we warmed up until Mr. Vance inevitably decided that we weren't taking our Jack LaLanne–style butterfly flexes seriously enough and made us start counting aloud as a group. A blessing in disguise that probably prevented countless comments like this one.

"You're getting this, like, intense video-girl butt," Marielle said as she pulled her right foot up to meet her left thigh.

I was not the thickest girl on the team by *any* means, even with sliders on, but I *was* the only Black one, and Marielle never did walk up to our pitcher, with her full face of overdone makeup, and say, "You're getting this, like, intense drag-queen look."

At the time, I found Marielle's comment offensive not for its microaggressions but because it aligned me with the Black women I had been taught *not* to be. But in the same breath, it was also fucking *confusing*. If I looked like a video girl, why wasn't I getting video-girl action? Why was *William* the only boy who seemed to like me?

Hearing that I'd been called a video girl by a white person would have curdled each and every container of milk in my mother's refrigerator. It was *everything* she had attempted to avoid for her child. Having a goth in the family Christmas photo was sigh inducing, but infinitely better than having a video girl.

But the sometimes goth, sometimes just downright kooky way I dressed wasn't about actually *being* a goth or a plain weirdo. I could play the part, but I wasn't really one of them. It was just about standing out and trying to make myself seen as something other than just one of the four Black girls in our class.

By putting my personality out on my literal sleeve, I was asking people to make the effort to learn *anything* else about me. Ask me why I'm wearing this strange graphic tee that just says "IMF" on it. (It stands for "Impossible Mission Force," and see? You had to ask.) Or the significance of the paw print on my necklace. Did these Docs take a long time to lace up in the morning, and why did I keep wearing them if they did? You're a Legolas girl? I'm an Aragorn person, but anyway, have you read *The Silmarillion?* If you're from New York—sorry, New Jersey!— then why are you wearing that Cubs jersey, also why did you dye it black?

Mr. Fraser asked all those questions and more. He had to, in order to do his job as a college counselor. Also, I showed up in his office for our first meeting wearing a brown pinstripe three-piece suit from H&M, with a cheap brass pocket watch on a chain looped through the button holes of the vest, so I'm gonna go out on a limb and say he would have had questions, regardless.

● ● ●

Taft had three or four college counselors to handle the approximately one hundred students in our class, and while I'm sure they were all wonderful at their jobs, I maintain that Don Fraser is the single best college counselor in the whole of the continental United States. He knew more about me than any other teacher at Taft. He listened to me when I spoke. He heard what I *wanted*. But most important, he helped me get the fuck out of Wisconsin.

Juniors had their first meetings with college counselors after seniors' acceptances started rolling in during the early spring. The counseling office was a large but cozy space with multiple offices, one for each counselor and a multipurpose room where you might see one of them patiently walking a junior or senior through corrections on an essay, or tempering the onset of an "I didn't get into my first choice Ivy League but a classmate I perceive to be less deserving than myself did and so Daddy and I will be suing Yale's admissions department" meltdown.

Sometime after an art class trip to the city that had convinced me I desperately wanted to go to NYU, I arrived for my first meeting in Mr. Fraser's office. He was smiling—the man was perpetually in a delightful mood, a cherub in a sweater vest—and welcomed me with a promise. "This is going to be *fun*."

"I *don't* want to go to Rutgers," I said firmly after getting settled. "I don't even want to *apply* to Rutgers."

"I had the feeling you'd say that." Mr. Fraser laughed, clicking a few things on his computer before turning around in his desk chair to face me completely. "I've been thinking about you. You want something either extremely large, or smallish and proportional to Taft, I bet?"

"Kind of, I think. Yeah."

"Are you going to skate in college?"

I was a bit surprised. "What?"

"Ice skating," he said. "Your winter sport is skating, and since you've been volunteering with the Watertown club at night, I was wondering if you wanted to keep skating in college."

My friends and the woman who supervised the rink on Wednesday afternoons knew that I skated, and I spoke to Mrs. Gallagher about skating, but otherwise it never really came up with the adults in my life at Taft. Mrs. Gallagher didn't even know I was volunteering with the Watertown Skating Club's beginner synchro team in exchange for a discounted club membership rate; Taft students weren't supposed to have after-school jobs, and sometimes it was hard to tell where the *Non ut sibi ministretur sed ut ministret* line was drawn. She'd already lecture-warned me about putting in an application at Starbucks.

But Mr. Fraser knew. "The University of Delaware has a synchronized skating program, which is why I'm asking."

"Oh! I know about that one. One of my friends looked at Delaware for synchro too." I didn't mention that that friend was online, a college junior whom I'd never met in person.

"What about softball?"

"I don't know." Esther was still considering joining the softball team once we got around to tryouts, but even if she did, there would still only be two of us; a long and lonely season. I wasn't sure yet if I would play again in my senior year, which would ruin any chances I had at serious play in college.

Mr. Fraser nodded and reached to grab a piece of paper from the mouth of the desktop printer. "I'm guessing athletics aren't going to be your first priority, but your sports are so darn specific it really helps narrow things down while still getting in the academics you're going to want."

"What do you mean?"

"Well, for instance." He glanced down at the paper in his hand and trailed his finger down. "A friend of mine, an admissions counselor at Haverford, was telling me that one of the students at

Bryn Mawr—that's their sister school—just started a synchronized skating team."

"Oh! That's Emily—*she* was on my team in New Jersey, and my mom told me about how she started a team at Bryn Mawr last year!"

"Bryn Mawr and Haverford share a lot of resources and facilities, and I think Haverford—something tells me you're not interested in all girls? No, I didn't think so—would be a good fit for you. It's smallish, and liberal arts focused, but has that international relations track you want. You should also think about what you're going to want to do outside of your major, and I have the feeling that a liberal arts school is going to help you fine-tune those interests."

It didn't occur to me until years later that the sheer novelty of an algorithm was a key part of the "fun" Mr. Fraser had been talking about. Facebook didn't come to Taft until our senior year, and Twitter and YouTube were still a ways out from existing, much less becoming the casual companions of an entire generation. The average high schooler had no idea how much of our lives—what we ate, what we purchased, what we posted, and more—the ubiquitous "algorithm" would eventually control.

But Mr. Fraser knew *everything* about me—or that's what it felt like, at least. He was the algorithm. And he was correct: Talking to someone (someone who was not another student) who could immediately see me as a person with interests, wants, and desires that stretched beyond the first impressions formed by race *was* fun. Or at least a novelty, in its own right.

"Nope," I confirmed firmly. "Not all girls, at all. Ever."

"I thought so. You, Yara, Jason, Sam, Tabitha, and Mike—quite the group." He chuckled. "Here's the deal. I've heard you loud and clear. No Rutgers, and no same-sex. *But.* I wouldn't be doing my job if I didn't tell you this: Rutgers is going to cost you nothing, and you're going to get in. Next, I assume you're planning on applying to Brown?"

"I don't really want to apply anywhere above Connecticut."

That one made him laugh too. "Got it. Well, again, I have to tell you…it's going to be in your best interest to at least *look* at either Brown or Smith. You'd be applying as a legacy to both, and especially at Brown—coming in as a double legacy, sort of on the same track as your dad? It's going to look *great*."

I wrinkled my nose. Smith had no men and my mother had been part of a sorority there. I loathed the idea of Greek life; frats and sororities went against the entire aesthetic I'd cultivated. I was not a *sheep* and I did not *join* things like that. I could barely tolerate the dress code I lived with now, and I assumed any campus with Greek life fostered an environment in which I'd have a hard time finding a place. Much like Taft.

When I mentioned this, Mr. Fraser simply grinned and said, "Well, you're going to *love* Reed and Oberlin."

He handed me the paper from the printer then, a detailed sheet with my name and graduating year in bold letters at the top. In five columns he listed twenty colleges, along with the cities and states they were in, my level of interest, and the expectedness of my acceptance separated into three categories: Likely, Reach, and Possible. I would end up applying to around ten or twelve of them.

For the first time, I was to have the majority share in the choice of what my education would look like. I had chosen Taft, yes, but it wasn't as though there'd been other options. Unlike many of my classmates, I'd only applied to one independent school—the one we knew I could get into. While my parents would certainly be paying for this latest decision, it felt as though it was wholly mine to make. I would do the narrowing and winnowing. I would pick not only the winner but the final two, three, and more.

They couldn't *force* me to go to Rutgers. "Though, if Rutgers feels like it might be the right choice for whatever reason," Mr. Fraser suggested gently when I once again reiterated that I simply was *not* going there, "there might be some negotiation you could try with your parents. Think of it that way—you could have a car at Rutgers, maybe, if your parents weren't paying tuition in addition. That would be an amazing amount of freedom, and it could open up more job opportunities for internships in the city. Plus, you could drive home to do your laundry—can't beat that!"

"I didn't come to Taft to just turn around and go back home and go to college with the same people I went to elementary school, middle school, and did freshman year with. What would even be the point?"

Around us, the counseling space was dotted with college brochures, pennants, little mascot figurines, and more. Many of them were the heavy hitters one expected to see—Harvard and Yale were well represented alongside some of the other Ivies (Taft had a tenuous relationship with Princeton, and very few acceptances), the Little Ivies, the Seven Sisters, the military academies, the three HBCUs prep schools are willing to acknowledge (Howard, Spelman, and Morehouse), and some other well-regarded private institutions. The expectations to exceed that I felt as a Black student at this school, a legacy at that, and as the daughter of Brown and Smith alums, meant that I simply did not think that Rutgers—an excellent school, frankly—was good enough.

"Do some research before the college fair next week, and remember to keep an open mind while you're there," he said. "We'll start narrowing after that, and you and your parents can decide where you want to visit this summer or over any breaks this spring."

It had not occurred to me that the college process might amount to a vacation or two. My dad's midlife furniture-repair franchise career detour meant that we hadn't really been on a blowout trip in quite some time. "Do you think I should visit the ones in California?"

"I think you should *definitely* visit the schools in California before you make that kind of decision."

"Are you willing to put that in writing in an email addressed directly to Andrew and Lynn James?"

Mr. Fraser laughed loudly. "That is what I'm here for." The man was an ally in the truest sense of the word. "The other thing I'd like you to do is take a look at the Common Application essay questions. We should get one of those chosen and start outlining before finals hit you."

"I can do that." If there was anything I wasn't worried about, it was writing a college admissions essay. I'd done it for Taft, after all, and before one even counted schoolwork, I was writing an average of three to four thousand words of straight prose a day in my "writing games" and fan fiction.

"Great. I'll email you, and we'll set another meeting time right after the fair. This was a great first meeting, Kendra. Send Callister in next, would you?"

I folded the school list and slipped it blindly into a folder in my backpack before standing up to leave. "Thanks!"

I don't know what it was like for others; the students who would be the first in their families to attend college, those who couldn't afford things like far-flung college visits, application fees, or more, or those who flat-out weren't encouraged to apply, much less attend, by the adults in their lives back home. I had a leg up as I started to think about college, but because I *had* those things and didn't really have to think about where money or support was coming from, Mr. Fraser felt like the biggest advantage of all.

I would end up telling what felt like several white lies and obscuring a lot of experiential truths at Scholars Striving 4 Success, but the feeling of being incredibly seen and heard by our college counselors was not one of them. At least not for me.

4.

ESTHER WAS HANGING out in the Harley Roberts Room after my meeting in the college office. I settled into one of the ornate couches in front of the fire with her for a bit, where we gossiped about the softball team and made small talk with prospective parents who sat waiting for tours until the younger girl had to leave.

I left my backpack by our seats and made myself a cup of tea in one of the paper cups Mrs. Frances kept out for refreshments before stepping back out into the hall. The mailroom was just steps away, and I was expecting a package.

"Give me just a second," said Ms. Harris before vanishing with my package slip into the back room, where the larger boxes sat.

There were two stools behind the mailroom window, and Callister Hamilton, now finished with her own meeting with Mr. Fraser, occupied the second. Eyes down, she was methodically peeling and smacking Forever stamps down onto a stack of donations mailers from the development office.

"Here you go, hon." Ms. Harris reappeared, holding a brown box.

I cut it open immediately, greedily grabbing at my order: DVD copies of *Kiss Me, Kate, Some Like It Hot,* and *The Band Wagon,* and *Intermission, The Recruit,* and the director's cut of *Daredevil* (2003). Last was a hardcover of the burgeoning phenom, *Twilight.*

"Now, I don't see many of you ordering the classics!" Ms. Harris nodded approvingly. "I saw *The Band Wagon* at the movie theatre when it was released again in 1963."

"It's my favorite movie," I said as I stacked the DVDs. "*Some Like It Hot* is number two."

"Mine is *Kiss Me, Kate,*" Callister offered, glancing up from her pamphlets.

I met her eye almost suspiciously. "Movie or stage show? This is *different* from the stage show."

"Oh, the movie. That one," she said, pointing at my pile. "I like Bob Fosse."

"Ann Miller's the real star."

"You mean Carol Haney."

"I don't. You know it was shot in 3D?"

"Yep, that's why that one scene—you know, 'I Hate Men'? They have her throwing the plates toward—"

"Toward the camera because when audiences saw it in 1953 it would have felt like the plates were being thrown at them," I cut her off.

The other girl smiled. "It's a good movie."

"Yeah." I paused. "Do you want to…watch it?"

"I would! But my mom is going to be here soon to pick me up. I'm having dinner at home tonight."

As a Black day student at a largely white boarding school, Callister Hamilton was doubly removed from the larger student body. Even I, someone who felt on the outskirts of Taft's social sphere, had no clue what day students even did with their time when they weren't in class. I'm sure Callister had friends, but I had no clue who they were. She hadn't been to one students of color orientation, and while I didn't go to *every* meeting, I'd never seen her at TAALSA. That she favored *Kiss Me, Kate* and Bob Fosse were the first hard facts I learned about her.

Callister had full cheeks that glowed with undertones of red clay and persimmons. We were of a height, but while I was skinny and lanky, she was thick and far more rounded than I, sticking out yet again, as one of the very few heavier girls in a school full of athletic stick figures. She and her family were devout Christian Scientists, which was reflected in her modest dress. Callister was always in a pair of Gap khakis and a collared shirt or church-appropriate blouse; we didn't share a struggle with the dress code.

What we did share was a love of old musicals. Modern secular music wasn't really a *thing* in the Hamilton household, but musicals and classic Hollywood films had been deemed all right by her conservative mother. She liked *The Band Wagon* all right too, I'd learn later on, but like me, preferred Gene Kelly to Fred Astaire overall, so *Singin' in the Rain* was her preference. We were both fascinated by Cyd Charisse's legs and the ways she used them to lure men into her web, and at Taft? Well, that was plenty to form a friendship on. It was practically a bounty.

● ● ●

Day students were more than welcome to stay on campus at night; whether they wanted to eat dinner with boarders or needed to use the library during study hall, the facilities were open to them the same as they were to the rest of us. The night of the college fair, juniors were told we could opt out of study hall, just this once, so that we could get up to the field house, where admissions officers from what seemed like nearly every respected college in the country had set up on rows and rows of folding tables.

Whether you were boarding or driving in each day, the whole point of Taft was never having to leave campus for a thing. Like the sliders Mr. Vance handed me on the softball field, the fact that colleges came to *us* was part of the concierge high school experience. I never had to see the inside of another school's gym unless I was there to put a ball through a hoop, and God knew that wasn't happening.

I invited Callister back to Voge that evening after we'd eaten, but before we were due up at the gym. Yara turned down the invitation when I told her what we'd be watching, and again when I showed her a picture of Howard Keel in the elfin red onesie donned by the company for "We Open in Venice" and declared him to be extremely hot.

She waved my laptop screen away. "This man has no idea where a clitoris is."

"You liked *Seven Brides for Seven Brothers*," I reminded her.

"My *sister* likes *Seven Brides for Seven Brothers* and my sister was my babysitter. I have *seen* it. I don't *like* it," she shot back. "I'll see y'all at the gym later."

She peeled off before we hit Voge, where Callister and I made a beeline straight for the common room. There, a messy stack of blank tapes belonging to Yara and me sat on the media console— *Lost* was a true novelty of a show in its first season and we wanted to catch each one, but my mother had her hands full recording new episodes of *Buffy* and *Angel* for me back home. Hence the tapes.

Watching things with Yara had its own rhythms. I had to be quick, which I found easier when it was just the two of us and the well-trodden material and characters we both loved were the targets of our verbal livetweet. We watched everything on DVD with subtitles (yes, even pre-Netflix) because we both just talked so damn much. When we were watching *Dogma* for the hundredth time, or I was trying to convince her yet again that *Firefly* was a show she would enjoy, that was fine. But I couldn't abide someone talking through a musical, which I tucked into with the same seriousness as I would a Broadway show I'd paid orchestra prices to see.

"I *do* like Ann Miller in this, a lot," Callister commented after the sultry tapper finished "Too Darn Hot," and then didn't speak again until I mentioned once more that I found Keel to be quite the specimen of a man, because that's just where my mind was that year and it wasn't budging.

She grinned as wickedly as I would ever catch her. "The goatee probably makes it better."

"Makes what better?" I asked.

"When he *does* find your clitoris," she said, raising an eyebrow just as Keel's Fred began to spank his wife, Lilli, right there on the screen in front of us.

Callister, I was beginning to learn, was a true delight. Every so often she would drop a line that made me genuinely sad that it had taken me *this* long to find her. She'd been lost to the day-student gathering space near a third-floor tower, which, as far as I'd been concerned, moved around more often than the damn Room of Requirement.

We had to pause just after "Brush Up Your Shakespeare" so that we could begin the long trek up to the college fair, stopping to pick up Yara on the way. She and Callister had known each other (vaguely, at least) since freshman year and got along just fine.

The layout of the gym forced us to part ways once we entered the fair. Colleges were set up in alphabetical order by name so that students could easily go through their printed lists. I wasn't the only one clutching a piece of paper from their college counselor tightly in my fingers, but we all had different priorities. Yara was looking at several larger schools, places where she would be able to play basketball and study sports medicine. Many of the tables I visited were more sparsely populated—small liberal arts schools that had events like Drag Balls and Safer Sex Nights were not high on many of my classmates' lists.

We had about two hours to get through the maze of tables, and by the end of the night I'd collected brochures from most of the schools Mr. Fraser had presented me with, though I was discerning in my own way. NYU, I learned, was going to be *wildly* expensive; I skipped Rutgers on principle and breezed right past Vanderbilt when I noticed that one of their admissions reps was wearing a bow tie. I knew *that* prep school trap when I saw it—no, thank you.

Sam, Santiago, and Mike were waiting by the field-house doors when Callister, Yara, and I approached. Between five of us, we held a forest's worth of trees in our hands.

"Do you want to come to the student union with us?" I asked Callister.

"My mom'll be here in fifteen minutes; I'm going to wait in Harley Roberts," she said. "But we should finish watching *Kiss Me, Kate* soon, maybe tomorrow?"

"Absolutely."

Together, we all started walking out of the field house, making a beeline for the path that led back down the hill to the main campus. It was pitch black already, and the buildings below us glowed; each dorm window seemed its own hearth, warm light coming from within as most of the campus continued on with the business of nightly study hall.

After a moment, Callister nudged me. "Can I hold anything for you?"

"Oh, I'm good, thanks."

"You got so much stuff!" She glanced down at my stack and shook her head. "How many schools were on your list?"

"*So* many," I said. "But I got some extras too. Places that looked cool. What about you?"

"Oh, I didn't bring mine, but it was a lot too."

"You remembered *all* of them?"

"No. Gosh, *no*." She laughed. "I'm probably not applying."

My jaw dropped; I was instantly jealous. "Oh my God, your parents are letting you do a *gap year*?"

A friend of mine back home had already been *promised* a gap year by her parents, and when I eventually gave my parents the requisite "Well, Jane's mom and dad are letting *her* do one" during college, they'd laughed and said something about "white nonsense." When I reminded them that Jane was half-Chinese, their scoffs altered. "You're not wasting that kind of time," they answered, laughing as though a gap year was simply the most hilarious concept they'd ever been asked to consider.

Callister's laugh echoed Lynn and Andrew's. "I guess you could call it that? I'm not going to college."

I stopped in my tracks. We all did, as though the choreography had been blocked out in advance.

Sam, holding his brochures from some of the best premed tracks in the country, looked like he'd seen a ghost. "*What?*"

"Yeah." Callister shrugged, and as her shoulders traveled toward her ears I finally looked down at her hands—suspiciously empty, I saw now, even in the dark of night. "I had to go to the fair or Mr. Fraser and Mr. Martinez would *kill me*."

"Mr. Martinez?"

"Oh, he's my advisor this year. Totally freaked when I told him I wasn't applying, and he and Mr. Fraser said that I had to come and keep an open mind," Callister said, as though this was the most normal thing in the world.

Which, to be fair, in the world—not *our* world, but the actual real world that existed just outside the iron gates and down the road in Watertown proper—that was a completely reasonable and normal thing to say.

But not here; not *at* Taft. "You didn't find *one* school?" I asked, incredulous.

"I just kind of walked around. I think I did the mile, actually, 'cause I went around the gym at least four times!" She laughed.

"You have to apply to college," Sam insisted.

Callister shrugged again, fully bemused. "You're saying that like it's in the Bible."

"It's in the Taft bible!" I exclaimed.

"Well," she said, still chuckling, "luckily, I only follow one God."

Yara smirked, laying a hand on my shoulder. "Bart," she said pointedly, "she's just fucking with you." She glanced over at Sam, who still looked horror-struck. "You too, dumbass."

"We're *all* going to college," Santiago said. "Whether we want to or not."

"Well, of course we *want* to!" I shrugged Yara's hand off. "But, it's okay. I mean, we all have a year *and* there are going to be more fairs *and* you already took the ACTs, so it's fine. No one is behind. This is all exploratory at first anyway."

"Exploratory is the perfect word!" Callister agreed, smiling at me. "I guess I could change my mind."

Eventually, Sam and I were forced to breathe in the cool night air again as we resumed our march down to campus. When my friends turned toward the Jig and the student union, I announced that I would meet them there in a moment, and walked with Callister to the Harley Roberts Room, where she would wait for her mother.

Mrs. Frances was long gone for the evening; the room was dark and chilly when we perched across from each other on two formal chairs. I placed my armful of pamphlets on an antique coffee table while Callister fiddled with the pull rope to turn on a small banker's desk lamp, hooded with green glass. In the verdant light we flipped through the brochures in a comfortable silence, occasionally piping up to point out a fun program or amenity one school offered over another. When she smiled while dragging her finger down one of Sweet Briar's sheets, I was relieved. Yara was right—Callister had just been fucking with me. She was going to *apply* for college at the very least.

"That's my mom," she said, glancing up. A pair of lone headlights shone through the windows, a single wood-paneled station wagon sitting in the main roundabout. "I'll see you at lunch tomorrow? Maybe?"

"Yeah!" I said. "Do you want that one?"

"Hmm?"

"Sweet Briar. It's not one of my top choices because it's all girls, but it's like…*so* pretty? I don't know, I'm thinking about it now. But you can take that one if you want."

"Oh gosh, keep it! *You* might change your mind," Callister said with a wink. "I'm not applying."

"Right, right," I said. "Well, I'll have it if you want."

She thanked me and after she'd slung her messenger bag across her body I waved goodbye.

● ● ●

"She's definitely applying for college. She's just not starting her admissions essays *now* because she's not an anal-retentive psychopath like you, Bart."

"Cool, thanks."

"*Ow!* Pay attention."

"'Ow' is like the bare minimum when you're taking out *ten fucking years of locs.*" There was just as much hair on the floor underneath Mrs. Gallagher's family room couch as there was on Tabi's head and still a million or so locs to go. I was more than through with this plan. "You have *got* to buzz this."

"We've been working on it all afternoon. You might as well finish."

"*We?*" Yara yanked the loc between her fingers. "The fuck do you mean *we?* You didn't do any of this. Jaz and Gina did more than you."

To Mrs. Gallagher's young daughters, Tabi's insistence on unlocking her neck-length hair rather than cutting it off had been a fun, hour-or-so-long diversion with a "real-life Barbie head!" and the promise of snacks—straight sugar, brought in by yours truly, from the drugstore down the street. Plying the girls with Skittles and Nerds Ropes had worked until about ninety minutes in, when the full effects of five bags of tropical-flavored treats hit their bloodstreams all at once. They were upstairs now, playing with actual Barbies and swearing up and down that everything was just fine every time we heard a particularly loud *thump*.

"I'm not cutting them," Tabi said again, insistent. "My hair would be the same length as *Sam's*."

"And?" I asked. Tabi shot me a look that might have unlocked her hair all on its own. "Fine. *Fine!*"

"You're afraid of having shorter hair than a guy you're not even having sex with. Relationships are dumb." Yara stabbed the bottom of a new lock with the pointy end of a thin comb and began to drag it through, breakage be damned. What Tabi wanted was technically possible, but two impatient high schoolers who had never had to deal with their own natural hair were not the people to be doing it.

"Anyway," my best friend continued. "Kendra, Callister is *definitely* applying for college. Her brother was a monitor and he went to Harvard."

"Really?" It had been a few weeks since the college fair, and while I'd learned the basics of my new friend's family (she had an older brother, Trevor and a younger sister, Sienna, who was applying to start at Taft as a day-student freshman the coming fall), I had missed the part where her brother had been a monitor. "I didn't know day students could be monitors. 'Monitoring' dorms is kind of right there in the title."

"He wasn't a day student," Yara said.

That one got Tabi's attention. "Wait, what?"

"He lived on campus for his senior year, at least," she said, raking the comb through another loc. A little dust bunny of dry hair fell to the ground. "Their mom had a phone installed in his dorm room that could only dial out to *her*. And if she called and he didn't pick up she would freak *out*."

"How do you know?" Tabi asked.

"S'what everyone in the boys' dorms says," she answered as though it should have been obvious.

"That sounds *very* fake," I said.

"Whatever. They're super religious," said Yara.

"*I'm* religious," Tabi pointed out. "And I got the same calling cards with the same amount of minutes y'all do."

"You're a Baptist. That's normal." Yara rolled her eyes. "You know what I mean. You're not a Christian Scientist."

"The only really weird thing about that is the amount she's at church. Like three services a week. You know God, She has quotas," I said. "Our neighbors used to have to do it too. Can I have the pink stuff?" I reached out for the bottle of moisturizer we'd found among the girls' hair stuff in the kids' bathroom upstairs. Tabi's hair needed far more help than the bottle could provide, but the fact that we were moisturizing it at all as we impatiently worked was notable.

"You had Christian Scientist neighbors?" Yara snickered.

"Mormons. They're in church a lot *and* forever. Like, eternally."

"Of course she knows Mormons," Yara and Tabi mumbled simultaneously before both succumbing to laughter.

It was my turn to roll my eyes. "Have you ever read about Joseph Smith? He had visions from God! In his hat! Like, *while* fording rivers and battling cholera. There also may have been some murders. Shit was crazy. It's *very* interesting."

"Sure." I knew Yara well enough by that point that I was able to catch the interest piqued on her face before she fell into her comfortable role of straight man to my enthusiasm. Later, probably after dinner that evening, we would go back to my room and she would almost certainly allow me to lay out a brief history of early Mormonism—knowledge I had mostly collected from the C plots of paperback romance novels set in the nineteenth-century American West, and an unfinished read-through of a Howard Hughes biography, which I'd picked up in an aroused fugue state the weekend after seeing *The Aviator*. I loved our friendship.

"I didn't know her brother went to Harvard," I went on. "That's good. She's *definitely* applying to college, then."

"You wouldn't pay $35,000 for high school, turn around, and not go to college," Tabi offered, rather sensibly I thought. "Even if you're on financial aid, that's so much money to not do anything with the diploma you're paying for."

"Right," I agreed. "It doesn't make sense. We're a college *prep* school."

"Or it makes all the sense in the world." Yara looked at me, raising an eyebrow as she countered. "You're spending the money now that you'd spend for college knowing you're not going, but making sure you at least get the best high school diploma."

"The *best* high school diploma? She's not at Exeter."

"Yeah, but she's also not at Choate," she said, smirking. "I d'know. I still think she's going to apply, but I'm just saying I get the logic."

I shook my head, focusing instead on the tangled task at hand. I had to agree with Tabi on this one. What was the point of subjecting yourself to this place if you weren't going to try to escape into the best college you could at the end of it? The idea that Callister simply didn't feel the pressure or have the need to get into college was a completely foreign concept, and became all the weirder knowing that her *brother* had not only gone away to school, but an Ivy League at that. Surely her parents expected the same from her.

"Yara, you have to detangle from the bottom up! Even after they're out!" Tabi exclaimed, flinching and pulling her head away from our hands.

"Then *you* do it!"

"Let's just keep going." I sighed. "Tabi, we're choosing a movie to put on, though." Ten years' worth of locs meant we could watch whatever the hell we wanted to, without complaint.

I checked on the kids before we pressed play (that $12 an hour was technically mine, after all) and then settled in for another hour or so of working our fingers to the bone. By the time Mrs. Gallagher and her husband returned, we'd managed to get through almost a quarter of her head.

Our advisor promptly handed Yara her broom and dustpan.

"Tabi, sweetheart…" Mrs. Gallagher cupped a hand around her own cheek, staring at the scene before her. "Are you going to take care of this before classes on Monday?"

"That's the plan?"

"Uh-huh." She sighed and pointed at Yara and me. "You two, do as much as you can before dinner. Tabi, I will be back from church by 2:30 tomorrow afternoon. You will be here, and we will go…fix this. What even— Your locs were lovely, Tabitha."

Tabi shrugged. "I wanted to change it up."

"Ah."

"My mom said it was okay."

"Did your mom know you were going to take them out yourself?"

"I d'know. It didn't come up."

"I'm sure it didn't." Mrs. Gallagher sighed again. "Kendra, were Jazmine and Gina fine?"

"Yep, they were helping for a while."

"Of course they were." Our advisor looked as though she wanted a stiff drink, a brick to the head, or both. "Tabitha, you're welcome to join us for dinner. Kendra, Yara, you two will eat in the dining hall as usual, and afterward one of you can run a bonnet or a scarf from Tabi's room back over here before you get distracted for the night, thank you."

It was the pointed "thank you" in a tone that only a Black mother could produce—a deceptively calm voice that still managed to be imbued with generations of ancestral disappointment—that ended the conversation.

About ninety minutes later I was crouching in front of the couch, dustbin in one hand and head of the broom in the other. Yara had sprinted off moments ago, back across the street to campus and Tabi's dorm, Mac House on the back roundabout, to grab the required bonnet before she "got the 'itis and forgot" after dinner. Tabi had vanished upstairs to watch *SpongeBob* in the play-room with the girls, half of her hair undone and defying gravity. I was jealous of the options she was going to have at her visit to the salon tomorrow.

Whatever was going on with dinner reached its peak when Mrs. Gallagher reentered the living room, something crackled on the stovetop, and the smell of properly seasoned, non-FLIK food wafted in behind her.

"Here you go." The older woman handed me a folded wad of bills. "By the way, I spoke to your dad the other day, about the alumni of color meetup on Alumni Weekend—"

"Yep, I'll be there," I said, cutting her off. I had already discussed it with him. There had been much talk during his time as a trustee about the importance of alumni of color legacy retention, something that both he and Mrs. Gallagher believed started with positive experiences at alumni weekends and examples to follow.

I, the first Black American legacy, was one of those examples. Is it any shock that I went into school admissions professionally?

"Well, it's a closed weekend, so I expected nothing less," Mrs. Gallagher said dryly. "I was going to say, we also spoke about the internship opportunity that I announced at TAALSA a few weeks ago."

I stopped sweeping. "Oh."

"Yes, he and your mom were thrilled to hear you'd be participating."

"Uh-huh."

"Do you need anything ironed before the interview session next week?"

"Not really." I looked back down, focusing very intently on getting every last stray piece of hair into the bin. "I wasn't really planning on interviewing, since it's banking and I'm studying international relations in college. I already talked about it with Mr. Fraser."

"Uh-huh." Mrs. Gallagher echoed me with a short laugh. "How about that gray skirt you have? *Without* suspenders."

"The suspenders are attached."

She laughed fully this time, shaking her head. "They are not. A blouse and tights too. It's an excellent opportunity, and you're going to interview."

"I thought it was just for Prep 9 and NJ SEEDS students."

"Interesting, your parents seemed to be under that impression too."

In all fairness, most of the kids at Taft who would be interviewing for Morgan Stanley's students of color internship *were* from Prep 9 and NJ SEEDS, but that was just because those were some of the only places Taft knew how to get Black and Latinx kids from in the tristate area.

A Black boarding school alum who had risen through the ranks at Morgan Stanley was paying it forward now, using her influence to help set up and run an internship program for students of color from a handful of the top New England college prep schools. She personally traveled to each school and met with students to give them their, oftentimes, very first experience with a corporate interview in a setting far less intimidating than the high-rise buildings the bank occupied in New York City. Because Mrs. Gallagher screened those chosen to interview in advance, most of us got in.

This sort of thing did not happen at Columbia High School—or most public high schools in New Jersey, I suspect. When I'd been younger, my father had worked at Barclays and then J.P. Morgan Chase, and had he stayed in finance straight through, I probably could have found my way into a paid internship like this one. But he hadn't, and, more important—to me, at least, though not Mrs. Gallagher, apparently—I had no interest in *any* department at Morgan Stanley. I could barely handle Geometry, where I was one of the oldest kids in my class, after repeating Algebra 1 my sophomore year, which Mrs. Gallagher surely knew.

"And," I said, my internal monologue continuing as though she'd been privy to the thoughts in my head as well, "I have *a lot* to do this summer. I have to write all my college essays, *and* we're visiting. I have to go to LA."

"That's what June and those last two weeks of August are for." She wiped her hands against the denim on her thighs and sat down. "Sit."

I did, leaving the broom at my feet.

"This is a good opportunity, one to be *thankful* and *grateful* for," Mrs. Gallagher said.

"I *know* that I don't want to be a banker," I insisted.

"You don't. You've never done it," she said. "Besides, you know good and well that's not all Morgan Stanley does."

"They're a *bank*!"

Mrs. Gallagher laughed. "God forbid you have an experience that opens your eyes to the fact that a company doesn't become a billion-dollar international player without diversifying the services they offer. Just a bank…" She scoffed, shaking her head. "Bring your things over to be ironed before they get here on Wednesday, yes?"

I nodded, scowling outwardly and plotting inwardly. Much like loading the dishwasher back home or living with a certain sophomore-year roommate, I could make anything I did not want to do unpleasant for *everyone* in my orbit.

Yara announced her return to the Gallagher household with a banging screen door and heavy steps, as she bypassed the living room entirely and sprinted up the back stairs to the playroom. Mrs. Gallagher shot me a final stern look before she stood up and headed back into the kitchen.

We gathered the last of our things and shouted goodbye to Mrs. Gallagher before letting ourselves out through the front door. It was chillier out now than when we'd walked over together after lunch. I set the pace, walking quickly to the four-way intersection that separated this grouping of faculty housing from Taft's front gates.

"Yara?"

"Bart?"

"No, wait, this is a real question," I said. "Are you doing that Morgan Stanley thing?"

"Ugh, you too? My Prep 9 counselor's been on my *ass* about that one."

"Mrs. Gallagher just told me I have to. Or I guess my parents told her I have to."

"You're at boarding school. Your first mistake, as always, was telling your parents literally anything," Yara answered as though she was speaking to a brand-new lower mid.

"I mean, my dad'll be here in three weeks. He was gonna find out."

"Your parents are here too much." My friend rolled her eyes, stepping off the curb as the light turned green. "You have to apply, sure. No one said you have to get *in*."

5.

THERE'S NOT A single decent picture of me in a *Taft Bulletin*, our quarterly alumni magazine. We have covered, extensively, why you should not assume that this was Taft's fault while I was a student there. Wearing my body weight in handmade hemp jewelry dedicated to dead fictional characters wasn't against dress code, but it wasn't exactly photogenic either.

I have a fraught relationship with this publication. It covers all the news of the school from the season prior. With images of students arriving on campus in the fall and then celebrating their departures for college in the spring, the summer and winter bulletins tend to be the most robust. I've found myself dotted through the magazine since graduating, here and there, usually after returning for an alumni weekend. My favorite is a blurry image from summer 2013 in which I am correctly identified by name, yet labeled as "enjoying my ten-year reunion" with a group of people I've never seen before a day in my life. I graduated in 2006.

Having your picture taken as a student was not an uncommon occurrence. Though I do suspect that it was mostly us nonwhite kids who really got the full experience; the strange sensation that you were being watched as you sat in a private corner of the library, wondering where that faint *click-click* noise was coming from, looking over your shoulder every few seconds until you finally spotted a camera lens peeking out from between the *N* and *M* volumes of the *Encyclopaedia Britannica* on the shelves three rows over capturing images of you and your friends studying that the admissions office would then slap across every brochure like it was that iconic shot of Britney, Paris, and Lindsay in the back seat of a car.

Our paparazzo's name was Mr. Duncan, and he *always* got his shot. Just enough to make sure smiling and studious Black and Latinx kids were peppered through each magazine, somehow more visible on the page than we ever were on campus. That was, of course, the point.

I was obviously feeling myself in the picture that appears in the summer 2005 issue. Dressed like an early aughts *ANTM* contestant out on a go-see, I'm the only person in our group of sixteen wearing heels. I distinctly remember the brown and beaded Steve Madden mule sandals I'd chosen for the occasion of Alumni Weekend. My dad, also pictured in the large group, had come to campus for the alumni of color reception that Saturday morning and, jeans aside (it was a *weekend* after all), I'd made the extra effort to dress rigidly within the boundaries of the school dress code so as to mitigate any potential embarrassment or ruffled feathers. I knew some photographic evidence of this gathering would be taken and used for at least the next year.

"Morgan Stanley is going to be amazing for all of them," Mrs. Gallagher leaned over and said to my father as we gathered on the steps just outside the Harley Roberts Room. Mr. Duncan wanted his photo before the bagpipes called for the start of the class reunion parade.

Out of the corner of my eye, I could see my advisor gesture to me, Esther, and Georgia, another Black student, pointing us out to my father. "The three of them were accepted," she said. "And then Charles too, he's in Kendra's class—I think he has a warm-up at the track, or he'd be here. They're going to have a great summer."

While I couldn't speak for Esther and Georgia, I knew where I stood and fully intended on causing irreparable damage to the stock market as soon as the opportunity presented itself, thus hopefully cutting this internship short. Unfortunately, there weren't many students who had interviewed for the program and *not* gotten in. As with everything else she did, Mrs. Gallagher had selected her applicants deliberately, and despite Yara's practical advice, I'd not been able to tank the interview. Morgan Stanley wasn't looking for applicant savants—just ten to twenty students who could be trusted not to royally fuck up an office copy machine.

"So, are you two going to take the bus together into the city this summer?" My dad asked Esther and me.

Click-click-click.

"Maybe partway?" Esther answered. "Newark Penn is closest for me."

"Yeah, and I'm probably gonna take the local 107." There was an express bus too, but I liked the longer local route that left more time to read my library books.

Click-click-click.

"Ten dollars an hour, so you'll be working hard, I'm sure," he said. "But you'll have fun."

Click-click-click.

I nodded unenthusiastically. The only fun I had that summer was the evening I convinced Esther to leave the office early so that we could sprint up to the *War of the Worlds* premiere at the Lincoln Center movie theatre and meet Tom Cruise.

Done grabbing his candid shots, Mr. Duncan issued a series of quick instructions that boiled down to "smalls to the front, talls to the back, and squeeze in," which took another five minutes to arrange despite the fact that surely we'd all been doing this since kindergarten. After a bit of jostling on the stairs I found myself standing next to Georgia and Esther and directly in front of William Abdi, who (perhaps not realizing that he, in turn, was standing next to my father) "playfully" drummed his fingers against the small of my back before Georgia moved to stand in between us.

"All right, great—let's get smiles! One...two..." The repetitive click of the shutter staccatoed once again across the spring breeze.

"Thank you, sincerely," Mrs. Gallagher said, once Mr. Duncan had collected his final evidence of our existence. "Thank you to those of you who've traveled to be here, and thank you to our current students who are out here and giving up their lunchtime with friends." Yara, Tabi, Sam, and Santiago had not chosen to do the same, and I couldn't really blame them.

"This is important to me," she continued. "And should be important to you, especially current students. It's—well, it's a little sad how few of us are here on a weekend like this. And I hope you remember how nice it's been to connect with older alumni, and consider returning to campus—and returning the favor—once you've graduated too. We should be here. We should be seen here. This weekend is just as much for us as it is for everyone else, and you should want younger students, even the ones who aren't here yet, to see you."

Of the sixteen in the final picture, only ten were alumni who had returned to campus for the weekend. The rest were students or teachers. Two more not-pictured alums had attended the reception, bringing the number of alumni of color who had returned for the reception to a grand total of twelve. The other pages of the bulletin celebrating the festivities that weekend do not feature a single Black face; not a sighting in the crowds marching in the parade, not one Black alum seated at a dining hall table with a group of old friends, no images of any of us walking the halls and visiting old teachers with looks of fond nostalgia on our faces.

It's not that the Black alumni who returned didn't do those things. I'm sure they did, especially folks like Josiah, who had just graduated the year before and made sure to stop by the dining hall to see everyone left behind before accompanying Esther, Georgia, and me to the reception. Every teacher he'd had was still on campus; several of his younger friends were set to graduate after finals in a few weeks' time. But somehow our presence at this alumni weekend was relegated to this single instance. It didn't matter what these twelve alumni of color had accomplished, how successful they were, or how successful we current students were, perhaps, to be as we headed off for the sort of prestigious summer internships that high-achieving students clamored for. We were still as segregated on the page as we were on the average Taft day.

"I had such a good experience that I sent my daughter here," reads a quote from my father next to the picture, printed in the *Bulletin* that summer. "She hears this from me daily."

● ● ●

During my mid-twenties, "What did you do?!" started to become "Will you send your kids there?"

The answer now? No. Probably not.

I won't lie and pretend that was my first answer. That my future children (Tiberius, Luc, and Lafayette) would apply to Taft was all but an inevitability while I was still at S³4, as it had felt for me; I loved that campus, and had from a very young age. But things began to change when I spent that single year in southern New York, confronting how the realities of race were still playing out on prestigious independent school campuses. One parent, an EGOT contender themself, went out of their way to speak to me, a twenty-five-year-old nobody, the few times we saw each other. They had no reason to—their kid had been admitted years before and my financial aid expertise was no concern of theirs, in the least—but more often than not, we were the only two Black people in a room at school events.

That feeling of being the Only One isn't something I will be able shield my kids from, but I certainly don't have to actively seek it out for them. Especially if I am more than a fifteen-minute drive away. Especially if I've turned my parental duties over to a faculty and administration who claim to be able to act in loco parentis despite not having a single clue of what it is like to be a Black parent in America. I want Taft to be better, but I'm not yet willing to allow my own children to be part of that great experiment.

Maybe I'm selfish. After all, the education that I received at Taft was excellent, tailored to my needs and interests in a way you just don't find at high schools with two thousand kids in attendance. I could probably do those three years over again and, bolstered with everything I've subsequently learned, have the time of my fucking life on that campus, a country club for privileged teens. But would it be worth it, even if Taft is trying to make things better? Because they are—they are trying very hard.

In 2020 an open letter signed by more than nine hundred alumni and current students was sent to Mr. Mac and the school's board. Compiled with suggestions from Black and POC alums, and chaired by alums of all races, the letter asked that (among many things) Taft actively strive toward a safe, supportive, and antiracist community for BIPOC students.

This list of actions included several observational points as well, including this one: *Many alumni have cited trauma as a main reason for disengaging with Taft after graduation.*

I don't believe that the graduating class of 2020 will be the last class to deal with the fallout from the trauma Taft can inflict on its students of color, because white people—the majority of the people who run Taft—are playing catch-up and have been for years. Even then, Taft's handbook did not have language specifically addressing racism and the consequences of racist actions *after four years of Donald Trump being in office*, a fact that feels bafflingly irresponsible.

Mr. Mac and the school's board of trustees responded to the open letter separately, though aligned, in two letters of their own, respectively. Mr. Mac wrote, *We will need to really dig in. This is a really daunting, exciting, powerful moment for us, and Taft is committed. We will need the urgency that leads to immediate action and the determination that leads to long-term change. In other words, we will need to measure our work not only in days but also in years.*

I was struck by the reference to the "moment" we were in. The board went further than just that word, opening their letter by stressing the need to understand *where we are as a society*, writing, *It is clear that we are at a critical socio-cultural transition as a nation. There are extraordinarily complex challenges facing society as we confront racism and discrimination embedded in our society and institutional structures as seen most clearly in recent incidents of police brutality.*

I remembered that summer of 2013 when my coworkers at S³4 and I kept actively abreast of the George Zimmerman trial, watching individually as we worked through the day, and gathering at lunch to watch and discuss as the prosecution pressed on, seeking justice for Trayvon Martin, who'd been killed simply for being Black and wearing a hoodie. His death was also a "moment."

There is no mention of Trayvon Martin in Taft's lengthy alumni magazines from the fall or winter following that trial. No articles about the emotional reactions I am sure the Black students on campus, especially the boys, might have been having to George

Zimmerman's acquittal; the weight of being fifteen and watching a jury declare that it is right and just for a man to shoot you simply because he feels "threatened" because you are in a place he perceives you should not be. What must that have been like, to be a Black boy living in the white enclave of Watertown, Connecticut? What was it like walking down to the drugstore for a snack with a group of Black friends after that verdict came in? Perhaps discussions were held on campus—in fact, I'm sure there were. But I still wonder, why wasn't Trayvon Martin's death or the acquittal of his killer enough of a moment to consider making a wholehearted and enthusiastic commitment to "diversity, equity, and inclusion"?

Why wasn't Sandra Bland a moment? Eric Garner? Philando Castile? We all saw the footage. Chanted their names.

Distance, time but also literally three thousand miles of physical distance, has helped me translate that feeling of "ownership" I preached to prospective students every weekend into what it's been all along: responsibility. If anything, that's the one true and lasting legacy I have inherited from Taft. Perhaps it is a combination of the ways I experienced racism in high school being benign in comparison to those of others, and that my ability to just bury everything deep down was both unhealthy *and* unparalleled, but I never did fully disengage from Taft, as many other alumni of color have.

I do not donate, but dutifully, I have attended reunions, alumni fundraising events, memorials for beloved teachers, and more. I've gone to be seen, not only by current students, but also by the faculty and staff. A reminder that while so many have rightly disengaged, others are still watching closely. And the fact that I *can* endure the simple act of repeatedly placing my body in that space is not something I take lightly, especially knowing now how many alumni cannot bring themselves to do even that. Taft will have to reckon with that absence, eventually.

These absences are as much a part of Taft's foundation as the brick exteriors and the soft Connecticut soil they were rooted in. This is not a place set up for nonwhite students, and I have never expected an apology from a building, an aura, a moment in time, or more than half a century's worth of harm, starting with Taft's first Black student, Wayne Jackson in 1954—absences not always tangible, but always *there*.

I don't think any school can apologize or change or protect their Black students until they've heard the full breadth of stories. Mine is just one, but I never lived through racism in the infirmary (there have been accusations of everything from the mishandled racist pain management we often see reflected in the broader American medical system, to dangerously handing out the wrong medication because telling the difference between two Black students was too difficult), and no one ever called me "nigger" to my face. I never had a case mismanaged by the counseling center out of a lack of understanding of my different socioeconomic status or an "untraditional" homelife. I wasn't harassed by male teachers who thought they could get away with it due to the color of my skin. I didn't have a college counselor who lacked the context of what it might be like to be the first person in your family to apply, much less attend, or took it upon themselves to refuse to send my application documents in to certain schools where they simply couldn't *imagine* my admission. No one in the administration ever advised me against studying cultural anthropology or African American studies in college, insisting they weren't viable career paths.

But, according to the accounts of hundreds of students, those things *happen* to Black and other nonwhite children at Taft and other independent schools. To this day.

SENIOR

1.

WHILE SITTING AT one of the desks I rotated through in Morgan Stanley's corporate gifts and graphic design department, I penned a screed justifying the decision a friend and I made to close our *X-Men* RPG (it was nothing sinister, just out-of-control player egos and flouncing, mostly, with a side of moderator boredom; once again, if you know, you know) and posted it to my LiveJournal, ending with the message, "If you feel the need to question this decision from *my* point of view about the closure of X-Axis, you can reach me at Kendra.James@morganstanley.com."

Gmail? I had two of those, and account invites to spare (and at least two classmates at Taft had been dumb enough to *pay me* to get their hands on them). Hotmail and Yahoo? I had those too, because where else were my friends from the Shoebox Project comment sections supposed to contact me after new chapters dropped? Then, of course, there was the account set up on the FirstClass server that Taft used to run our school emails from. Nothing was keeping me from offering up any of those emails to players who wanted to come at me over the closing of an online superhero game (where I was mostly, by that point, just alternating between writing fluffy romantic moments and writing huh-how-would-*these*-powers-make-sex-better?! sex scenes) outside of a pure and undiluted disdain for Morgan Stanley and his goddamned bank.

(Not a singular he? Not his name? Not even the original name of the bank? Didn't care to learn then, don't care now.)

It was a valuable experience, sure, and like so many experiences at Taft, one I was glad to get over with sooner rather than later. The opportunity to intern at a major financial institution as a seventeen-year-old, and to get into the program so *easily*, was not something I would have stumbled upon back in New Jersey—even with my dad making his way back into the world of Wall Street. I probably would have come across a similar opportunity in college, and it's also likely that my parents might have once again forced me to take it, had we not already been tortured by the experience together as a family.

The summer of Morgan Stanley was a long one. The bright spots of college trips were interspersed with fights about work-appropriate clothing, fights about whether or not I was on drugs or just tired like every other teenager (fall asleep at *one* eleven-year-old's soccer game on a muggy eighty-five-degree day in northern New Jersey and you ruin the entire summer), fights about whether or not I could hang out with Yara and Margot in the city on weekends, and fights about how I could spend the money that *I* was earning at the job I didn't want to be at.

But now that we'd gotten through it—both parties having had a miserable time, as I'd fully intended—my parents could no longer say, "You don't know you don't like it, because you haven't tried it yet," or, my mom's favorite, "I know the WB has brainwashed you, but *most people* work a corporate job if they want a reliable paycheck," when it came to flashy internships.

More important (and, perhaps, the spin Taft itself might give in an admissions pamphlet), I'd learned to trust myself and my voice a bit more. Perhaps it was a self-fulfilling prophecy (many things with stubborn teenagers are), but I emerged from that summer content that not only did I know myself *damn* well; I had a sense, even then, of what I wanted out of a job and a career. So much so that I avoided taking another corporate job until my thirties. Knowing then that I could trust my instinct and say "absolutely the fuck not" to something, no matter how prestigious it seemed, was a valuable lesson, and a privileged one.

It was an absolute relief when Mrs. Gallagher told me later that year that I could please *not* bother showing up to the next summer's round of interviews. Falling asleep, again, during a presentation on the 101s of fixed market incomes on the second-to-last day of the program had apparently been the final straw. Worse somehow, I guess, than when I'd asked the manager of the corporate gifts department flat out why anyone would want an engraved piece of cheap crystal (I spent the summer centering Lucite engraving designs in Photoshop) as a gift of accomplishment from a company that surely had billions of dollars tied up in assets around the world. Wouldn't they just want a check instead?

God, I hated that place.

● ● ●

Mr. Huston, my history teacher that year, called our fall schedules "college-lite." With classes infinitely more spread out across the week, *two* sleep-ins, on Monday and Thursday (meaning my classes didn't start until 8:35 a.m., so because seniors could skip breakfast, I could sleep until 8 a.m.), only two classes on Thursdays with a three-hour break in the middle of the day, and being done with *everything* by 12:35 p.m. on Fridays, I called my new schedule "fucking sick."

The dread I'd felt over living in Centen dissipated as soon as I saw the huge super-single I'd been assigned on the first floor, near both the front and back doors and the first-floor common room, with a window that looked out on the courtyard that touched Congdon, the Upper School Boys Dorm, and the library and science center. It was a bright and cheerful space on nice days, and perfectly and broodingly atmospheric each time Watertown had a bit of weather. I started hanging up my usual menagerie of posters, though this year the space above my desk was reserved for a *National Geographic* map of World War II's European theatre, a large poster featuring Fred Astaire and Ginger Rogers, and several smaller images of Lena Horne, Gene Kelly, and Dorothy Dandridge. I'd started a new 1940s-era *X-Men* RPG with my friend from Australia, as you do.

At Morning Meeting on our first day of classes, Mr. Mac addressed the devastation of Hurricane Katrina and announced that Taft, along with many of the other ten schools, would be opening a few slots to accept Louisiana independent school students who now found themselves displaced for the year. In doing this, our headmaster reminded us, we were all living up to the school's motto, "Not to be served, but to serve."

"Whatever. As long as they don't try and give me a roommate," Yara muttered after we'd found each other in the stream of students leaving Bingham Auditorium that morning. "Do you want to hang out in my room until your next class?"

"I only have an hour," I pointed out. "And my next class is *your* next class too."

"Oh, good call."

I raised an eyebrow. "Yara, you, like...have your schedule, right?"

"I mean, it's in my printer, but yeah. I *said* I have to go back to my room," she said, as though it all should have been obvious.

I had plans of my own for the next hour. Callister and I hadn't spoken since finals in June. The last on-campus SAT test had been the day after my last final, Latin, and while I'd held out hope of seeing Callister in the gym that day, she'd stuck to her word and simply wasn't taking it.

She had no social media either, no AIM account or LiveJournal, and as far as I could tell she hadn't checked her FirstClass school email during the summer. Or, if she had, she'd not deigned to reply to me. I hadn't the slightest clue as to how her summer had been or even if, frankly, she was coming *back* to Taft. I wouldn't have been surprised if she weren't, after all, given her ambivalent attitude toward matriculation.

("Ambivalent" was, of course, my word. Callister had told me several times with her whole chest that she *wasn't going to college*. She was all set; I was just bad at listening.)

On the second floor, above the student union and the Jig, were several band rehearsal spaces, a screening room with a projector alongside a DVD player, the photography darkroom, where Margot spent a lot of her time, a few empty classrooms that the English department occasionally used, and, I think, the dance studio—a room I never actually saw with my own eyes. That floor also housed the day-student common room, a sun-filled space with many pieces of brightly stained wooden furniture and a whiteboard, the latter of which made it look more like a repurposed classroom.

I doubled back to the circular stairwell where the stairs spilled out into a castle-like turret space, where freshly polished, chestnut-colored day-student lockers lined the walls with the exception of one, which housed a single, ominous classroom door. I hadn't noticed the lockers the last time, when I'd approached that door for Honor Court. Or perhaps I had—it was impossible to know between the dark that had fallen over the campus that night and because I'd done such a thorough job of trying to forget overall.

The vibe upstairs was much calmer than in the common room

below. I recognized a few other day-student seniors from classes, and another classmate, Katherine Escher, whom I was surprised to see sitting next to the friend I was searching for.

Callister, wearing a light salmon-pink button-down shirt, her usual inoffensive light-to-dark-brown-to-black dress pants, and a new pair of Steve Madden loafers, beamed when she saw me.

"Hi!"

"*Hiiiiiiii!*" She clambered up from kneeling in front of her locker and rushed over to give me a hug. "It's nice to see you!"

"You too!" I said, returning the squeeze. "How was your summer?"

"The usual. Service." Being in service, she meant, *and* attending them. "Weirdly, I was in the city for a weekend. There was a canteen for everyone in the church youth groups in the tristate area. It was so much fun, *and*"—she leaned in, grinning—"it's a *really* good place to start looking for a husband."

"Did you...find a husband?" I asked, unsure if this was even the question to be asking.

"No, but I have time and the prospects were strong," she said, laughing. "Do you know Kat?"

Our pale, raven-haired classmate looked up from the bench where she'd remained sitting and waved briefly. I knew her from art classes, but only from behind. It was a surprise to finally put a face to the long, dark plait I'd spent a year staring at.

The sleeves on her red-and-black plaid shirt were rolled up neatly to the elbow and she wore her straight-legged pants tucked into a pair of brown boots, laced up to her calves. Like Callister, Kat carried her belongings in a messenger bag, but hers was an overflowing brown canvas, or maybe a dulled leather. She looked like she'd styled herself after a young Indiana Jones.

(Or that was what I told myself so that I had the flimsiest of excuses later when I clicked buy now and had a bootleg set of

Young Indiana Jones DVDs sent to the mailroom from a nice eBay seller in Japan.)

"Nice to meet you."

"We're in AP Studio Art together this semester." She paused before adding, "I spent junior year in Paris."

"Kat and I were talking," Callister said, excited, "and we think we're going to do the musical this year!"

"Like, auditioning?" I asked. "I hate *Grease* and I can't sing."

"So do I. It's incredibly sexist," said Kat. "But, no, we're not going to be in it. You don't have to sing; we're doing stage crew."

"Kat ran the light board for *Les Mis* and *Noises Off* sophomore year, and she's doing tech for Morning Meetings this year." That explained why I'd never seen Kat outside of Mrs. Myers's studio. It also probably explained why she, a boarder, was up in the day-students' locker loft. She was a true Theatre Kid, and a Stage Crew Kid at that—a subspecies of an already rare breed within Taft's confines. "And Mr. Lane's favorites graduated last year, so there's no ADs, casting directors, or stage managers left. That could be us."

"I've never—"

Callister grinned, reaching out to place her hand on my arm. "I haven't done stage crew either, but it's going to be *fun*."

Some leeway for Taft's three semesters of sports or arts could be garnered, especially during senior spring, but for the most part the rules held firm. The prior fall, I'd halfheartedly participated in an aerobics class run by Mrs. Mac, our headmaster's enthusiastically fit, sweatband-clad wife. Anything to avoid managing a field hockey team again. I didn't have plans for this fall's extra-curricular yet.

"Does it start today?" I asked.

"Three thirty in Bingham," Kat said, standing up to leave. "Auditions start immediately."

Callister and I waved after the other girl as she disappeared down the steps.

"When did you and Kat become friends?" I asked, as soon as the click of the door on the second-floor landing had echoed back up the brick stairwell.

"Freshman year! Spanish class. She's from Miami, so she's been learning since elementary school," she said, smiling. "You should sit with us at lunch!"

"Where are you eating lunch?" I asked. There were two places to eat lunch, as far as I was concerned: The Black Table and The Black Seniors Table, and I was looking forward to eating with my fellow seniors later.

"With Aggie in the lower dining hall, probably."

Agnes Kim was a senior from South Korea who had been attending American boarding schools since middle school. She often ate at a table with some of Santiago and Sam's friends from the boys' dorms and several other Asian students I didn't know (sometimes called The Korean Table or The Chinese Table or just The Asian Table, depending on where you fell on the axes of Lazy and Racist), which stood out in the dining hall almost as much as the two Black ones. I cannot count how many times I heard, in passing, various versions of the same terrible advice: "You can't eat there, and they don't want you to—that's why they don't speak English."

To no one's surprise (as often happened at Taft), once I took Callister up on her offer I found their table to be absolutely delightful, and immediately bonded with Agnes (in English) over our mutual love of the Korean boy band Shinhwa, after she got over the shock that I knew who the band was, much less that I had multiple pictures of Lee Min Woo up on my wall and glue-sticked into one of my many journals.

"Day students can be friends with anyone," Callister confided one evening as we waited in the Harley Roberts Room for her mom to arrive. The floorboards groaned and settled in the chilly night air while we passed a bag of Jelly Bellies back and forth between us. "We're invisible, most of the time, so when we pop up in something or someplace we're usually not, you guys treat us like a novelty you've never seen before. But then you get bored when we can't spend the night or gossip after study hall, or whatever. Wash, rinse, repeat."

"You have a bunch of boarder friends," I pointed out.

"I do," she said. "And I love all of you guys, but it's sort of like…"

"Yeah?"

"I don't know how to say it without insulting you."

"My best friend is *Yara Harris*," I reminded her, deadpan. "I have heard it *all*."

She laughed. "Okay. I guess I mean, I kind of feel like once we're done being a novelty, day students just end up with all the friends no one else wants. It's sheer luck that we all also happen to be the coolest people in school."

"That's not insulting; that's the plot of, like, *every* single good comic book!" And also similar to the plight of every Black student at Taft, but I wasn't quite up to making those connections just yet.

"Really?"

"Oh my God, yes," I assured her. "We're getting *powers*."

●　●　●

We did get powers. Or, rather, *power*, bestowed upon us by Taft's theatre director, Mr. Lane.

As a Capricorn, I am comfortable confessing that I am, more than a decade later, still riding the high from the power ascribed to me as the assistant director of a high school musical.

Our theatre director was a tall, wiry man, with two tufts of gray hair at either side of his temples. He wore round glasses and had the face of an emaciated but inquisitive owl. In the pursuit of creating student theatre, Mr. Lane was known to get occasionally snappy and he certainly had his moods. And, of course, there was the time he asked me to "go up to the track" and "get some of my *friends*" to fill in the Negro Section of the courtroom he was creating for our spring production of *To Kill a Mockingbird*—a show that, along with *Once on This Island* and *A Raisin in the Sun*, to name a few, no school where students of color make up only 23 percent of the student body should ever try to stage. (I've heard tell that when you get to 35 percent, your school gets to do *Hamilton*. As a treat.)

But in the grand scheme of the numerous ways Taft's faculty and staff could be casually microaggressive or racist, Mr. Lane was low on my list of grievances. In fact, we got on quite well, and Callister and I would often work and study in his office with his two giant border collies between classes and rehearsals. The space was built to look like a tree house, a quirk that, much like building your own home amusement park and calling it Neverland, is considered fun and whimsical up until the exact moment you are arrested and convicted on multiple charges of possessing child pornography on your personal computers...as Mr. Lane eventually was.

"There's one at every independent school, guaranteed," a colleague would tell me years later in a disturbingly matter-of-fact tone. "It's just a matter of whether or not they've been caught yet."

Callister, Kat, and I knew none of this at the time (nor were we the subjects of any predatory behaviors), and so we happily sat with Mr. Lane and helped run auditions for *Grease*. By the time the afternoon was over, Callister and I were co-assistant directors (co-, because the other girl's mother had historically not *loved* to have her on campus late into the night) and I was the sole stage manager, in charge of keeping the show bible. Kat, an AV jack-of-all-trades, was named head of sound design for the entire show.

"Kat, you and Ian will coordinate on mics and general AV needs. At least two of you should learn how to run the light board," Mr. Lane instructed once auditions were done.

"Who is Ian?" she asked.

"Ian," he repeated, pointing to a man, perhaps in his early to mid-twenties, whom we could only *just* see fiddling with something in the stage right wings. "Ian!"

Ian looked up and stepped forward. He was tall. He had blue eyes. He had neck-length black hair pulled back into a small pre–hipster culture man-bun. He had a beard. He wore collarless shirts and *denim*. He had a pulse. He very clearly did not go to Taft.

And, most important, unlike the attractive boys at Taft, Ian had to talk to us. He was paid to.

"I can help with AV stuff too," I said.

"Me too," Callister added immediately.

"Great!" said an oblivious Mr. Lane.

I nodded slowly. "Shawn Hunter up there can teach us how to run the light board, definitely."

"And I can supervise," Kat murmured, eyes fixated on Ian like the rest of us.

I have since found pictures of Ian-from-New-Haven, many of them clearly taken from hidden corners and angles as I tried my best to not be actively horny on main during rehearsals. He was not as mind-blowingly hot as I remembered him being. But to three teens, starved for attention from the opposite sex, he was basically Rider Strong.

Mr. Lane waved Ian down, gesturing for him to leave the stage and join us where we sat in the auditorium. Auditions were over, but we still had to deliberate on role assignment before dinner.

"Ian is playing Gaston in a *Beauty and the Beast* production in New Haven this winter, and last year he played Radames in—"

"*Aida*." Callister sighed softly. She found my hand underneath the seat and squeezed me into her sweaty palm.

"Yes," Mr. Lane said. "So, he'll be helping with casting."

"He can sit here." Kat pushed her bag from an otherwise vacant seat to the ground.

Somehow, *Grease* got cast that afternoon.

In the time between auditions and the long walk from Morning Meeting the next day, down the stone hallway from Bingham to the bulletin board just in front of Mrs. Gallagher's office, where Callister and I each hung, with an air of grave importance, one of the two pieces of paper Mr. Lane had handed us, I managed to recruit a small stage crew.

Jonathan George was one of three new Black legacies who'd enrolled that year. The short, bespectacled freshman had arrived from Washington State with his sophomore sister, Taylor (the second legacy). Another freshman, Athena Hernandez, had already bonded with Jon at orientation and followed, joining him under our wings and behind the stage's.

Callister bestowed Jon with the nickname "Simba," and Kat showed Athena and me how to run the light board for *Grease* and a variety of Morning Meeting setups. Ian took it a step further, one afternoon handing me a physical light and sending me up a skinny trellis bolted to a piece of ceiling and wall far too high above Bingham's chairs while he shouted instructions on how to hang that one and adjust the others to align with his lighting design plan. I could have died! I was delighted!

By the time October rolled around, I'd dropped my one AP class, studio art, after realizing that I simply didn't *care*, but between the classes remaining, the musical, and the few pieces of college applications that still needed tweaking, I was busy by my standards.

Rehearsal on October 18 was a particularly good one—an already amazing day of classes in which I'd been awarded a 5.0 on my paper on the themes of class in Curtis Sittenfeld's *Prep* for our Boarding School Literature senior English class (yes, really), and finally hit send on my early action application to Tulane. My parents soured on the choice of school after Katrina, but the idea of setting down roots in a city in the midst of rebuilding appealed to my sense of adventure, and my proposed budget. (I later learned that this is called "gentrification.") Regardless, it felt amazing to have my first application out and done with and to know that, God willing, I'd have at least one not-Rutgers school to go to by December.

A freshly mailed college application also meant an excuse to engage in my favorite pastime, alongside Kat—bothering Callister about her poor attitude regarding higher learning. Kat was just about done with her McGill application, and she'd already mailed off St. Andrews over the summer.

"Going to college in America is just doing yourself a disservice in the long run," she explained once again that afternoon, her voice practical as ever as she untangled a thin lav mic wire. "You don't want to end up in debt, all to live in a city that won't even *be* there in twenty years because we don't give a shit about global warming because it's inconvenient." She looked over her glasses at me, pointedly.

"I'm literally just trying to get into law school," I said.

"Not a very persuasive argument today, guys," Callister pointed out.

"You told me once that you were thinking about an overseas mission, Callie," Kat steamrolled on. As liberal and politically aware as she was for a Taft student, even Kat couldn't comprehend that someone would simply choose not to go to college. Neither of us could make it make sense in our Taft Bubble minds. "You could do a mission *and* enroll somewhere in the same country."

It was a smaller group filing in for rehearsal that day, just the Beauty School Dropouts with us, each draped in a temporary costume of salon capes and plastic shower caps while they worked on the blocking for their big number.

Down in the orchestra pit, Ian was checking the floor mics that would amplify the band. Every so often, Callister, Kat, and I would sigh softly when the mics picked up a spare note as the older man sang through the Rodgers and Hammerstein catalog under his breath while he worked. He'd clearly played Curly a time or two.

A paint-covered Mr. Lane stopped by our aisle toward the end of the afternoon to drop off a musicals mix CD he'd made for Jon—"Simba's Broadway Mix" it was labeled, and yes, signs *were* missed—and as soon as the Dropouts vacated the stage we commandeered the boombox and hit shuffle. As Ian helped us reset the space for Morning Meeting, he performed the entirety of Gaston along to the music, gaining the rapt attention of everyone on our crew and the stragglers left behind and prompting an echoed murmur of "Thank you, Mr. Lane" that surely sounded more lecherous than it should have coming out of the mouths of several high school–aged girls.

It was an excellent and, moreover, distracting rehearsal. Sienna, who was one of our Dropouts (for the time being—neither girl had told their mother that the youngest would have to wear *red* lipstick in the role, and a lot of it), asked her older sibling if they had time to grab a small dinner from the dining hall before going home. It was clear that she was angling for a few extra minutes with her friend Tomasina (legacy number three), a freshman Dropout from Atlanta.

Callister agreed that they did have time, so we gathered our things and left. Dinner, even FLIK food, sounded appealing.

We walked over to the dining hall quickly, stopping only to wave at Mrs. Gallagher through the glass window of her closed office door and then to the mailroom counter to pick up fresh copies of the *Papyrus*, the school newspaper, which had just dropped that morning. Occasionally a student journalist would review a movie they'd seen at the Waterbury mall or at the second-run theatre down the road in town. Inevitably, I would disagree with their opinion and would spend the next forty minutes at dinner talking Yara's ear off about why *Alexander* was bad, yes, even if Angelina Jolie was in it.

To my surprise, everyone at our usual table also had a copy of the *Pap* out. The table was subdued, eyes intently scanning the black-and-white print. The dining hall was notably quieter; a tension was palpable, though it didn't emanate *just* from our table. It felt as if the whole room was waiting for something to happen, as though a table were about to collapse underneath too many plates and bookbags, or the arcing children in the giant *Snap the Whip* painting were going to become real and topple out onto us all. Something was wrong.

"Have you—oh," Sam said before I could even sit down, pointing to the paper in my hands. "So you *did* see it."

I shook my head. "See what?"

"I heard the little racist bitch cried already," Tabi said. We slid into empty seats at the end of the table. This late into October, no one gave Kat a second glance anymore—just another misfit who'd been accepted within our ranks.

"Sienna, Tomi's over there! Go!" Callister glared at her sister, who was trying to squeeze in as well, and pointed to the table behind us, where a bunch of Black and Latino mids and lower mids were already gathering, heads down and pouring over *Papyruses* of their own. "Who cried?"

"Emma Hunter." Mike's tone was as gossipy as I'd ever heard it, and I was shocked to hear him give a shit about something that wasn't the GameCube and antenna TV he and Santiago weren't supposed to have up in their room.

"The junior?" I asked.

"Yep," said Santiago.

"Oh my God, did she get kicked out?"

"No, no—" Kat tapped her copy of the *Pap*, which she already had open on the table. "I think I found it. Page 3?"

"*Yeeeep*." Santiago drawled his word with a smirk. "She called *us* the only racist people on campus and then *she* fucking cried."

I opened my paper quickly and flipped to page 3, the first of the Opinions section. There was only one opinion in that issue, just the second of the school year. Callister read the headline aloud. "'Do We Take Advantage of Our Diversity?'"

Mike gave a dark laugh. "Keep reading."

It was a short piece, no more than seven hundred words or so, that would have been just as at home on a Breitbart page as it was in print at a school that had no language readily available about the consequences one might face for committing acts of racism on campus. Acts, for instance, like publishing an article in the official school paper that asserted that the Black and Latinx students on campus were, actually, the real segregationists, refusing to integrate into the white norm, and purposefully keeping white students out of our spaces and activities. We were unfriendly, intimidating, and granted too much special treatment in the form of specialized orientations and dances; and we had, according to Emma Hunter, quite a bit of power and influence for a group of people whose presence in each grade you could count on your fingers alone.

This was news to us!

● ● ●

"Fuck Hermione, first of all."

Santiago set the tone for the emergency joint TAALSA/UTC

(United Cultures at Taft) meeting two days later, and I dutifully typed his words into the official minutes.

I don't remember why I was the one to take notes at this particular meeting. I had been an enthusiastic but unreliable attendee of both groups during my sophomore and junior years. Meetings were held in the evenings before study hall, generally on days when I had either skating lessons during the winter, or extra Latin tutoring. Between the musical and giving school tours, I was about as "involved" with the school community as I felt the need to get for the benefit of college applications.

So while I was many things during my senior year—student, assistant director, stage manager, tour guide, group mom, and sometimes condom procurer—I was not, as far as I can remember, a TAALSA secretary.

Meetings were held in an empty history classroom. Black and Latinx kids would pour in and we'd shut the door. If we gathered on a Wednesday evening the room would quickly turn ripe; we were teenagers, and very few of us showered immediately after games and practices. Occasionally an adult was present (usually Mrs. Gallagher or, that year, Mr. LeRoy Freeman, the new history teacher), but for the most part we were unsupervised—an issue that, judging by Emma's article, clearly plagued the club running the school's paper as well.

TAALSA had been founded with a mission, something about support and unity. We were supposed to be there for one another, in this sea of whiteness. Maybe occasionally plan out some sort of diverse programming that wasn't for Martin Luther King Day for the rest of the students on campus with the aid of our advisor, because if we didn't, who else would? Plenty of that happened, I'm sure, but what I remember most is a constant stream of cackling laughter. Kids dissolving into mirthful tears, shooting the shit back and forth at each other, getting everything out that was too risqué for even the safe space of our lunch table. No one was safe, from the teachers ("I'd get As on my papers from Mr. Hastings, too, if I had blond hair and bulimia") to other students ("Duh, she has gonorrhea of the throat. She goes though white PG dick like freeze pops") to kids sitting right there in the same room ("If it wasn't statutory, you know she and Kat would've double-teamed that theatre assistant already").

That last one was quite bold of Tabi to say, given that I'd been buying her those condoms that fall for her on-again, off-again relationship with Sam because she was too embarrassed to buy them at Brooks herself.

That day was different. It was an unusually solemn meeting, well banked in my memory thanks to extensive records: journal entries so rife with emo rap lyrics and typos that even if I managed to forget in the decade plus since graduation, I would still find myself swallowed, sucked under by the same ravenous anger. Clipped, urgent instant messages lacking the extraneous LOLs: "Meeting. 7pm." Terse emails between students and teachers. Meeting notes, meticulously written. The complete text of Emma Hunter's article, which none of us, still, could believe had actually been published in the *official* school paper.

Santiago called her Hermione because the Emma in question happened to look just like actress Emma Watson. The physical resemblance was uncanny, but the similarities stopped there. The fictional Hermione was written, however strangely, to care about the feelings and treatment of those who found themselves marginalized by society.

Emma, on the other hand, sat through a single Morning Meeting about Black students that had not taken place during February, and she'd just about had a stroke over it.

"'I felt a little uncomfortable listening to Mrs. Gallagher speak about why only four African American Taft alums have sent their own children...the easy conclusion is that white students and teachers made their African American and Latino peers feel unwelcome...but the barrier created between white and African American students is as much—if not more—a creation of the students of color than it is that of their Caucasian peers.'" I read aloud. "She's saying the segregation on campus is our fault—like we want it this way. She's basically saying that we swallowed the keys to our own shackles," I concluded. It was an analogy I'm sure I felt was quite awe-inspiring at the time.

The speech in the crosshairs of Emma's op-ed was nothing more than a short history of Taft that left the student audience with a bitter truth in the end. Of the handful of Black students who had graduated in each class each year since the 1950s, only four of them had sent their children back to attend as legacies. The first, Wayne Jackson, the Bermuda native (not actually African-American, as Emma had identified him; just saying 'Black' did not come so easily to some, back then) who had arrived as a mid in '54 just after *Brown v. Board of Education*, called his time at the school "the loneliest three years of my life." And he did so in our alumni magazine, where his white classmates couldn't miss it. His daughter, the first legacy, Alisa, also from Bermuda, graduated in 1989.

The other four of us, those legacies from three other alums, were sitting in the audience during that Morning Meeting. It was the fall of 2005, sixteen years later.

"One of our current seniors is going to be our first African American legacy to graduate. Why don't more Black and African American alumni send their children back?" Mrs. Gallagher asked her audience of students, teachers, and administrators.

It's not hard to guess why there would be more white legacy students than Black at a New England prep school, but Mrs. Gallagher laid it all out in plain-speak for those who needed it: Black students—especially Black *American* students—were running at a deficit of both attendance and generational wealth, and Taft's boarding student tuition was upwards of $35,000 that year. And what did that money buy? An education, yes, but also isolation. Could any of the white students on campus imagine what it might be like to be one of three (if you were lucky) white students in their class, Mrs. Gallagher had asked, as Black students often were? Perhaps it was ostracizing to not only be one of two or three Black students in your classroom, but to feel like the only one for miles in the sea of whiteness and farmland that was Watertown, Connecticut. Maybe that feeling of isolation came down to the little things, like literally having to get onto a bus to go to another city to get your hair done.

None of this information was revelatory to me by this point, nor Taylor, Jon, or Tomasina, not to mention our nonlegacy friends. Frankly, until Emma's article made its way to press, I was more concerned about the fact that Mrs. Gallagher had shown several pictures of my father in the 1970s wearing a pair of terrible glasses during her PowerPoint presentation. As far as I was concerned, that was the absolute height of embarrassment. But, delivered with such honesty and very much Not in February, the speech was a shock to our white classmates.

So, Emma took to the *Papyrus*. And I took notes.

Our combined group agreed to go through the op-ed point by point to craft a response. Someone else read aloud, directly from the *Pap*, "'Moreover, Black and Latino students tend to keep to themselves; many pass up the opportunity to socialize with the rest of the student body.'"

"Fuck her," Santiago repeated. I glanced over at Kat (who, as a good white ally, spoke only once according to my four pages of minutes) and agreed.

Santiago went on, "That's fucking outrageous. We have friends. Kat is sitting *right here*! My *report card* says I'm too social during study hall and 'rambunctious.' To say that we don't socialize—" He shook his head. "That's a blatant lie. Just because there's a minority of us and we make friends with each other…there's less of us so it's more noticeable than when white kids have white friends. Which they do. That's *all* they do! Well…not you, Kat."

There were murmurs of agreement, and a freshman named Daufin piped up. "I try to branch out, I try to meet white people. I'm trying to get a white girlfriend and stuff, but none of them are interested in talking to me, even in class." The fact that no one cracked on him for that comment alone shows how deadly serious this particular meeting was. "But if this is what they think of us, then why should we branch out?"

It's a strange thing, looking back, to have so many primary sources surrounding one single incident of anger. Notes this thorough are meant for history, not the drama of a small high school. Yet this was history, of a sort. It wouldn't be until years later that I realized we were all stuck in a cycle that had repeated itself at Taft since Wayne Jackson's arrival and will likely continue forever— or at least until Taft actually succeeds at the work of sustained antiracism. But there's no such thing as a school year of Februarys, you know?

Odder still was the lack of a fully developed mind present to help as we parsed through Emma's article. While there was, somewhere in the senior class, another nearly twenty-year-old PG, I may have been the oldest in the room that night, three months from eighteen. It was just us, ten children sitting in a room, surrounded by whiteness on all sides, attempting to solve the racism of a 115-year-old institution.

I looked around, taking stock of the students sitting behind and on top of the classroom desks. I wasn't close with every person there. The freshmen were still very new, green and living away from home for the first time and confronted by Emma's article in their second month of school. But I could tell you something specific about each of them, some character trait or something they had said, done, or mentioned in passing. Taft was a small place; it was hard not to know a little something about everyone. Even before her article, I could have at least said, "Emma Hunter: Looks like Hermione. Writes for the *Pap*. Lived in Congdon during my sophomore year."

"Could she say the same about any of us?" I wondered out loud.

Esther nodded in agreement. "I've never seen Emma try to befriend the 'minorities' she mentions in her article."

"Do we have to try harder to make white friends?" Maura asked. "Because we already have to prove to them that we're smart enough to be here. Why should we have to do even more work to make friends with them?"

Because we have to work twice as hard to get half as much.

The oft-repeated line hung in the air. That's how life worked for us, in the classroom, in the dining hall, in the small safe space that was TAALSA. Good to comprehend that lesson early on, I guess. High school is, after all, a place of learning.

The woke student, the activist student, the empowered student, is commonplace now, but their emergence is treated like an aberration each time. As if students of color dealing with racism in historically white institutions was unheard of; as if it were one of those new norms in America that could be blamed on the popularity of twenty-four-hour cable news, the effects of cancel culture, and too much screen time, or 9/11.

Published today, Emma's article might have gone viral; at the very least it would have been passed on among students of color throughout New England boarding schools with a subject line reading, "Karen Tried It," and a link to the article in the body of the email, punctuated by the Confused Mr. Krabs meme and nothing else. In solidarity, a Black student from Northfield Mount

Hermon would make a series of green-screen TikToks, standing in front of paragraphs from Emma's piece, annotated with hand-written notes, as she dismantled it, and Emma herself, point by point. Emma would then become the subject of a profile in the *Cut*, sending the story national, at which point Jada would call us all to Red Table for an open and honest conversation on the path to healing, which Gammy would attend, but only under duress. And after making a show of public-facing compassion in the wake of this PR disaster, Taft would quietly go back to business as usual, but at least we would have had *something*.

In 2005 we were alone. We didn't have the backing of Twitter or even (the) Facebook. Without any outside help—not even a final exam or grade for effort to tell us if we'd gotten it right—we had to figure out how to respond to accusations of self-segregation, to the argument that we were somehow perpetuating racism in a school that hadn't admitted one of us to attend until sixty-four years after its founding.

Of course, Black children are asked to do this constantly, no matter the setting. Karen doesn't like the way Annie's hair smells, and so Annie is sent home with a note from the teacher telling her mother that she needs to lay off the Pink lotion when braiding her hair. Karen's mother buys all the tights for the school dance recital that week, and even though they don't match her skin, Annie is expected to wear them with a smile. Karen and Annie turn in their papers at the same time, and Annie is accused of copying off of Karen instead of the other way around, because Annie's paper "doesn't sound the way she talks." Most of us begin dealing with this the very moment a white student enters our classroom. Hell, even our day care.

We are expert, if involuntary, pioneers in these spaces; we navigate situations like this one with grace, because we must. Black kids hear some shit *every single day* from their white peers in America. The fact that there aren't two or three viral videos per week of white students catching hands is a minor miracle, one that only further demonstrates the full breadth of our patience as a people.

Of course, Black students can't get away with reactionary behavior in the same way our white peers can. When faced with a Karen—or an Emma—we must demur, retreat, and solve our problems quietly. *Appropriately.* And if the problem cannot be solved to the satisfaction of the institution's white majority, we must learn to accept the possibility that the problem will not be solved at all.

● ● ●

This story—the *Papyrus* article, and the meeting that followed—stayed with me. It certainly helps, however, that the cyclical nature of racism at Taft is more dependable than my period. This story has been stewing in my mind since I began writing professionally in 2011, a job whose skills I must ironically give credit to Taft's English and history teachers for. Their classes, harping on outlines and revisions in a way none of my teachers had before, sharpened my pen over three years. This experience, however, was one I could never suss out how to write about until now. But a lack of inspiration has never been the problem.

I've yet to meet a single racist Taftie, Emma wrote. *And if any Taftie were going to discriminate against another it would most likely be on the basis of gender rather than race or religion.*

I considered writing about Emma, her article, and the fallout for the first time in my early twenties, when I found a photo taken that winter of our senior year. The image is too dark to tell who it was exactly—or, like with so many of my white classmates, I simply don't recognize the person in the picture—but it clearly shows a white student standing above us in a fully extended stage crane with his right arm raised, ramrod straight and palm flat. If you could touch the image and be drawn in, you would hear him in the middle of giving a speech impersonating the fascist European dictators of the 1940s during an impromptu dance party in the Black Box theatre. As a joke.

I considered writing this piece in 2016 when I scanned the school's annual donor report and noticed that one of the year's top donors was the known racist, misogynist, and overall trash fire of a human being Roger Ailes. His son attended Taft at the time, and he had also been invited to speak at a Morning Meeting in April of 2015. There's simply no way to foster an environment of diversity and inclusion, or even to claim that's an environment you want, when you're even slightly financially beholden to a man who spent decades running Fox News and sexually assaulting women. *Allegedly.*

I considered writing this as an essay in 2017 when nearly the exact same article appeared in a winter issue of the *Papyrus* in response to another op-ed attempting to address the conservative racism at play in the election of Donald Trump. The student author decried claims by students of color that Taft could feel "unsafe" and urged the school not to "take the beliefs of minority students as fact."

When I sat down in 2018 thinking that this was the moment to finally tell the story, it was after receiving a lengthy letter via email from our headmaster, still Mr. Mac, explaining the latest incident on campus. It had, once again, occurred around MLK Day. Some-one (no one knew who, we were told) had written *Go back to Africa, nigger* on two African soccer players' dorm room whiteboard. The letter was board-member appropriate, promising punishment for the students once they were found out and detailing a "day of healing" that the school had participated in after the message was discovered. Knowing the man who wrote this, I'm confident in saying that Mr. Mac likely meant every word and deeply believed that *these acts were at odds with all we believe in, that there is no place for hatred at Taft, that all students must feel supported and safe, and that we can move forward in productive ways*, even if it had never proven to be true.

Tales of other incidents in that school year trickled in through a Facebook Messenger thread. Rumors that a Chinese American hockey player had her displayed artwork destroyed after giving a speech to the school about her experience at Taft as a Chinese American during the MLK Day multicultural celebration. Whispers of allegations that a lesbian student had been told, "Fags don't belong here."

The dams finally broke open in 2020 in the wake of the murder of George Floyd, when, seizing the moment, several incredibly brave students and alumni of independent schools across the country took to Instagram to start a series of accounts with names like BlackAtPolyPrep, BlackAtChoate, BlackAtTrinity, BlackAtHarvardWestlake, BlackAtPingry, and BlackAtTaft. Through these accounts, Black students were invited to anonymously submit stories about the racism they'd had to endure from fellow students, teachers, administrators, health center nurses and doctors, and dorm parents alike.

The stories, crossing decades, were painfully familiar and, unsurprisingly, tended to skew female. Black girls who felt invisible. Black girls who felt hypervisible. Black girls who had trouble fitting in. Black girls whose bodies were policed. Black girls calling out the Black boys who'd benefited from being able to use a sport or the racist appeal of being "dangerous" for a white girl to date in order to climb their school's social ladders, leaving everyone else worse off in their wake. Black girls doing the work and taking to the front lines by reporting their own stories while *also* standing up for Black boys and other students of color as they took their administrations to task.

But as always, it was the familiarity of certain posts—the way the stories rang true without hesitation no matter who they'd come from—that I found the most disturbing.

Throughout the first month of my sophomore year, my assigned roommate would consistently call me the N-Word. [Having dealt] with it throughout freshman year, notifying teachers and getting no response, I ignored this silently until it was overwhelming.

I rowed Crew. At a regatta, a Taft parent said, "I always know when your boat is coming down! Just look for the black dot out there!" felt so uncomfortable in my own skin.

I was in AP Chemistry one year, and my teacher referred to me as "pale-face" and referred to the other Black girl in the room as "darkie."

My senior year, DeRay Mckesson was invited to speak at Morning meeting. After the MM, in the public dining hall, a football PG was overheard calling this speaker "a f*ggot" and claiming that DeRay was "chatting bullshit." At the time, this was overheard by the only openly gay man at Taft. The student then proceeded to go to Prentice [a dorm] and very loudly blast Future's latest album with fellow football teammates. How's that for hating Black people but loving our culture? When confronted, he claimed he was being bullied, and I was brought to the dean's office.

I was told by the headmaster that I would never get a job studying African American studies in university and that it was best I picked a different major. He completely dismissed and failed to acknowledge the relevance of Black studies in any white spaces.

One year, I was gifted a watermelon for Christmas.

I once asked my Asian friend why the people in our majority white friend group were talking to me less frequently. She told me that I didn't act white enough for the people in our friend group.

I watched a grown female teacher put her hands on a Black Muslim boy during Ramadan, in the middle of the dining hall because his shirt was untucked. I confronted her and she took no responsibility and instead claimed that she, in fact, was not in the wrong. When I asked her how that child's parents would feel if they saw her put her hands on their son, she replied saying that she doesn't tell other people how to parent. When I approached the boy's advisor, she did not do anything to comfort the boy. There is no comfort in knowing that his body, and so many others, have been subject to being hypervisible and physically policed by others.

People like to blame this on the climate of the 2020s; the divided nature of the Trump era, this time we live in when the explicitly bad whites—the ones whose racism feels like traditional, old-school, nigger-calling American racism—feel bold enough to gather and march without their hoods because white privilege means they expect no consequences. I've no doubt that those recent shows of strength have emboldened certain students, along with knowing that they are safe in an institution that welcomes dollars from men like Ailes with open arms. But I have two hours' worth of words in those TAALSA meeting notes, all spoken by Black and Latinx students who felt unsafe and unwelcome in this place even then, that say otherwise. Racism is not welcome at Taft, and yet it manages to reserve several slots in each freshman class just the same.

"Until white people make an effort themselves, Taft's race stuff won't be fixed," Maura said. She was right, I think, and if we'd been more capable—or supervised—we might have made a list of the "efforts" we needed our white peers to make. Nothing too extreme, just the basics: Don't sing the "nigga" in Kanye's "Gold Digger"; stop using "Well, what if there was a club for white kids at Taft, huh? Huh??" and other hypotheticals like that shit's the Konami Code for Reverse Racism; and maybe, if we were feeling ambitious, they could all commit to participating in some "Black stuff" during a month that is not February?

More than a decade later, after observing how race is lived at Taft, I've finally realized that our definitions of "effort" are simply very different. White effort is canceling school for a day of healing, allowing students to sleep in that morning, reemphasizing that this behavior is unacceptable, and vowing to punish the perpetrators. White effort is earnestly trying to diversify the student body, as if simply having us there will change the very foundation the school built itself on. White effort never gets to the foundation of the problem itself, because that would require acknowledging that the foundation of whiteness is the problem and that, in turn, might hurt the endowment.

Black effort is being a sophomore, all of fifteen years old, like Esther, and asking just as earnestly, "What do they want from us? There're five hundred white people here and like forty of us, so what do they want? I can't fix Emma's racism! Or white people's!" Black effort is being seventeen, alone in a room without an adult, and trying to answer Esther's question.

Black effort is having to answer her question in order for you *both* to make it to graduation.

Black effort is gritting your teeth and persevering when the answer to that question turns out to be that what they want is for us to pat them on the back and appreciate their efforts. Black effort is being more than a decade out of high school and receiving an email about the latest racist event on campus, and willingly giving up part of your Sunday morning to parse through the details and come up with a plan of action for the students on campus. Black effort is being thirty and trying to figure out how you can show solidarity with current high school students from three thousand miles away. Black effort is doing all of this for free. Black effort is sitting down for a dialogue about race on campus weeks after the shooting of another Black man, six months into a global pandemic and two years after that Sunday of free labor, and knowing that despite it all, still, the problem will not be solved.

Emma was "unnerved" by the idea that we engaged in our own students of color orientation at the start of the year (she wouldn't be the first white woman to get jumpy at the thought of too many Black people gathering at once) and lamented feeling "overwhelmingly out of place" on the way to an interschool dance with several Black and Latinx students—not because she didn't know the kids at the other schools, but because she didn't even know the kids at her own. It could be that her word count didn't allow for it, or that her deadline was pressing, but not once did Emma stop to consider why we didn't all go out of our way to socialize with the white majority—or why, more to the point, I suppose, we didn't go out of our way to socialize with *her*.

The human condition comes with (often not enough) empathy. I'm capable of it, and it's why as often as I've thought of this night on campus, I've also allowed that Emma has changed since then. The human condition also comes with growth after all. There is every chance that she looks back on this article and is horrified to know that she ever thought like this. After all, who among us didn't find ourselves on the wrong side of history at least once in our teen years? I certainly did. And forgiveness was, after all, at the crux of Taft's disciplinary system—we were taught that so long as you didn't lie about what you'd done, there was an opportunity for redemption.

But to allow for the possibility that perhaps Emma "didn't mean it that way" or that she's "different now" is just another example of the effort Black people find themselves exerting on a daily basis. We are all too often expected to come to empathize and meet the people who have harmed us with a handshake and a smile.

Besides, when given the opportunity to face the students she'd insulted—the one concrete and implemented action that came out of our hurt that night—Emma refused to participate. Esther and Maura organized a meeting in the Black Box theatre a week or so later, presented as an "open dialogue" between nonwhite students, white students, and specifically Emma herself, but the author of the article declined to show up. She reportedly told campus administrators that "emotions were running too high" and she didn't feel that it would be a productive conversation. We sat waiting, but no adult felt it necessary that she be made to attend.

I wonder, often, if Emma ever thinks about her article. She has the luxury of being able to simply forget an incident like this, to call it an adolescent mistake and move on without its specter hovering every time she thinks about her high school years. My own memory of this article and this TAALSA meeting is crystallized with a clarity and accuracy generally reserved for grand slams, prom nights, and first Beyoncé concerts.

Regardless of how Emma feels now, her damage was done. Fixing her fingers to use a private white institution's official press to blame Black students for not doing enough to solve said private white institution's diversity issues was a Rose Armitage–level move. And when you're a Black student attending a white institution like Taft, your *Get Out* radar is always on. We didn't have such a perfect name for it back in the day, but we all knew whom to trust, what to trust, and when to trust it. Shit, maybe we just knew instinctively that Emma was the type to write an op-ed calling us all part of the problem and lamenting about the Black and Latinx students she wrote she "wished she knew better," instead of approaching our dining hall table (we were pretty easy to find, and she clearly had no problem seeing us all seated together). Why would we want to be friends with that person? And why, with major incidents of racism on at *least* a semiannual basis, would *any* of us want to send our kids back?

I would love, again for both the sake of narrative and my own dignity, to finally offer you a triumph. I'd love to say that in the end, we won. That even with her refusal to show up for a dialogue, Emma and the *Papyrus* were forced to print a retraction. That someone—perhaps whoever was advising the *Papyrus* at the time—came through to offer us an apology for the hurt the article had caused.

But as subsequent incidents at Taft attest, I've already told you the truth: We didn't win. We did not surgically remove racism from the school after Emma's article. Life at Taft simply kept going, and if we wanted to stay, if we wanted to succeed and graduate, we had to keep going too.

That was an important lesson to learn, this time in a way less traumatic, one that would allow the memory to really *stick*. Racism and ignorance are a reality. More often than not, you, as a person of color, will simply have to grin and bear it and keep calm and carry on. If life stopped every time a white person's ignorance impacted us or our communities directly, none of us would have made it to graduation. We'd be perpetual sophomores, running in slow motion through a swamp of microaggressions toward a graduation ceremony just out of reach.

By its very existence, Emma's article answered the question she'd balked at being presented with. I was one of only five Black legacy students to attend Taft in more than one hundred years because by the time October rolled around, every Black freshman had already met at least one Emma Hunter, with three more Octobers left to come.

2.

CALLISTER WASN'T AT TAALSA that night because her mother wouldn't let her or Sienna stay on campus late enough to join.

Yara wasn't at TAALSA that night because she was making out with Kallister in her dorm room. Or so she claimed.

Callister Hamilton and Kallister Hennery (yeah; *yeah*) were in fact two different people.

Callister, the day student, maintained her positive, good-natured attitude even under the pressure an approaching opening night could cause. She always had a smile on her face, and I was jealous of the way her grin set off her cheekbones and perfectly placed dimples.

The other Kallister was understandably standoffish in the way you might also be if you had to switch schools for your senior year because the president had completely mismanaged the response to a national disaster that flooded your city a year before college and forced you to move a few thousand miles north to finish out your high school career in the snow.

I did not have the necessary emotional intelligence yet to deal with that kind of backstory, and so I did not handle Kallister's arrival, or her instant connection with Yara Harris, very well at all.

● ● ●

Much like when a Blue Checkmark shares some overly precocious observation about social justice that their toddler has managed to communicate in exactly 280 characters or less, I tend not to take the wilder exploits shared by most teens at face value. That instinct took seven years in and out of various school admissions offices to develop and was not one I possessed myself as a high school senior.

So when Yara regularly IM'd me over the summer, describing the various exploits she and Margot were getting up to around the city—a party with Poly Prep kids one Saturday, a Long Island blowout for July Fourth at the empty vacation home of one kid from Lawrenceville, even getting back in time for one of the last Waldorf Astoria senior proms of the season and, more important, the afterparty at a Spence girl's penthouse on Central Park West—I fully believed her. And slowly, I began to panic.

Not only had I not been able to join them; I wouldn't have been able to keep up if I had. Partying was not my speed. Maybe in New Jersey, but definitely not at Taft, a place that had made its stance on alcohol and drugs as plain as puritan dress: Get caught doing either and the door would be hitting you on the way out.

I already had my one strike, and Yara knew this. Yet, "Do you want to go in on a bottle of Grey Goose with me and Margot?" was September's constant refrain as we clambered on and off the buses that took us into Waterbury for the weekend.

Margot, it didn't occur to me until much later on, never extended the same offers, never talked too much about her summer adventures. Either she played her cards much closer to her chest or, as I suspect is more likely, there were fewer parties than Yara was letting on. And Margot, determined to come off as a chic Manhattanite, knew better than to run around flashing a fake ID at just any liquor store clerk in the greater Watertown area. Those things were expensive.

The school musical was an excellent distraction from Yara's new "adult" energy, which I simply did not know what to do with. Every cigarette lit up while we waited for the bus after a movie pushed me closer to Callister and Kat. Every esoteric diatribe from me, annoying enough that it deserved a drag from a freshly rolled Spirit (Yara rolled her own cigarettes because it was 2005 and Johnny Depp, then at the height of his powers, rolled *his* own cigarettes), pushed Yara closer to the new girl in our Baby Boomer Generation (American History of the 1950s–1960s) class, Kallister.

As Mr. Mac had promised, three or four students arrived at Taft from various parts of southern Louisiana in mid-September. The addition of another Black girl to our senior class was deeply welcome. Kallister's arrival brought our number up to six: Yara, Harriet (the Francine of the class of 2006), Akinyi (a new PG student from West Africa, using the extra senior year to acclimate to life in America before starting at Yale the next fall), Callister, Kallister, and me. With the boys, there were now ten—ten!— whole Black seniors at Taft. Even Harriet, whom I rarely spoke to, had expressed some excitement upon seeing Kallister in our Adolescent Psych class.

Kallister quickly proved that she wasn't a Harriet, or a Francine— she barely looked twice at the other tables in the dining hall before confidently sliding into ours.

We'd been told that morning that we had to submit our personalized yearbook pages for review soon. Yara and I had agreed the year before to do ours together, and so that summer, with access to Morgan Stanley's Photoshop CS2 license, I'd mocked up and laid out a sample of what our pages would look like. We'd agreed to make it *Dogma* themed, and I'd even included the handwritten lyrics to Lauryn Hill's "I'll Get Out" that Yara wanted to border the two pages we'd share.

"Because we're getting out," she explained gravely to Kallister while we ate lunch. "Out of *Taft*."

"Why've you got Ben Affleck on your yearbook page?" the other girl asked, pointing to the printout I'd handed Yara. Ben Affleck and Matt Damon were indeed the centerfolds of our page.

"*Dogma*'s our favorite movie," Yara said. "Have you seen it?"

"No," said Kallister. "This food's disgusting."

"Yeah, that's FLIK for you," I said, taking the mockup back.

"You should come watch it with us," Yara continued. "*Dogma*'s great."

I scowled. No one *ever* watched *Dogma* with us. Well, only Tabi and only after she'd absolutely *begged* at one point that we bestow her with a nickname from the film for fear of being left out (and then threw a fit because she didn't like being called "Rufus"). "Well, I have rehearsals after classes mostly, so I don't know when I'm going to have time."

Yara shrugged. "We can just borrow it from you, right?"

"Are you going to pay for it if you scratch it?"

"She gets like this," Yara said to Kallister. "During sophomore year she started making people sign DVDs out for the last month of school because someone on the softball team lost the 'classic'— direct quote—Freddie Prinze Jr. movie *Boys and Girls*. Like she was the fucking public library."

"She's just careful about stuff," Callister offered in my defense from her side of the table.

"Anal-retentive," Yara clarified.

"I'll trade you *Dogma* for two episodes of *Deep Space Nine*," I said.

"Done."

I stared at her suspiciously. "That's *Star Trek*."

"Bitch, I listen to you!" She laughed. "I know it's *Star Trek*."

"I get to pick the episodes."

"I wouldn't know which episodes to pick!" I had to laugh, too, at this response, which Yara recognized as her opening. "So, I can borrow *Dogma* this weekend?"

I was annoyed but also out of excuses that wouldn't come off as petty. "Sure."

"Whatever," said Kallister.

To hear Yara tell it, *Dogma* was the first of many movies that would go unwatched between her and Kallister in Voge, where they *could* close the doors while inside together, simply by virtue of being the same gender. One semi-out lesbian, much less a Black one, at Taft was noteworthy—two was unheard of. The fact that they immediately found each other makes all the sense in the world *now*. Not because Black lesbians all flock together, but because the uniqueness of our circumstances meant that like often found the most comfort with like.

Even taking Yara's stories about their hookup sessions with many servings of salt, she and Kallister were clearly a matched pair. They looked alike, first off, with the same athletic builds, short permed ponytails, and disdain for skirts, dresses, or anything else traditionally feminine. Yara had always been a smart-ass, even sometimes with teachers, and Kallister's pure, unfiltered derision for all things Taft amplified Yara's keenly tuned fuck-it attitude.

"Did you do the reading?" Kallister asked a few days later. We sat in a row on the far side of the room in our Boomers class: Yara, Kallister, me, and Callister. (Yes. Mr. Huston did weep.)

"Did you do the reading?" were my five least favorite words to hear as we settled into a classroom, and Yara, having been in classes with me for three years now, absolutely knew this. "I'm the Shawn and you're the Cory. It's just our thing," she'd say as a gentle follow-up, patting my arm while I rolled my eyes but geared up anyway to hastily explain Archduke Ferdinand's death and the start of World War I.

Yara shook her head at Kallister's question and pointed at me. "Hell, no. Kendra probably did, though."

Feeling less like a Cory and more like a third-wheel Topanga, I glared back at her. "Try doing it once in a while."

"Fine," Yara shot back. "Callister, what was the reading about?"

"Guys, it was thirty pages on the Korean War. I can't explain that in two minutes—do your homework."

"You're not even going to college; why are you doing yours?" Yara muttered.

"Did any of *y'all* do the reading?" Kallister asked, gesturing to the rest of the classroom.

A few of our classmates nodded.

"So what was it about?" Yara asked the room.

There were snickers and rolled eyes, but no answers.

"Losers," Kallister huffed.

Yara nodded. "*Seriously.*"

I can't do this for a whole year, I typed into the blank Word document where I planned on taking notes. I angled my laptop screen toward Callister and scowled.

My friend shrugged, a what-can-you-do? motion that doubled as a simple instruction: Just leave it alone. Callister was far more calm and, I think, just a more empathetic person. She never liked Kallister any more than I did (and if anything, she had the right to—the girl had taken her *name*), but she knew how to extend a bit of grace.

"I'm praying for her," Callister said on our way out of Boomer class. "I mean it *must* be hard; everything is new and she was caught up in that sinner's storm when she didn't do anything wrong and it ruined her senior year. But that doesn't give her the right to be such a"—she inhaled sharply, casting her eyes around to make sure no one would hear her—"bitch."

"Callie, Katrina wasn't because of sin; it was because of global warming."

"If global warming—the manifestation of our inability to take proper stewardship of this beautiful world God gave us—isn't a sin, then I don't know what is," she answered promptly. "Anyway, I'm just saying that I get why maybe she's not super nice and we have to make her feel welcome, at least, by being better than that."

"Better than a bitch doesn't take much," I grumbled.

"Kendra!" Callister shook her head.

"Sorry. You're right, I guess."

"Kendra!"

It was Yara this time, hustling out of Mr. Huston's classroom without her Kallister.

"I'll see you at rehearsal," said mine, before taking her leave, probably back to the safety of the day-student lockers.

"What?" I turned around to face her.

For her part, Yara looked sincerely confused. "What's up with you today?"

"Nothing." What was I going to do? Tell her that I was mad because she was becoming good friends with someone who brought out her worst impulses and habits, but who also didn't have Margot's sense of self-preservation? Was I going to confess that I found it incredibly suspect that she'd gone out and found another Kallister just when *I'd* found a Callister to be friends with? There was no good way to explain that I resented her behavior around Kallister, in part, because she was proving my mother *right*, and that—other than feeling like I was watching a friendship fail—was something I simply could not abide. I *hated* having to meditate on my own complicated feelings; Yara knew that, and I disliked that she was making me experience them.

Instead, I simply retorted, "What's up with *you?*"

"Nothing." She frowned and paused for a moment before pointing down the hallway that led toward Voge. "Can you come chill before Latin?"

"I don't have my textbook for Psych after, so I have to go back to Centen."

"If you skip buying Jelly Bellies before class you'll have time to go get it. Promise."

"If I don't get my Jelly Bellies, Pete's gonna think I'm dead." I had an understanding—going on three years—with the man who ran the school store in the basement. I bought two bags of jelly beans every day. If I didn't show up for my bags of candy, Pete was to alert the health center; either I was dead or I'd summoned something I shouldn't have while burying a gris-gris bag in Emma Hunter's honor and death was probably looking like a blessing in comparison.

Yara reached out for my hand. "Please—I have to ask you about something."

"Okay, well…" I gestured halfheartedly, meaning for her to simply ask.

"It's *private.*"

"Fine, *fine.*"

At my cue, Yara began dragging me down the hallway. I followed her to the second floor of Voge, where she lived in a room almost identical to mine the year before. I'd done a better job decorating, I thought. Yara's penchant for the tear-and-stick method, as I'd dubbed her habit of mauling magazines, lived on that year. Her walls were an assortment of rough-edged images from copies of *Rolling Stone*, *Entertainment Weekly*, and *XXL*. Large posters of Lauryn Hill and Aaliyah were pinned reverently above her desk.

Yara pushed a pile of clothes from her bed to the floor and offered me her desk chair before climbing up to sit cross-legged, facing me.

"So what's up?" I asked.

"Mr. Huston said my Morning Meeting speech is ready to go," she said. "That's what I was talking to him about. I'm on the schedule for after Halloween."

"I'm glad you're doing it," I said, which was the truth.

"Yeah. So what I wanted to ask—can I just give you my walk-on and walk-off music to play, or does Lane have to approve them first?"

"*That's* what you wanted to know?"

Yara rolled her eyes. "No, dumbass—I'm saying I *want* you to run tech for my meeting."

"Well…thank you. But you know everyone else can press play on a song and stuff too."

"Yeah, but they won't *get* it," Yara said. "I'm gonna walk out to 'Run's House.'"

That one, another overused *Dogma* reference through the course of our friendship, got me. "That's a good choice."

"And then when I'm done, I'm gonna leave to Led Zeppelin."

"Good Zeppelin, I hope."

"Not 'Staircase' Zeppelin."

"Hobbit Zeppelin?"

"It's in contention."

I nodded. "Okay. I'll see what I can do."

"Thanks. It's my coming-out speech, so I want it to be perfect, and you're the one I trust to make it perfect because you're an anal-retentive bitch who'd definitely fight God for me."

"There is a good chance that's how our lives end, yes."

We leaned toward each other, clasping hands briefly. I *got* this, and Yara knew that well enough. The fact that she was not straight had never been a mystery to me; rather, it was more a question of whether or not she'd land on the L or the B of the LGBTQ+ spectrum. Despite having had gay friends back home (a group of us had almost been suspended in middle school for a string of revenge-driven events that started when another girl idly threatened to out one of our friends to their über-religious parents), I did not put enough stock in how astounding it was that she wanted to come out to an entire New England boarding school. We didn't have so much as an out LGBTQ+ teacher, much less a functioning Gay Student Alliance.

But adding queerness on top of already being Black and female and on financial aid at boarding school was to begin treading water with spent limbs. I wish I'd understood that, just a bit more, at the time. But "intersectionality," as it pertained to identities, was not a word that was top of mind. I understood fully that the experiences of white students were not the same as the experiences of Black students. That being a Black girl who played sports at Taft was wildly different from being a Black boy who did the same. But drilling down further than that was difficult; Yara was the *only* gay student at Taft I knew of.

Well, until Kallister. Whom she had *not* asked to run her Morning Meeting.

"I got you, Loki," I said, gripping her hand firmly again. "I'll switch for tech if I've gotta."

"Thanks, Bart."

"It's not a problem." I shrugged and offered an olive branch of my own. "Sam and Santiago and I are going to finish our college essays at Starbucks after classes on Saturday. Do you want to come?"

Yara nodded. "Yeah. Our Amherst applications are due like next week."

"I know." I sighed. "It's all *really* close."

"It gets us out of Wisconsin, though."

Yara crawled up to the headboard of her twin bed, pushed up to the room's high inset window, where her massive CD player rested on the oversized sill. She hit play, and Lauryn Hill started singing, midway through "Mystery of Iniquity" off her *Unplugged* album, the song that Kanye West had sampled for "All Falls Down"—my favorite track on my favorite album at the time. A peace offering meant to offset the hand-rolled cigarette she was now lighting, leaning against the window to blow the smoke away.

It worked. I opened my backpack and took out my Latin homework. We sat in a pleasant silence, smoking and studying until the warning bell rang for the next class.

● ● ●

Sam and Yara were both deferred to regular admission for Amherst. A very thin envelope from Tulane came for me a few days later, pushing me back into a date range they called "Early Decision 2." Santiago heard the same from NYU by dinner.

Mr. Fraser confirmed the next day that this was, indeed, proving to be an unusually rough year for admissions. But he wasn't worried. "*You*," he would say to me pointedly, "are going to be absolutely fine."

After about a week of fretting, several repeated visits to his office, and news I had dreaded for nearly a year—an acceptance with a full ride to Rutgers—I forced him to elaborate further. "Kendra, if I'm going to be very blunt, you're a diverse student with decent grades and glowing recommendations from your teachers. You may not get in everywhere, but you're going to get into an amazing college."

"Diverse student" was the politically correct way of saying what our white classmates would often overblow and state bluntly when they received a rejection to a school that one of us had gotten into: "Well, you got in because you're Black and they had to meet a quota."

I was spared some (not *all*) of this, but only because I wasn't applying to schools that were necessarily considered "competitive" by my classmates. The only Ivy League school on my list was Brown, and, well, I *was* trying to take advantage of my status as a Black legacy with that one. Half my white classmates applying to Yale and Harvard who had my average grades or worse were doing the same.

I told my mom and dad about Rutgers in person when they came up for Hotchkiss Day on Parents' Weekend. During a family dinner at the bank turned steak house on Watertown's Main Street before the final Saturday night performance of *Grease*, my mom said, cheerfully, "Well, this is *great*! At least you have a place to go!"

"Over my dead body!" I replied, equally chipper in tone.

My dad, probably running tuition numbers in his head, just sighed.

The fall musical went off without a hitch and we all hung out in Bingham afterward until curfew, as close to a closing-night party as we could manage without access to alcohol. I took cast pictures and candids for myself, marveling over the ways in which Taft's social rules somehow did not apply inside the theatre as one of the sophomore chorus girls placed her wig on Jonathan's head and carried him across the stage on her back.

While we sang showtunes at the top of our lungs that night, a group of boys, most of whom lived in the detached senior dorm, decided to take advantage of the lax rules and restrictions that a Parents' Weekend brought with it.

James Richards and Chip Sutherland weren't fall athletes or performers. They had the time that night to sneak off campus to a nearby hotel with a group of recent graduates who had returned to celebrate Hotchkiss Day. After driving back (drunk, said some rumors) they were supposedly busted trying to sneak in through a dorm window. By midweek, Richards was gone. Chip received a weeklong suspension. Some theorized it was because his varsity sport started in a matter of weeks.

"Y'all's MIA list is gonna be *something*," Tabi said. It was already rumored that the length of the class of 2006's list broke school records. We were certainly in contention for losing the most legacy students. George Miller Jr. hadn't made it out of his time as a mid, and now the class of 1974 was losing another legacy kid in Richards.

"Mmm," Mrs. Gallagher said, pursing her lips together. She clicked something on her computer screen and pushed back from her desk to look at us both. "Tabi, please get the door."

"I didn't do it."

"Tabi, close the door and sit down."

Tabi, with a keen sense of self-preservation as it related to Black Mom Voice, did as she was asked and shut the three of us inside. She even twisted the blinds closed.

"Thank you. Listen…" The older woman folded her hands. "The Hotchkiss Day incident was embarrassing. The administration is going to be cracking down on drinking."

"We don't drink here," I said immediately. "Like, not even at the movies or anything."

Mrs. Gallagher nodded. "I know that, and I believe you."

"Okay."

"You might want to pass the message on, though," she said. "To your friends. Especially the ones who have college applications out. *We*"—here, Mrs. Gallagher pointed to herself and then gestured around her office, eyes resting on the many pictures of our classmates that she had displayed—"are not getting caught up in this. Smoking too. Yes?"

"Yes," Tabi and I said in unison.

"I've talked to—" I started to add, but Mrs. Gallagher held up her finger.

"I don't want to hear about it. I've also talked to certain members of your class, Kendra, but I don't want to hear names."

"Well then, what are we supposed to do if you already talked to them?" Tabi asked.

"Share our conversation. I'm sure you understand the subtext; you're Taft students," our advisor said. "Other than that, keep yourselves out of it. Graduate. Go to college. That's all."

"Yes, ma'am," Tabi said.

"Thank you." Mrs. Gallagher nodded and gestured to the door again. "Go on, class is starting."

The Saturday after Richards was kicked out, Yara, Maura, Esther, Tabi, and I boarded a public bus and headed out to play catch-up. We had a double feature planned. *Serenity* was up first, and over lukewarm Panda Express in the food court afterward, Yara declared that it was "*Way* better than *Revenge of the Sith* last year," before asking if the series it was based on, *Firefly*, was sitting on one of my hard drives, conveniently forgetting that she'd complained every time I'd tried to show it to her before. Once we finished eating, I walked into *Elizabethtown* feeling like a proud parent watching their child take their first steps.

"...and so Fox, being Fox, aired all the episodes out of order, which made it *infinitely* harder for fans to connect with the stories or characters. We would have had episodes as good as *Serenity* if it had just gotten a second season, and Wash wouldn't have died and—"

"Kendra."

"*And* it would have been able to build a larger fanbase, even though it was on Fox, which didn't even make sense in the *first* place—"

"*Kendra!*" Yara interrupted me again. After sitting through two features, we were ready to head back to school and squeak in just before curfew. "What time is it?"

I dug around in my canvas 1940s Red Cross bag for the Nokia brick mobile my parents had gotten for me that summer. "It's 4:14."

"Okay, so we have time."

"The bus is at 4:25," Tabi confirmed. We huddled just steps away from the mall bus stop, outside the Ruby Tuesday that'd once given me the worst food poisoning of my short life.

"Cool. I'm gonna walk over to the packie." Yara pointed across the parking lot to a series of tiny stores lining the thin sidewalk, including one state-sanctioned package store. That's a liquor store, and a phrase you can be forgiven for not knowing if you've never lived in a state where burning witches was once an acceptable pastime.

I pursed my lips. "The bus is going to be here in ten minutes."

"Yep." Yara nodded and grinned. "Be right back."

No one would have ever dared describe the Waterbury bus system as punctual. But we all had enough general sense of the way it ran to know that the 4:25 bus was the last *safe* resort. Technically—*just* technically—the next three buses would also get you back to campus before 5:30. That said, whether or not you wanted to risk a Sunday morning study hall, or worse, was none of *my* business. But I knew that for my part? I did not.

Besides, it was a Saturday; the internet would be on all night. There was a dance that evening (Hollywood Night—'80s Night, but with a John Hughes theme), but I had plans in two separate RPGs with friends on three different continents.

I looked at Tabi, Maura, and Esther. "Well, I need to get on the 4:25 bus. She's probably just buying cigarettes." I could still cover, at least, and to be fair I didn't know for sure if she'd be buying anything more than that. "It's fine, I just need to get back—I already have grades for dress code bullshit."

"Me too," Maura agreed. "Mr. Safi threw my flip-flops out the window *and* gave me grades for them."

Esther looked worried. "I don't want to be late…"

"Oh, you won't be," I said easily. "We're getting on the bus."

"How's Yara getting back?"

"I'm not her mom; I don't know." Annoyance was clear in my voice. I could still *see* Yara as she made her way across the large parking lot to the sidewalk side. There was no way in hell she'd be back within five minutes. Even if the bus was late, she'd be cutting it close.

I took a breath. "There's another bus. She'll get on the next bus. Worse comes to worst, she'll get a cab."

As cutthroat as it may sound, when one is trying to get back to a boarding school campus before the proverbial streetlights come on during a New England winter, the bus schedule *always* trumps whatever version it is of girl code you follow.

"Good, because I think it's on time." Maura pointed to the ramp leading into the parking lot down by the Sears. My eyes darted back and forth as Yara slowly vanished from sight and the bus moved closer, eventually pulling in right in front of us. Four twenty-eight, only three minutes late.

I dropped my five quarters into the meter box and stalked to our usual seats in the back of the bus.

● ● ●

I expected the person behind the knock on my door that night to be Tabi, likely checking one more time, as she was wont to do, to make absolutely sure I didn't want to walk over to the main building with her. Even if she and Sam didn't go to the dance, they'd end up in the student union with Maura and several of our other classmates.

Instead, when the door opened that night after my hasty greeting, Yara walked in and Kallister followed.

"Whatcha drawing?" she asked in lieu of a hello, flopping down next to me on the bed. A waft of stale cigarette smell flew up in her wake.

Kallister, who had never been in my room before, took the more demure route of inviting herself to my desk chair while taking several long stares around the space. Her eyes lingered on the wall behind my desk, decked out in 1940s memorabilia, before traveling to the wall against my headboard, where the more contemporary images lived, and my bureau, messy with belongings and random odds and ends.

"They know you have those?" Kallister asked, pointing to several half-melted candles that took up one corner of my dresser.

"Told you she's witchy," Yara said. She tapped my sketchbook. "Shit, is that for us?"

"*Yes*," I said pointedly. "I still need you to write out those lyrics, by the way, if you want them to actually be in *your* handwriting. These are gonna go at the bottom of our page, by our names."

Like many earth signs presented with a group project, I'd ended up doing most of the work on our yearbook page out of equal parts convenience and frustration. And so, I was drawing out figures in a sketchbook: my own versions of the characters from *Dogma*, but animated. The project, which had started as a happy distraction, especially while procrastinating over college applications that summer, was now something I was speeding through to get done on time.

"Cool!" Yara said.

"You're welcome." I set the sketchpad aside. "Nice to see you made it back to campus, by the way."

"Nice to see you waited for me, Bart." She grinned and punched my arm.

"*Dude.*"

"What? The next bus was only like five minutes late back here. Ms. Greene is in charge of sign-ins this weekend; it's fine, she's not gonna assign a Screw Crew for five minutes."

"It's not just being late." I took a pointed sniff. "What was at the packie?"

"Grey Goose and Spirits."

I rolled my eyes. It was *always* Grey Goose. "Richards just got kicked out, and he played a varsity sport and he was a legacy."

"And?"

"Well, you play *girls'* basketball and you're…not a legacy. So, like, be careful."

"Well, that's rude," said Kallister.

"No, that's Mrs. Gallagher fucking pulling me and Tabi into a room to ask about you after the whole Richards thing happened." I looked Yara directly in the eye, ignoring the other girl.

My friend didn't look as worried as I needed her to. "She asked about me specifically?"

"She didn't want to talk about names, but she said she talked to everyone who *needed* to be talked to, and then like—I don't know, Loki, the message was pretty fucking clear," I said, exasperated.

"Okay, so she didn't ask about me specifically."

"Can you please treat this like I'm having a conversation with an almost eighteen-year-old, and not like we're celebrating your fourth birthday again?"

"Dude, chill," she said. "I already talked to her and it's not that big of a deal, unless you told her something."

"I didn't. And it kind of is going to be a big deal if you get kicked out of school senior year. Colleges pull acceptances for that."

Yara rolled her eyes. "This is a lot for a friendly 'are you going to the student union' visit."

"I don't know what you want me to say. I don't want you to get in trouble!"

She held her hands up, palms forward. "Okay, so you have your anal-retentive side wound fucking tight tonight. Cool, so, you're not going to the student union."

"I'm *not* going to the student union," I shot back. "I've got shit to do, including finishing our yearbook page."

"Which absolutely needs to be done on a Saturday night. Got it." Yara smirked, rolling her eyes before she stood up from the bed. "Okay, well, since I *don't* have study hall or a Screw Crew tomorrow because I was *only* five minutes late back to campus today, I'll see you at brunch tomorrow morning."

Kallister looked more bemused than anything as she followed Yara out of the room, slinging an arm around her waist just before the door closed behind them.

I wanted to scream.

That anal-retentive side in me has mellowed since Taft created the monster in the first place. How ironic that a one-week suspension was more effective in curbing any temptation toward rebellion and good old-fashioned misbehavior than any of the tactics involving a belt or a brush my father began employing in the second grade. I was not the model Taft student by any means, but I was more of a rule follower. I preferred pushing against cracks in the foundations that were already there, rather than looking to create any fissures of my own. It made me seem more buttoned-up and, yes, anal-retentive than the average seventeen-year-old. I was just constantly scared, plain and simple.

But as you age, the fear begins to abate, replaced instead by various notes of resentment—the second inevitable result of a botched consequence. The step after fear and resentment though, *healing*, revealed something more complicated, forcing me to admit that I never handled any of Yara's supposed drinking in a particularly empathetic way. It was black-and-white for me: Don't do that. You'll get kicked out and *that* is the worst thing that could possibly happen to a person, right? I'd also quickly decided Kallister was the problem. Yes, Yara and Margot (supposedly) spent a whole summer partying, months before the girl from New Orleans entered the picture, but *she* was the poor influence, I'd decided. Margot, at the very least, had campus discretion.

I blamed Kallister for the gnarled tangles in Yara's and my close friendship simply because I was jealous and fearful of losing my closest friend and because I was too scared to do any of the things my peers back in New Jersey had spent their teen years doing: the normal experimental boundary pushing of adolescence.

Their physical closeness pained me as well. Just last year, Yara and I had been *that*. The fact that I was the straightest, most dick-obsessed girl in the world never seemed to matter when we leaned against each other in bed, watching a movie or just staring at the ceiling, limbs tangled as we discussed the gossip of the day. But I wasn't going to leave a room with her, arm casually draped around her waist. And, for the life of me—no matter how many times she said, shouted, or laughed it out in my direction—I could not "chill."

I should have gone to the student union that night and, if not apologized, at least sat down and acted as though everything was normal, extending the bare minimum of kindness. Instead, I exchanged my sketchbook for my laptop and logged onto AIM, where a friend I'd never met in person was waiting on the other side of the world. That was easier.

3.

FOR THOSE APPLYING to college in the regular admission pool that year, the Common Application was due by MLK weekend. From the jump, I had no intention of spending the weekend of my eighteenth birthday filling out last-minute college applications, and so by the time we left for Christmas break in mid-December, I'd washed my hands of the whole process. Deferrals and all, for better or worse, each of my too many applications had been sent out, complete. There was nothing I could do but wait.

They did this every year, this waiting game, and so most teachers at Taft were quite adept at managing senior stress from the period of January through early April. Mr. Fraser sent us a constant stream of "not to worry" emails and someone left enough *How to Have a Productive Gap Year* pamphlets stuck between the wood slats of Callister's locker to start a Hotchkiss Day bonfire. Mr. Freeman, the only Black male teacher on campus, started having us over to his apartment for Sunday night movies, starting early in January with *The Inkwell* and homemade chicken and waffles. Mrs. Gallagher began making plans for a February trip to Hartford so that we could see a local production of *For Colored Girls Who Have Considered Suicide / When the Rainbow Is Enuf* and maybe take our minds off the stress.

After catching me scrolling through Pitzer's admissions page during class, Mr. Cobb rapped the front of my desk with his knuckles and said, "Well, if I'm remembering correctly your dad went five and one. Got into Harvard, Yale, Brown, U of Illinois, and Morehouse, I believe. You'll be fine." I have no idea if he was remembering correctly, but Mr. Cobb had been teaching at Taft so long that the textbook I was pointedly not paying attention to had his name on the cover. It was *only* available in our school bookstore and the level of work inside made the Ecce Romani series look like *Sesame Street*.

Every senior managed their stress differently. We lost yet another classmate before January was out: plagiarism, it was rumored when Joey Graves vanished seemingly overnight, probably from the stress of trying to get one last grade up before college admissions offices took their final look.

Santiago, Sam, and Mike proclaimed one night at dinner that by spring they were going to dominate the campus Frisbee golf scene, and started playing every afternoon after classes and before wrestling practice. In January. In Connecticut. We left them to it.

Yara joined up with the varsity basketball team again, and Callister took her usual position as basketball manager, assuring Tabi, Sam, and me one night that Mr. Huston ran a "tight ship" as a coach. "No one's getting into trouble during basketball season," she said with a firm nod.

Our stage crew group was a well-oiled, cohesive unit as we continued to tackle the school's AV needs. Most mornings, you'd find two, sometimes even three of us (even though only one was required) piled into the booth at the top of the auditorium, whispering through whatever lecture was being given.

Poor Callister got an earful straight through the winter, as I continued to fume over Yara. I griped at Kat too, cautiously. I trusted her and she was probably the most levelheaded, mature person I knew, but Yara's business wasn't mine to spill to a white girl; not at Taft. And so Callister sighed every time I huffed down next to her, arms crossed, angry about whatever it was Yara had done that day.

"You'd test Jesus's patience with this. On the cross," she'd reply flatly, shaking her head.

Our day-student friend was a good sport, listening to Kat and me complain nonstop about the virus of admissions deferrals sweeping through the senior class, or, worse yet, the radio silence most of us had heard.

"At least you got into Rutgers." Kat repeated her favorite refrain.

"And you got into Florida State," I pointed out.

"So you're both *going* to college," Callister said, rolling her eyes.

Kat's lips pressed into a thin, flat line. "If you can call FSU that." I gave Callister a knowing look. *See. She gets it.* "Callie, are you coming in on Saturday?"

"Yes. MLK workshops are mandatory, even for day students."

"Which workshops are you guys doing?" Kat asked.

"I'm thinking about going to the one about Black comedy," I answered. "But there's the possibility of me coming out of that one pissed off, depending on who else is in there. I don't want to hear Justin O'Brian laugh about blackface."

"Fair. His thing about Mexicans in history yesterday was, um…insane?"

"That's a word for it," Callister agreed. "What was it?"

"Dog zap collars, or something."

"To keep people from crossing the border, yep," I said. "I wrote it down."

"Of course you did." Callister patted my shoulder knowingly.

"You know he only says things like that to get a rise out of people. You reacting feeds the beast."

"Yeah, notice how he's never trying to get a rise out of us in front of Mr. Huston?"

"Well, he's not a complete idiot," she said. "He got into Taft."

"I was going to do African Americans and the death penalty," Kat offered. "That one starts with a documentary."

I made a face. "You really want to hear what Justin has to say about Tookie Williams?"

"If we have to wait to find out what workshop Justin O'Brian is doing before we sign up for anything, we're all going to end up stuck watching *Crash*."

"Don't forget Louis D'Aria, Scott Peltzer, Topper Johnson, Grant Phipps, and Tripp Macintosh." When Kat and Callister both simply stared at me, I elaborated. "Everyone I've ever heard sing along to the nigga parts of songs. I don't want to be in a session with them either."

"Did you write that down too?" Callister asked sarcastically. Kat might have as well, but she was too busy looking scandalized that I'd said the N-word aloud and in her presence. Not entirely sure what she was expecting to hear in a documentary about Black people and the history of the death penalty in America.

I did write everything down. I shoved it all into the same brown manila envelope where I kept each precious handwritten letter, postcard, book jacket, and candy wrapper sent to me from my gaming friends around the world. Sometimes I'll go through that envelope, worn and fragile now, and surprise myself when I find something as simple as a ticket stub from the Brass Mill movie theatre. *Casanova* (2005), 2:15 p.m. stamped on the front; reviewed, succinctly, on the back in a black .3 pen, "fuck yes; love a shapely calf."

Even though I kept my online journals locked, I knew there

was always the possibility that someone from Taft could get in and see what I was writing. I'd uncovered Delores's Friends Only DeadJournal the year before (to much drama), after all. But even without the promise of complete privacy, my documentation occasionally turned ruthless. *I've decided to just keep a log of every stupid thing Justin O'Brian says in history class,* I wrote that fall. *Then at our 15-year reunion, when everyone's drunk, I'll rise slowly from a trapdoor in the floor and read it all out loud.*

For as healthy as my fear of Taft's punishment was, there were no rules on campus that actively deterred racism; nothing to put the fear of God into them as had been done to me. Justin was thrown out of class once when Mr. Huston finally overheard him. A Screw Crew got tacked onto the end of his weekend for his "edgy" comments. Ms. Greene, the science teacher who sometimes supervised us AV kids, looked bemused when I brought it up along with the house lights one morning, as students filed in for Morning Meeting.

"Are you Mexican?" she asked, and when I shook my head she repeated Callister's advice. "You have to stop reacting, Kendra. You're not offended and he doesn't believe what he's saying. He's just trying to get a rise out of you and you're giving it to him good."

So much for encouraging allyship.

It was easier to confront these attacks when they were abstract, or directed at us Black and Latinx students as a group, rather than when they flew at us individually. We were supportive of one another always, as Yara had been when she'd helped me "hex" Jenna out of our room. But an action against *one* put the onus on that one person to beat the drums of war first, and some of us simply weren't up for that. Embarrassment, shame, trauma, the desire for privacy while processing, or simply not wanting to— there's no wrong reason for choosing not to tell someone about an act of racism perpetrated against you, personally. Especially not when you have no promise that anything will be done after you've finished pouring out your heart to the person who is supposed to be in loco parentis, and they don't act as your Black or Latinx parent *would*.

When Emma wrote an op-ed for the whole school to see, or someone made a snide remark in class that floated through a full room, it was an easy choice to allow the anger to bubble over. These were things everyone was seeing. Words that everyone could hear. I was not a valued commodity at Taft as an individual, but I did think, for whatever naive reason, that Emma would face consequences for attacking *every* Black and brown student in the school paper outright.

And then she didn't. And the school year kept moving. And she, and most other students, simply went on about their lives. And I wrote, *If Taft can't handle all this, someone has to.*

Rachel Buchanan didn't radicalize me. But maybe Emma Hunter had started to.

● ● ●

Shani Davis won two medals at the Turin Olympic Games in speed skating that year. A few weeks later we watched as Three 6 Mafia took home the Oscar for best original song, and Ang Lee was awarded best director for "a movie about gay shit," as Yara described it, with a proud nod. "Niggas on ice. Gay rap Oscars. These are signs. We'll all get into college."

A few days later, Yara's prophecy bore fruit. I received an email from Tulane letting me know that I'd been accepted to the class of 2010.

When I got into Pitzer on March 22, I wanted to send in my commitment immediately. My parents, who hadn't paid multiple college application fees for nothing, instructed me to wait until the rest of the letters came back.

On March 28 I got into Oberlin and they were thrilled. I held Oberlin's acceptance letter in my hand alongside my only two rejections, from Haverford and Brown, which arrived the same day, and fumed inwardly. I was absolutely rankled, having been just brainwashed enough by the narrative some of our loudest classmates loved to spin every spring.

"Of course Sam got into MIT; he's Hispanic and from the ghetto."

"Quotas." Girls like Laura and Olive relished the opportunity to use that word. "They're just meeting *quotas*."

"Jason Santiago *and* Yara Harris got into Amherst. It doesn't make sense. You don't just get to go to college with your best friends. Unless it's just because…you know."

"Mike? *Duke?!* See, this is why affirmative action should be illegal."

"It's not fair—Kendra's getting into Brown because they need her. She's Black and I heard Mr. Fraser say she's a legacy."

My earliest cases of imposter syndrome were imparted by kids who couldn't keep their fucking mouths shut. The word "reach" had been very clearly printed next to Brown on that first list Mr. Fraser handed me, and so some of my disappointment in not getting into Brown boiled down to pure entitlement. Like any student applying somewhere as a legacy, I assumed, just a little, that my name would give me the edge I needed. The whispers from our classmates bolstered that, and the lack of pushback from our teachers meant that our so-called advantage was stalwart and unquestioned.

My parents were thrilled with the options I did have, and after a long weekend at home I went back to school with a short list, ultimately trying to choose between Pitzer and Oberlin: places where I would not have to see a Vineyard Vines whale or a Lacoste alligator for the next four years.

I visited a nascent Wikipedia for the first time in that last week of March, opening the pages for each school in two separate windows and scrolling through Oberlin's listing, looking for dirt.

One name listed in Oberlin's alumni section, sitting innocuously between two musicians I'd never heard of, jumped out at me: *Avery Brooks, '70.*

Mrs. Gallagher tried to take the Black and Latinx students on campus to one play per year. Just before spring break she'd delivered on her promise of making sure we saw *For Colored Girls…* She'd taken us into New York City to see Sanaa Lathan, Audra McDonald, Phylicia Rashad, and P. Diddy in *A Raisin in the Sun* in its last Broadway revival and, in that same late winter, she'd bundled us up for a trip into New Haven to see Avery Brooks at the Yale Repertory Theatre, leading an all-Black cast in a production of *King Lear* set in the Mesoamerican Olmec civilization. I had little interest in Shakespeare that hadn't been turned into a musical, but I was the first person on the bus to New Haven, and the last one off.

I grew up with Avery Brooks. He played Captain Benjamin Lafayette Sisko on my favorite TV show of all time, *Star Trek: Deep Space Nine.* Born into a family of Trekkies, I had no choice, really, and four months after Captain Jean-Luc Picard's crew had their encounter with Q at Farpoint in 1987, I showed up to join my parents in their viewing sessions. But *Deep Space Nine*'s 1993 premiere marked the start of an *obsession.*

The Shakespearean-trained Brooks was the first Black actor to lead a *Star Trek* series, and one of the few Black leads starring in any genre media. Plus, DS9 was quality television, one of the first shows to serialize storytelling over the course of twenty-plus-episode seasons in the 1990s. Instead of the plot-heavy two-part cliffhangers that were often used to advance stories in between standalones and bottle episodes, or even the season-long Big Bad arcs that *Buffy* and *Angel* used so effectively, DS9 was well on its way to figuring out how to tell a fully realized *Game of Thrones*– or *Breaking Bad*–esque story of war, feud, and intrigue over seven seasons before Bill Clinton was done getting impeached. I could watch and actually enjoy a deliciously unapologetic, straight science fiction show where a Black man was in charge. I didn't have much interest, at the time, in the real-world-based sitcoms and few dramas where Black people starred and thrived. But *Star Trek*? I *wanted* to be in that world.

I idolized Brooks and Captain Sisko. The character was many things throughout DS9's run: a captain, a war hero, a 1950s science fiction writer, a baseball enthusiast, even a god of sorts. But before any of that, we learn one thing: Sisko was a single Black father in a future where being a Black man was not inherently life-threatening. A single father who loved his son, Jake, more than anything, balancing the demands of his career and his family. A world in which Earth's capitalism didn't exist, so when Jake confessed that he wanted to be a writer and reporter instead of entering Starfleet Academy, it didn't take long to win his father's support. A love interest for the captain was introduced, eventually, who *actually* looked like me—not some light-skinned, WB factory brand Black girl, but a dark-skinned woman with a cheeky independent streak and hair that looked as thick and time-consuming to manage as mine. A three-person Black family unit on a nationally broadcast television show that I never had to fight with my parents about watching, because *they* loved it so much that if I'd lost TV privileges during a week with a new episode, they would make me eat dinner facing away from the small antenna TV we kept in the kitchen so that they wouldn't have to suffer for my misfortune.

When I called my mom back, twenty or thirty minutes later, I'd made my decision. "I'm going to Oberlin."

"Oh?"

"Avery Brooks went to Oberlin," I said. "If I go to Oberlin, I may be able to *meet* Avery Brooks. So I'm going to Oberlin."

She was silent for a moment, and I heard her take a breath. "Kendra."

"Mmm?"

"This is a good decision."

"Great. Let's get that deposit in."

"Kendra."

"Mmm?"

"Avery Brooks…" Was she *laughing*? "Avery Brooks *teaches* at Rutgers, Kendra."

"Well, you should've led with that last April, then," I said before hanging up the phone.

● ● ●

In *Booksmart*—that 2019 movie about two girls' last hurrah before college directed by Andover alum Olivia Wilde—one of the main characters explains that their graduating class has decided not to tell each other which colleges they've been accepted to. Not only that; they mostly stick to that promise. I gasped, overly loud in an otherwise quiet theatre. It was the single most shocking thing I'd heard uttered in a piece of teen high school media—and I say that having seen all eight seasons of *The Vampire Diaries*.

Every single thing you do while at boarding school is predicated on the assumption that you will eventually attend a college— the guarantee of a college education is practically promised upon recruitment. And not just *any* college, but a good college. One you want to tell people about. One you absolutely *will* tell people about.

Like most high schools, public or private, Taft took pride in publishing its year-end matriculation list in the school paper and alumni bulletin. That list was *technically* supposed to be our first official word as to where every senior would be attending college the next fall. It never was.

No one could actually keep their mouth shut; everyone at Taft wanted to be seen succeeding. Plus we were teenagers and this next step of life was supposed to be exciting!

And so as of April 1, we were allowed (via tradition, not the student handbook) to start wearing the sweatshirts from our school of choice. Bragging, loudly, to your table in the dining hall that you had been accepted into Harvard would have been uncouth. Casually draping a Harvard sweatshirt across the back of your chair, however, announced your matriculation plans without breaking any WASPy social norms.

Some parents FedExed sweatshirts to their seniors overnight once they'd gotten their deposit check in to the admissions office, and the larger wire transfer for the new dorm or science center or whatever they'd paid for their kid's admission with had gone through.

I waited for a week for an Oberlin hoodie to arrive, like a normal middle-class student. It arrived smelling overwhelmingly like lavender. My parents had placed it in a box with a Crabtree & Evelyn bath set and a season of *Batman: The Animated Series* on DVD, because they were keenly aware of the sort of child they'd raised.

Two of us were going to Oberlin that year: me and Alexa Edgar, a day student I knew a little bit after casting her as a Pink Lady in *Grease*. Mr. Fraser mentioned in passing that we were the first students from Taft to go to the small Ohio college in a decade, maybe more. This explained, I decided, a lot of my classmates' confusion, which led to many questions that simply boiled down to "*What* is Oberlin?"

I don't know what Alexa's answer was, or if she was even asked, but mine was consistent and succinct: "Not Taft!"

(I explained at length, just once, that among other things Oberlin had been the first college in America to admit Black students and women, pre–Civil War. Two members of the screenwriting critique circle Kat and I were leading looked puzzled before coming to the conclusion that it was, "Oh, Black only—like *Drumline*, or Morehouse.")

College was not presented as an option in the James household. Rather, it was the point of All This—the years of preschool before kindergarten proper (the moment I realized that not everyone *could* attend kindergarten, much less preschool, for free was an early "check your privilege" revelation); the time my mother had to devote to staying on the white women who taught us in grade school and thought that a second or third grader who'd finished every YA historical fiction book about World War II was to be looked on with suspicion and needed their library usage monitored; the fighting to make sure I was placed in Level Four classes in middle school; even the comparatively minimal effort my mom and Mrs. Gallagher had put in to keep Yara and me from living together. Each action was meant to push me further toward the goal: college. A third-generation Black college graduate.

I didn't care about that last part so much. I was looking forward to the parties, the boys, the freedom, the Avery Brooks of it all, and the chance to reinvent myself as a person without the baggage that came with Taft—my classmates, the suspension on my record, race, all of it.

Because I couldn't imagine being anything but excited about college, I took others' professed enthusiasm at face value. I never stopped to wonder if anyone was faking it, parroting the words that were expected of them.

My parents weren't perfect, but they successfully shuttled me through the American education system with relatively few issues. That's not nothing when you're putting a Black kid through school.

When I left to go back to Connecticut after that long weekend, my brother was on the second suspension of his seventh-grade year. When my mom talked about trade schools—as she eventually had to do when it became clear that a high school diploma, much less a college one, was not in his future—it was with the dejected air of a woman who'd been scouted to be a full-time cast member on a *Real Housewives* show, only to find out at the last minute that she'd been demoted to a Friend Of because the production couldn't insure her. Like many parents of their generation, they wanted us to follow The Plan (obtaining a diploma, and a degree) because they wanted the best for us.

It took time to understand what it might have been like for the kids who didn't grow up with The Plan, the kids who'd grown up with The Plan and wanted to reject it, or the kids who'd had to figure out The Plan starting from scratch junior year. Callister's goal of meeting a man at church and getting married seemed wildly impractical. Sam's genuine excitement about his coming semester at MIT made sense because it matched mine, but I wouldn't have been able to have a deep conversation with him about what it really meant to be the first in your family to go to college. I couldn't have that talk with anyone else either, but Sam was at least outwardly excited, and that was a level field where we could both meet.

I am quite sure I trod the line of maddening and unacceptable enthusiasm from that April straight through to graduation. If I'd had anything less than my first choice of college, full parental support and understanding of that choice, a plan to pay for that choice, and a generally positive outlook on the idea of college as a whole, things probably would have gone differently.

No one ever asked us to think about that part, though.

4.

One night, two or three weeks before graduation, Mike, Yara, Sam, Santiago, and I sat on the varsity soccer field behind Centen. A copy of our senior yearbook was in the damp grass in the middle of our circle, and we had a flashlight and several lighters to use while we flipped through the pages. I confessed that I'd always assumed that this "laser-cut field" the administration was always talking about was actually cut with real lasers, and that a plane or helicopter was necessary to do it. Santiago gave me the same look he'd given me upon finding out that I believed Margot's parents were diplomats.

"Ours came out so good," Yara said once we landed on our double page in the back of the book. It was, as we'd planned, anchored by our fictional avatars and bordered with Yara's requested Lauryn Hill lyrics. Pictures of her sister and mom, Margot, and Kallister dotted her page, along with long messages to friends; my written messages were more brief, and I had focused on pictures of the two of us, and our larger group—those who sat with us now, my own Callister, Tabi, Maura, Agnes, Kat, and more.

I was feeling sentimental that night, so close to graduating, and so I didn't jokingly bitch about how I'd ended up doing the lion's share of the work. I couldn't even muster the jealousy that had soured so much of the latter half of that year. Her message to Kallister on our page, *that* one written in her own hand and with love, was too sincere.

"I'm happy with it," I answered instead.

"It's definitely as weird as the both of you are," Sam chimed in.

Yara grinned and patted my shoulder. "She rubbed off on me."

"'I'm wearin' you down, baby. I'm wearin' you down.'" I smirked as I repeated that *Family Matters* refrain from junior year back at her. I hadn't thought about William Abdi since he'd left, the idea of dating at Taft having taken a back seat to the idea of straight-up fucking in college.

"Hey," Mike said. He pointed across the fields to the house abutting the varsity baseball field in the distance. "Cobb just turned his lights off."

"You're *sure* you know how to do this?" Santiago asked.

"We've got hairspray. We've got lighters. We're good."

Mike pulled out his promised aerosol cans. He held a spray can in one hand and a lighter in another.

"Count of three," he said, and we obliged.

Halfway through "three" a fireball erupted, shooting several feet across the field. Santiago had to dive out of the way as Mike pressed down on the nozzle again, shooting a stream of Aqua Net through the lighter's tiny flickering flame right past our friend's shoulder.

"Do you think the Xena thing would work?" Yara asked. I knew immediately what she was talking about—the giant fireballs Xena would blow off a torch after swigging from a bottle of hard liquor.

"Let's not find out," I said.

"Who wants next?" Mike asked, thrusting his tools out toward us.

Santiago pounced, then Yara. Sam and I followed, infinitely more cautious, but still deeply enthralled once we'd had our first go. Slowly, we moved farther from Centen, blowing fireballs until we flew too close to the sun and saw the light in Mr. Cobb's house click right back on.

"Run," Mike hissed. "Run, run, *run*."

Mr. Cobb was spry as fuck for a seventy-something. He didn't make chase, but he got to his front door mighty fast as we sprinted back across campus. And a good thing he did too; I never did pay attention in science class, and it wasn't until I was watching a YouTube video years later that I learned how lucky I am to still have all ten fingers.

This was par for the course for Mike. My memories of him in high school are largely noncohesive, and this is his own fault as he gave me several accidental head injuries during our time together. Even that spring, a week or so into our intramural softball league (I quit the varsity team as soon as I got into college), he'd accidentally hit me in the head with a metal bat while team Minority Report warmed up, simply because he wasn't looking where he was swinging. The number of concussions I had during high school total "more than is strictly healthy," due to Mike's thorough lack of impulse control and ability to think more than fifteen seconds into the future.

He was never *trying* to hurt anyone, no, but there comes a point in time when a teenage boy simply can't play-tackle people smaller than him to the ground anymore without someone getting bruised. Mike was wild; his rash decision-making paired with what seemed like (in retrospect) anger and behavioral management issues. But our choices for companionship were limited in our tiny, highly segregated class, and for every deep bond like the ones I had with Yara and Callister, there were also friendships of circumstance.

Yes, all friendships are of *a* circumstance. You meet at school because you happen to be standing next to each other in the recess four square line. Or you bump into a cool-looking girl at a local coffee shop only to discover you have a bit in common after a few moments of awkward small talk. A neighbor's new puppy escapes into your backyard, and when you return it you've gained *two* new friends for life. You reply to the right tweet at the right time, and three days of DM conversations later, you're planning to meet up for dinner. Those are normal circumstances.

In this way I *am* selfish; I value choice in my friendships. At Taft I was part of a monolith only visible when we stood together. I was a Black girl and that societal designation assigned me a specific group of friends—friendships we had to maintain both for our own sanities and to simply make sure we were seen. I am thankful to have had them. I valued them deeply, and still do. But I still knew something was missing. I knew this wasn't entirely normal. Blame *Grey's Anatomy* or blame "International Players Anthem," whichever one you want, but I want to look at my friends and think to myself, *I choose you.* Taft burned this desire into me, and I have had to actively work against that instinct even years after leaving the Taft Bubble, lest I seem too cold or aloof. I have to constantly remind myself that, while other circumstances like a job are, yes, a forced setting where the people I socialize with are not necessarily people I would have met or chosen in other circumstances, it's still okay to *try.*

I'd forgotten what it was like to have those friendships after four years at Oberlin. I deeply resented, by then, that high school hadn't been as easy. That Taft had left me so bruised by the overall experience that I'd pulled away from the emotional connections that would have tied me to it entirely. Going to a reunion or an alumni event is one thing; a few hours of waxing poetic over a glass of wine with people who don't *want* to hear how hard it was is something I can do. Maintaining friendships with people who might have wanted to dig into our experience eventually, talk about how difficult and painful it had been…that was harder.

Especially after I realized that Taft needn't have been that hard in the first place, a lesson I learned as the proverbial veil began to drop right after Mike jumped off the graduation stage once he'd received his diploma.

● ● ●

Graduation was a rote process for Taft. This was my third Taft graduation, in fact—we went every year to cheer on the Black and Latinx students receiving their diplomas. First the bricks, engraved with each of our names, went into the path that bordered Potter's Pond; then we picked up our red and blue robes from the staging area in the courtyard just outside my first-floor Centen window. I watched them lay out chairs in perfectly aligned rows next, finishing up just as invitations to a senior sit-down dinner at the headmaster's house arrived in our mailboxes. I wore a black corset, black fishnets, a black skirt, and chunky black heels for dinner and the senior picture that followed.

After I spent the night projectile vomiting in the infirmary (imitation crab, it turns out, has the same allergen irritants as real crab), we all piled onto a bus for a TAALSA year-end trip to Six Flags New England, where Sam and Tabi's relationship became on-again, just for a moment, when their car got stuck at the top of a Superman ride and they passed the time it took to fix it making out over a picturesque view of the Connecticut River.

Lynn, Andrew, and Kyle arrived the day after our Senior River Cruise, two grandmothers in tow. We had dinner at the bank turned restaurant and my dad had a good time, glad-handing with other legacy parents.

The next morning, I graduated. Exiting Taft felt like far less of an accomplishment than being accepted in the first place, relief replacing the excitement I'd felt three years before. I wish I could say that I remembered a good deal of the ceremony, or that what I do remember amounted to more than just the smell of putrid smoke wafting through the aisles as male graduates returned to their seats, diplomas and lit cigars in hand. I pointedly drew my robe up over my nose when Frank Jiordano and I sat back down next to each other, as we had nearly every day, and he blew a ring of smoke from his lips.

"What?" he said, shrugging and gesturing to his bare head. "We don't have strings to move."

Taft graduates didn't receive mortarboards and tassels. I vaguely remember being told it was because Horace Dutton Taft believed that graduation from his school was only the first step in a boy's well-rounded education; only college graduates had "earned" the full pomp and circumstance that a cap symbolized.

And some of us had no plans to become college grads. Callister caught my eye through the haze of smoke, pulling me out of a glare from across the courtyard. I smiled and waved across to her as Mike shook Mr. Mac's hand and jumped.

Later, after my parents had loaded most of my belongings into the Pathfinder and both grandmothers had pressed their cheeks to mine and checks into my palm, I found Callister in the Harley Roberts Room, as always.

"I'm so sorry I can't come to your graduation party." The words tumbled out of my mouth as my stuffed overnight bag fell from my hands.

"That's okay!" she said after we'd hugged. "I kind of figured you'd be back in New Jersey by Sunday."

"Yeah. Honestly, I'm shocked my parents were cool with *to-night*, even," I said, pointing to the bag. "Can you come to Mrs. Gallagher's place for a sec?"

"My parents are walking around with Trevor." Her older brother, the mon with the mythical one-way phone line, had returned for his baby sister's graduation. "I have a few minutes. Well, probably a few hours."

"Let's make the rounds first?"

"Yes." Callister nodded. "Should we—do you want to find Yara?"

"Oh, don't worry, she'll find me," I said. "Tonight, Kallister-with-a-*K* isn't going."

The floorboards creaked underneath our feet as we stood; the sound of them was one of the few memories, it occurred to me, that I wanted to hold on to. Sitting in this room had never been anything but a relief. We both hugged Mrs. Frances goodbye.

Callister and I moved slowly, deliberately through the main building. Mr. Fraser was first, where Callister gave the man the effusive thanks and farewell of a student who'd gotten a full ride to Harvard. I did the same. He'd done right by both of us, I suppose—we'd both gotten exactly what we wanted.

We covered most of the school to say goodbye, even getting up to the ice rinks. Back down in the basement, Bookstore Pete even let me take two bags of Jelly Bellies for the road, on him. Our rounds to Taft's faculty and staff were a wild contrast to the number of people in our class I made the effort to give personal goodbyes to. The inadequate ways the campus adults had handled various situations over the years felt like less of a betrayal than the ways our classmates had treated us. As peers we should have been able to rely on one another more than the teachers, I thought.

It took just two semesters at Oberlin, finding myself immediately pulled under the wing of professors of all races, for me to realize that I could, and should have, expected more from the adults entrusted with my education and well-being. It wasn't normal, it turned out, to arrive at class on pins and needles every day, terrified about what unquestioned "joke" might come out of an eighteen-year-old boy's mouth next.

When we finally made it to Mrs. Gallagher's house, Agnes, Sam, Santiago, and Theresa—a day student fac brat who frequented Agnes's table in the dining hall—were already waiting inside.

"Callister, you're really not coming?" Santiago asked by way of greeting.

"To an unsupervised co-ed overnight bacchanal at a ski lodge in New Hampshire?" She cocked an eyebrow. "I'm sure not. RIP to your nostrils, by the way."

Sam glared, jabbing his finger toward the living room window. His father, mother, and Mrs. Gallagher were still outside, chatting in the driveway. "*Shhh.*"

"No one is skiing tonight—slopes or otherwise!" Theresa said hastily. She was borrowing the family Jeep to drive us to this New Hampshire graduation party that a group of class parents were paying for. *Please don't do coke off the dashboard of my mom's car* was a perfectly reasonable and valid request.

Callister touched my arm, pointing out the window again toward the crosswalk that led back to school. Her family stood on the opposite corner, waiting for the light to change. She would have to go soon.

We excused ourselves from the living room, walking through the kitchen to the back door. Mrs. Gallagher had a small backyard with a swing set that bordered the school's general parking lot. The overflow of cars from the day's festivities had spilled onto the fringes of her lawn, presenting a perfectly brazen place to sit. I pulled a folded-up piece of notebook paper out of my back pocket before perching cross-legged on the hood of someone's Lexus.

"Here," I said, handing her the paper. "Phone number. Email. AIM. LiveJournal. You have to email me once you get a not-Taft account or a cell phone. Or get me on Facebook."

"My parents aren't getting me a cell phone," she said, laughing. "But yes—as soon as I get an email address, you will be the first to know."

"Also, if you're ever in New York City for a church thing and you have extra time, you can just find a pay phone and call me—I am literally just a forty-five-minute train ride away." I sighed. "I'm *really* sorry I can't come to your party."

"Oh, stop. You're going to have *way* more fun tonight. The quote-unquote full cast will be there, y'know?"

"I don't know that I like the 'full cast' enough to be excited that they're going to be there," I said, gesturing into the air with finger quotes.

I was excited at the idea of a real, honest-to-God high school party—the sort of thing the kids I'd grown up with in Jersey had access to every weekend. I wasn't particularly thrilled at the idea of the company; I was more excited to see Yara, frankly, than half the rest of the senior class. Finally, a night where I could meet my friend at her advanced level of debauchery, encouraged and unchecked by Taft.

Callister offered me one of her easy smiles, the sort that made her seem so unbothered by everything around her that I would wonder every so often if a relationship with God really was worth it. "You've got the diploma; your parents have all your stuff. You're going across state lines to what sounds like an abandoned vacation home. Did I tell you what my brother said?" When I shook my head no, she went on. "Well, like, it's simple—some of Taft's rules are really important. Like, it's cool to live with an Honor Code, in my opinion."

"I guess."

"But some of Taft's rules are stupid. And they just…evaporate as soon as you graduate. Like, Emmanuel said goodbye to me like he never called me fat outside the aerobics room that one time."

"Shit." I frowned. Emmanuel Plumber was one of those kids who could move through Taft's circles, just a bit, because he rarely mentioned his affiliations with any scholarship program, was brilliant in the right sports, and was good-looking enough that white girls were willing to risk a hidden dalliance. They would never date him outright.

We weren't friends because I wasn't the Francine of our year, and he'd never *had* to sit with us at meals. "I wonder what he's called me."

"That's the thing. I don't think it matters anymore."

"Does to me," I said.

"It won't. Taft's gone. Clean slate," Callister said as though this was all obvious. "Watch."

Even though I had been coming to Taft since the early nineties, with a parent who'd been coming since the 1970s, Callister saw the place for what it was better than either of us.

Somewhere around the front of the house, Sienna started shouting for her sister. It was almost four. We would have to get going soon, too, if there was going to be time to stop for food on the road. The vote had gone for Cracker Barrel, the sundown town of chain restaurants, but I was not one to turn my nose up at breakfast for dinner.

Callister and I got up and walked back around to the front door, where her family had combined with Sam's in a small conversation circle. I could see Sam in the window watching, clearly hoping no one ruined his chances at going out that night.

Her parents shook my hand, and I gave Sienna a quick squeeze too, before hugging Callister once more. She wished us luck and a good time again and then left after promising to email me as soon as she had everything set up on her end.

I never saw Callister Hamilton again.

● ● ●

How unaccustomed was I to the concept of a high school rager? Well, I wore a dress shirt. A brown button-down from H&M

purchased during my Morgan Stanley summer. I immediately spilled beer on it.

To this day I'm not sure whether this was a regular vacation spot or someone's private residence. I could do an axel and a double salchow and play a passable defense in a game of pickup hockey, but skiing was a bridge too bougie even for me. What I am sure of, though, is that rich white parents were the ones who secured this place for us. Otherwise, they absolutely would have been arrested and charged with some sort of reckless child endangerment statute, in addition to felony drug possession.

The sun had only just set when we arrived at the lodge on the New Hampshire / Vermont border, closed for the off-season. The bunny slopes just behind the main building were covered in verdant green instead of snow, and the lift lines had been taken down from the poles that supported them. Later a handful of boys got drunk enough to start trying to scale them, Mulan-style, to a raucous chorus of "I'll Make a Man Out of You." We all held our breath at one point, waiting for one of them to get up after losing his grip and falling off. He bounced back within seconds, spry in the way only a fucked-up seventeen-year-old can be.

Inside, someone had prepped several beer pong tables, stacks of red Solo cups, Ping-Pong balls, and dingy plastic pitchers, cloudy and cracked from too many turns in the dishwasher. On the way up we'd made our plan. We'd get drinks, find Mike and Yara, and then stick together, like we always did. Agnes and Santiago helped add to our group at the bar, waving over a number of Chinese and Korean senior boys who'd arrived in a separate car.

"Cheers!" Agnes proclaimed, holding up a Solo cup vodka shot.

The main floor of the lodge was warm already, full of sticky bodies and alcohol sweats and a thumping bass. But that was fine; there were acres to explore outside. I grabbed Santiago's hand so we wouldn't be separated on our trek back to the gravel driveway, where I assumed we would stay until Mike and Yara's car arrived. But before I could get anywhere near the door, a rough hand landed on my shoulder and we both stopped.

"Yo, you two wanna play us?" Frank Jiordano asked when we turned around. He wore a black tank top and basketball shorts, and a thick silver chain with a giant cross bounced against his chest. His grip was secure on the vodka bottle in his right hand, though less so on the beer pitcher pinned precariously to his side by the same arm. I had never seen a Taft student look so stereotypically New Jersey. "Winner keeps going."

Santiago looked as confused as I did, but we agreed after being told that Mike—who had apparently beat us there—had lost already.

While Santiago and I played (I shot and Santiago drank after I found a long brown hair in one of the repeatedly used game cups and refused to have anything else to do with a beverage that wasn't my own), Sam got Mike's attention, eventually pulling him down onto one of the lodge couches and coaxing out the story of his afternoon. It didn't take long; there wasn't much to it. Kallister was flying back to Louisiana the next morning, and so she and Yara—maybe Margot too, but Mike wasn't sure—had scored some alcohol of their own, and a bunch of her older sister's Ritalin at the last minute.

"They got a hotel room in Hartford or something. Maybe it was outside Boston, by Logan. Close to an airport," Sam reported back with a shrug. "Whatever, we'll see her this summer."

Yara and I spoke online all summer as we prepared for college. She worked an office job, adding watermarks to copyrighted images, while I sat at home and RPed, having told my parents that I couldn't possibly work the summer before college as I had to take time and prepare, mentally. Once our freshman year started, those messages between Yara and me slowed to a trickle, until one day in December when she informed me that she was going to visit me at Oberlin, as she'd heard the good word about the number of lesbians and drugs on campus, and that both were even easier to acquire than underaged alcohol. We spent the rest of the month, into Christmas vacation, planning for her to come for Drag Ball in the spring. But then, in February, I received a cryptic message that simply said, "going away in a couple of days so we're gonna postpone until I'm back. Kk, awesome, bye."

I wouldn't see Yara again until 2013, but even not yet knowing that, I was annoyed (and perhaps more maudlin about it than I might have been, thanks to the beer) that once again Kallister was stealing a moment that I saw as supposed to be *ours*.

"Is there anything other than vodka?" Santiago asked, oblivious to the deflation in my mood. "Yuck."

"There's Henny in the hot-box room," a classmate said, pointing us in the direction of the basement stairs.

We entered a small white room in the back of the bottom floor. Six or so of our classmates were passing a piece around, some giving a hearty "How," palm up in the air before inhaling. I think about them every time I have to read a tweet from a parent complaining about how their child's Disney+ account won't give them access to *Peter Pan*.

"Welcome," drawled a blond lacrosse star, Whit Hanson. He sat next to Alexa Edgar. "Peace pipe?"

"Definitely." Santiago joined the semicircle while Sam and I grabbed the bottle of cognac and refilled our cups.

"You want in?" Whit asked Sam and me, holding out the pipe and lighter a moment later.

We both shook our heads.

"*Kendra!*" Alexa said, her voice teasing. "Come on, we're going to *Oberlin!*"

"I've got asthma," I said. We weren't at Oberlin *yet*.

"Whatever." She grinned, before standing and grabbing me in a hug. "Ugh, I cannot *wait* until next year. You're so cool, I can't believe we're going to school together! I can't wait to hang out."

She wasn't sober, and neither was I. Taking anything she said to heart was massively unfair, but God, this dumb, drunk, and brief interaction in that smoke-filled room stayed with me.

There are pictures too. One of me and Alexa, hugging each other and staring straight into the camera with smiles as big as the Mr. Potato Head that'd been used to make the vodka turning our eyes so glassy. In another, Santiago and I watch, rooting her on through a long toke from the communal pipe. Finally, Agnes finds the hot-box room and after a shot of Henny, she and Santiago grab Alexa in a double bear hug just in time to meet the camera's flash.

No one could be blamed for looking at those pictures—any of the images from that night—and assuming that we were all friends. That our class was a tight-knit, solid unit.

For years, especially in college as I made friends so easily across classes and dorms and interests, I thought back to Taft and tried to grapple with the part I *must* have played in my small social circle. I was fully able to recognize where I'd gone wrong in my first year at Taft. Reading my journals, I swam through a word vomit of respectability politics and entitlement. It was embarrassing, red-hot and shameful, but I *got* it and I was unabashedly relieved to feel the shame. Shame meant I'd learned; I knew better.

I came to the conclusion for a time that it must have been my energy, and maybe it had enveloped my friends as well. Just a negative vibe overall, cloaking our dining hall table and pushing the rest of our class away like a force field.

But that theory never held. It couldn't. Eventually I reminded myself that there'd been a Black Table before I arrived and it stayed after we graduated. I only felt that way because if Black girls were invisible at Taft, then so were our problems. Maybe that was why no one—not my dad or Mr. Wandelt, the admissions officer I'd been meeting with since the seventh grade—had talked to me about what being at Taft would feel like.

And it *was* a Taft thing or, more broadly, a prep school thing. A private white institution thing. I can look back at those pictures and know that.

You're so cool.

I allowed myself time to sit with my resentment once the bottom fell out of my first guess. How many relationships had I missed out on because Taft had created an environment where it wasn't until the last day of school, in a basement in the middle of the woods, that someone I'd known for three years could tell me they thought I was an interesting person? Fuck—how many of *them* had missed out on relationships with *us*? They'd been denied just as much as we had, if not more: graveyard adventures, river hikes, my uncanny ability to pick a solid Saturday double feature at the mall *every single time*, hangs in the student union that ended with all of us doubled over in laughter after one insult too many, Mrs. Gallagher's seasoned food, perhaps learning how not to be a complete idiot about race at an early age.

I wondered how many people like Alexa that Yara, Sam, Santiago, and I had missed out on getting to know. Who would find Tabi at their class party next year and tell her how excited they were to hang out with her at college despite not bothering to do so for four years at Taft?

In that small room my nose burned, irritated by the smoke, and my blood was too thin with alcohol to remember what Callister had told me earlier that afternoon. I wouldn't think of what she'd said again until years later, when I was desperately typing variations of her name into Google, trying to get back in touch with her before our ten-year reunion.

Taft's gone. Clean slate. The rules were gone, out the window with the environment that had created them. They were gone at that ski lodge in Vermont. They were gone at every alumni event I went to in New York City, where classmates I couldn't remember ever having a full, meaningful conversation with would grin and offer enthusiastic hellos. They were gone in class Facebook groups and in the genial emailed reminders to send in class notes for the alumni bulletin. They were even gone at our five-year reunion; no one recognized me by name, but that didn't stop them from trying to talk as though it was normal, something we'd always just done. Suddenly, outside Taft's gates, I was a person.

Alexa was pretty cool too, it turned out. She transferred out of Oberlin after our freshman year and finished college somewhere else before becoming a tattooed pole-dancing enthusiast while working days at a tech startup. Nothing like the girl I'd known, but clearly not known at all, at Taft.

I couldn't be mad at every kid who hadn't made the effort to sit with us at lunch or hang out with us in the dorms, especially not the ones who were otherwise harmless. At fourteen to nineteen, none of us were fully formed; some kids, especially those who'd been misfits at their schools before Taft, were brave enough and able to "cross over," but most students were not. Maybe they would have been—maybe the need to be brave at all could have been removed—had Taft done better. I think it would have been nice to feel as though we were part of the community *while* we were there.

Maybe more of us would send our kids back if we did, eh, Emma?

EPILOGUE

THE FINAL SCHOOL I worked at was a baby in the New York City independent school landscape, where institutions like Trinity dated back to 1709. I saw that as an advantage and said so when I interviewed for the assistant director of admissions position. I saw an opportunity for the school, at just under ten years of operation, to be nimbler than others when it came to diversifying their recruitment methods. They didn't have to be so beholden to the usual programs, I thought. There were other places to find students of color. And while the school was still majority white (as independent schools tend to be), it was the first place I worked where I saw a comprehensive commitment to diversity enacted from top to bottom. The onus wasn't just on us in the admissions department; teachers were expected to create classrooms and curriculums that didn't center whiteness, and parents, even the nice white ones, claimed that they came there because that's what they wanted. It was not a perfect school, but it was a welcome breath of fresh air.

I softened a bit in that first year, this school's optimism smoothing

270 / **KENDRA JAMES**

down some of the calluses that had grown on my memories of Taft, hardened from the guilt of each lie during my time at Scholars Striving 4 Success. I allowed the glow of the campus at sunset, all red and pink hues bouncing from the brick buildings to the pond and back again, to color my experience. Literal rose-colored glasses tinting my memories. It was here that I started to allow for grace—grace to people like Emma Hunter, who had surely grown as a person now. Grace to administrators who thought it was appropriate to hold law enforcement over a student's head in loco parentis. It was 2004, I reminded myself; how were they supposed to know better? Grace to the Justin O'Brians and the Marielles, who I was sure would regret their words now, should they be faced with them. Grace, even, to a school that preached diversity and inclusion and yet took money from Roger Ailes; certainly they'd figure why that circle couldn't square soon enough.

Things *could* change at these schools, I thought when I watched the deeply empathetic work my boss did with every family who walked through our office doors. She would carry a family on her back through the admissions process if she needed to, and then continue to fight for them to receive every resource they needed, from threes to the eighth grade, once admitted.

She encouraged me to take time off that year, a long weekend so that I could drive up to Watertown for my ten-year reunion. She didn't want me to regret missing it.

This wasn't my first time back to Taft. Hardly. I'd gone up for my dad's thirty-fifth in 2009, because Jon and Athena were graduating a week later. Then, in 2010, Agnes came back from South Korea and she, Athena, and I drove up together from New Jersey.

Before the *Bulletin*-declared enjoyment of my "ten-year reunion" in 2013, I returned for my five-year in 2011, but, in a failure to properly coordinate, I was the only person from our core group of friends who attended. After saying hello to old teachers, taking a nostalgic turn across campus, and making sure that the group of Black and Latinx students the current diversity director gathered that weekend had seen my face, I went back outside to the main drive, where each reunion class was lining up for the bagpipe-led march up to the lunch buffet at the gym. The person holding our '06 sign in the parade did not look familiar, nor did many other faces in the crowd, so I did what any normal person would do and had a minor panic attack as people tried to engage me in conversation as if we all *really* knew who one another were. I fled the campus and its sea of salmon pink, brown loafers, and pearls before lunch. Like a good Jersey girl, I promptly drove down to the Palisades Center, then the largest mall on the East Coast, ate a full meal alone at TGI Fridays, saw *Bridesmaids* one and a half times, and ended the day crying in a Claire's while I waited to get three holes added to each ear.

This ten-year—my *real* ten-year—would be different. I was ready, after a successful and overwhelmingly pleasant year in my new admissions job, to see Taft in a new light. It was still fair to ask, I thought, why, in the year of our Lord 2016, we still even *had* places like Taft, a place filled with so much privilege that students hadn't even been allowed to have after-school jobs and everyone— everyone who mattered—was fine with that. But maybe, just maybe, I could check some of that cynicism at the door and just, as my mother often pleaded with me to do, *enjoy myself.*

The problem was, I'd spent years working for a place that used IQ tests to help determine whether or not fifth graders deserved a chance at success, years listening to the ways school administrators talked about students ("Why would I have my best students apply out to your program or school? That's *my* tenure on the line," one guidance counselor told me), and one school year in southern New York where middle school students could go days without seeing the face of a Black or Latinx adult who wasn't a janitor or groundskeeper, yet still bragged about diversity. Life experiences that had finally given me the freedom over time to admit that maybe my time at Taft hadn't been the glossy, privileged *Gossip Girl* book I'd been trained to present it as.

I'd written an essay the year before, one of my first forays into talking about Taft in a public forum. But instead of focusing on the darker side of Taft's racism, I gave it an empowering spin. Sure, it had been hard, but I'd gotten through it with the exaggerated plucky moxie of the WB teens I'd idolized in my youth. When I was asked to read something new at a live show, I returned to the same well. But writing about Taft after that reunion didn't come as easily as it had before.

● ● ●

I felt Taft's nine-figure endowment and all the strings that came with it the second I arrived. The few strands of optimism my new job had helped me weave severed instantly.

Memory is just as important as the dollar when it comes to keeping these institutions afloat; especially as millennials and other younger generations, who are more likely to eschew traditional old-money status symbols like a boarding school diploma, start having children of their own. And I'd kept my memories tinted by the pink-brick beams reflecting out of Potter's Pond intact each time I spun my experience for admissions. I'd been actively aiding the con.

I don't remember most of the people I graduated with, and I am sure the majority of them do not remember me—not in ways that matter. Emma Hunter did not officially speak for every white kid at Taft, but she'd summed up quite well the ways in which I and the rest of the Black and Latinx students on campus were known. The smallness of us as a whole made those of us who were different—Black, Latino, Asian, gay, fat, poor—stand out even more. Standing out is very different from being remembered.

Black students aren't really a part of the institutional memory—which, how can we be? How long have we been a part of the institution? Any institution? The times they've trotted us out to showcase their commitment to diversity don't count. More to the point, why would we be? Memory is currency, and historically we are not a people of generational wealth.

I got stuck in a small-talk loop while I stood on the lawn the morning of our tenth reunion, waiting for the procession to start. Of all the people I'd been close with, only Agnes and Theresa had come back, and they were skipping the processional. We would meet for lunch.

I couldn't find Callister. Yara was somewhere in California; as of three years prior, she and Kallister were still close enough to celebrate Thanksgiving together. Both she and Santiago had dropped out of college sometime before the end of their sophomore years. Santiago was back home in New York, and according to Facebook he'd gotten really into hand-forging knives. Kat was on assignment in Johannesburg. I hadn't spoken to Margot in longer than I hadn't spoken to Yara. And while I'd managed to get in touch with Sam, he was on call reunion weekend during his medical residency in Boston.

When the bagpipes began to scream, I fell in line next to Shep, a military academy graduate from my year who leaned over to me once the march got going and offered me a secret: "This is the most sober I've been on this campus since sophomore year."

With an opening like that, I was inclined to keep Shep talking. Eventually, as the procession passed by Congdon and Mac House, we got around to talking about the people who weren't there. "No one I was friends with," I pointed out after a swig of water.

Shep seemed surprised, so I went down my own reunion-themed

MIA list. It wasn't lost on me that absolutely none of my Black or Latinx friends had come back. I felt almost burdened to do so.

"Huh, haven't thought about Kat in years. She was hot," he said, when I finished my list. "Well, Sasse and JD aren't here either. They died."

"I know. So did Mike," I said.

Shep's reply was succinct. "Wait. What?"

And so I explained what had happened to Mike. I explained it to Shep, and then to a woman named Hillary as we walked by a memorial bench engraved with the name of another passed classmate. I told Lester and Craig about Mike's death while we stood in front of a plaque hung in honor of the classmate who'd died in a car accident in 2012. It went on and on, and by the time I left it felt like I'd detailed Mike's death to more people than I'd spoken to in my entire three years at the school. Not that that took much.

It wasn't lost on me that I stood in a place that held memory and memoriam above all else, and so few people knew my friend had died. High school tropes teach us that there's always that one person who isn't remembered. Usually the quiet, mousy girl who grows up to be Drew Barrymore. Not the kid who teaches his friends how to blow Aqua Net fireballs and jumps off the stage at graduation.

The last time I'd seen Mike was at an alumni event in Kipps Bay, and he'd been planning on starting a job on an oil rig. I'd assumed he'd done just that. Not so much. From what I'd been able to piece together, he ended up training to be a bail bondsman in Arizona instead, and was close to finishing the program when he allegedly shot a friend and then turned the gun on himself. The friend survived, but the whole incident made the local news.

I was gutted, but not completely surprised, to learn that Mike's last few moments in the world were chaotic. I remembered his reckless side and how it manifested as many things—the time a group of us had watched him angrily punch a cement wall in the basement, running across the soccer field with our aerosol cans, the baseball bat to the head, his body hitting mine and his arms tightened around my waist as he slammed me to a ground covered in barely a centimeter of snow.

I had been sporadic about seeing friends from high school. For as much laughter as there can be when we get together again, their faces also remind me of the worst of Taft. Memories that, in my twenties, I did not care much to parse. Even now, tendrils of Taft's trauma remain and I can feel them sneaking up on me, especially when I think about the people I simply can't see anymore, like Mike.

Black alumni create a crumpled ball of memories out of their time on campus and bury it like a curse at a crossroads, trying their best to escape the pain and just have a *nice time* in their college years. Perhaps others have also been unable to lend consistent, deep, and meaningful aid to current students because they have not yet helped themselves. Sometimes I wonder if everyone else is fine and I was just a pathetic excuse for a student and teen, if I'm so unable to let go of the shit that happened fifteen years ago. It could be that too, I guess.

The simple act of telling people about Mike that day was a strange sort of turning point. It dawned on me, after reminding some of them first who Mike was, that this felt like an extension of high school. Back on campus, back underneath Taft's rules. Mike was mostly invisible again.

Mike didn't get any scholarship funds in his honor. There is no memorial. He died in the worst way, making the worst choice, doing the worst act. But it still bothered me that more people didn't know, that the school hadn't sent out a notice of any kind. In that moment I wished they had, if not out of respect, then at least to save me the job of doing it for them.

I stood on a campus built on memories, walked down a hallway lined with the faces of men dead for decades who hadn't shot at their friend, but who also hadn't been on the right side of the Chinese Exclusion Act, the colonization of the Philippines, or a woman's right to vote. They were draped in crepe banners celebrating the completion of our multiyear capital campaign, which had met and exceeded its eight-figure goal, as if to say, "Don't get it twisted; you've always known who is valued here." I had my own double standards surrounding memory, and Taft had theirs.

All at once I remembered just how unseen I'd felt during high school. I was hypervisible, always being pulled into admissions photos to present the appearance of diversity, pushed forward as the first Black American legacy to graduate since 1891. Hypervisible, yet not remembered.

Seen by our classmates as a homogenous group. Through a Trumpian lens, we were all from the inner city. All scholarships. All poor. Reactions to Mike's death just confirmed that to be Black in a New England boarding school is to be touted for your statistical presence in the student body and ignored everywhere else, even in death. And there I was, six years into a career helping them do it.

● ● ●

Clad in clashing patterns, stripes on my torso and plaid on my thighs, topped off with a pair of mismatched Chucks on my feet, I was no longer the careful and compelling portrait of a woman who had graduated from any sort of elite prep school. The crowd gathered to hear us speak that night, a mix of New York City millennial hipster types and media Twitter, was much smaller than I'd once spoken to every Saturday morning. Instead of meeting in an Upper East Side chapel, we gathered in a SoHo bookstore, claiming seats in the form of everything from folding chairs to a winding spiral staircase in the corner.

But I was uncharacteristically nervous as I took the stage that night. Not my first time public speaking, by far, but my first time reading my own words aloud. Instead of a memorized speech extolling the benefits of boarding school, I clutched a handful of papers in my hands.

"Hi," I said, once introduced. "A friend of mine from high school died before our ten-year reunion. Here are some thoughts about that, and about my high school experience in general, delivered with far more levity than the situation deserves. But we laugh to keep from crying, right?"

My dad, class of 1974, was in the audience—one of only two or three Black men in the room—that night as I talked about Mike for the first time, reading a version of what this last chapter would eventually become. He'd invited himself, and had I known he was coming further in advance, I probably would have read something else. I'm glad I didn't. One of my closest friends was there too, a woman I'd met that first day at Oberlin screaming about the *X-Men*. She stood across the room from my father, finding a seat instead next to the man who would eventually become my husband.

It hadn't been my plan, and it certainly lacked the drama of the scenarios I'd once imagined—trapdoors in the floor and hydraulic lifts at a reunion aside. But for the first time that night I was honest—open and raw—about my time at Taft to the people I loved. The glasses were finally off.

ACKNOWLEDGMENTS

This book was written during a worldwide pandemic, from the vanity desk of the single bathroom in our one-bedroom apartment. And so first acknowledged must be my husband, Jon, who ended up peeing in empty Gatorade bottles more than once, as I often found myself lost in hours-long writing sessions, listening to music through noise-canceling headphones that prevented me from hearing him gently (so as not to disturb the genius he assumed was actually happening, rather than just panicked rambling) asking if I was done from the other side of the door. I'm a nightmare wife! And yet you still support me. I love you, and I am very excited to actually start spending time with you again in 2022!

Several people have touched this book, going as far back as spring 2016, when a few lovely commenters at *The Toast* noted that they would happily read a full memoir based on a short listicle I'd written called "A Black Girl's Manual to Attending a New England Boarding School." That piece, and one prior (a listicle concerning the dread I felt at attending my ten-year reunion), was commissioned and edited by Nicole Chung, who has ever since been a welcome and massive source of encouragement, support, and friendship. I'm so glad you're in my life.

Alongside my husband, Katie McVay heard one of the very first "official" drafts of the stories in this book (and plenty of unofficial retellings, throughout the many happy hours of our friendship). Since, she's also had the pleasure of listening each and every time I've started catastrophizing and worrying over whether or not this book was any good or mattered anymore. Her advice, "Don't let anyone gaslight you about your own experiences," really got me through the back half of this manuscript.

That event where Jon and Katie heard me talk about Mike for the first time was put together by the editorial staff of Lenny Letter, and I'm very thankful to that group of women, especially my editor there, Jessica Grose, and Dianca London Potts, a constant cheerleader.

Down the line, I was lucky enough to meet my agent, Jane von Mehren, at an event where I read a piece about American Girl dolls and dildos. She saw past that dubious introduction and took on a writer who knew literally nothing about crafting a proposal, much less writing a whole entire manuscript, and somehow got a whole entire book out of it. Jane is magical. And also *patient*. It took three jobs and a cross-country move to get a finished proposal, but she stuck it out with me, and now we're here. With more adventures to come soon, I hope. Thank you so much.

The whole team at Aevitas Creative has my thanks, with so much appreciation going toward Allison and Shenel, who worked hard to give this book multiple lives.

Twelve hours after the ten-year reunion I'd dreaded, I met Shonda Rhimes, who told me that I am a good writer and later moved me out to Los Angeles, first providing the confidence and then the distance that I needed in order to get started on this book. *Thank you.* At Shondaland, my writing was made even better by Jen Romolini and Gina Mei; be grateful for the people in your lives who make you realize the value of great editing. Alison Eakle was the first person outside of the publishing world to read the proposal, and thus the first person to tell me I had something here. She made me excited to keep writing.

Maddie Caldwell and I connected immediately the first (and only) time we got to sit across from each other in the Grand Central Publishing offices. I knew I liked her, but what would the editing process be like? This is the first she's hearing of this, but when I turned my first manuscript pages in, I was still recovering from a *terrible* experience with another editor on some online work. When Maddie returned the pages, marked up with notes, suggestions, and cuts, I almost cried—not because of the edits, but because of the *questions* she had asked. I think many writers of color have at least one experience when, in the pursuit of making your writing "palatable" for a mostly white audience, aspects of cultural specificity or your natural voice are diminished and pushed aside; and when you're freelancing there's often not much you can do about it. Or *time* to do it in. So when I saw questions like, "What does this mean?" or "Never heard of this before, what is it?"—seemingly simple words, but so fucking important— rather than just immediate strikethroughs and rewording based on unfounded assumptions about what I "really" meant, I knew this was going to work. And I was *relieved*. Maybe this is what other, more seasoned authors have come to simply expect, but for this debut author it was a shock, but a welcome one. Add to that the fact that she, at one point, had to deal with a manuscript from me that sat at around 120,000 words, alongside all the numerous bouts of nerves and, once again, catastrophizing that I love to do, and did so happily—joyfully, even!—and I am confident in my declaration that Maddie was absolutely the best editor and partner for *Admissions*. I would not have wanted to do it with anyone else.

My whole team at Grand Central Publishing has my gratitude as well, including Jacqueline Young and Roxanne Jones. Thank you for making this book happen. I'm immensely sorry that I cannot respond to an email on time for the life of me.

This book would not be here without my parents, who sacrificed to get me to Taft in the first place. In this book they're learning, for the very first time, that I broke that doorknob on purpose, the details of what went down at our graduation party, and my longform name for the dissolution of their marriage (A Very Stereotypically Nasty Suburban Divorce), along with so much more. Thank you for your support and your bravery for even making it this far.

And finally, the last you'll hear about Taft from me, I promise. Thank you to Mr. Wilson, whose classes taught me how to write *well*; to Mr. Le, who let me write fanfiction as a final once; to Mr. Hawes, who blew my mind by having us read the script for *Collateral* (2004) for our screenwriting class; to Ms. Williams, who did *everything* for us; to Bookstore Pete, who made sure I never had to go without my jelly beans; to Mr. McNeil, who helped get me the fuck out of Wisconsin; to whoever it was in the registrar's office who decided that I didn't have to go past geometry in math, or chemistry in science—I hope your life, especially, has been unspeakably blessed.

Thank you to Yara, Tabi, Sam, Santiago, Mike, Callister, Kat, Agnes, Maura, Esther, and the multitudes of real people they represent whose friendships made my time at Taft easier, even though I wasn't the easiest person to handle; to Kathy, Jenny, Jeff, Jenni, Melissa, Minisinoo, the Sys, and so many others, my online RPG friends whose long AIM chats, gaming sessions, postcards, letters, and international candy and book dustjacket exchanges were key to not only my survival and happiness at Taft, but my growth as a writer. Y'all pushed me like crazy.

A massive amount of thanks, too, to the current Black, Latinx, and other students of color who have attended Taft since my graduation, so many who have done far more than I ever did to raise the school's awareness about racism on campus, matters of diversity, and equity. The needle is moving. (And, hey, some unsolicited advice? Start going to therapy *before* you graduate; future you will say thanks.)

READING GROUP GUIDE

DISCUSSION QUESTIONS

1. What other boarding school narratives have you read? How did they shape your beliefs about life in these rarified institutions? After reading about Kendra's experience, how has your perception of these stories and the schools they exalt changed?

2. Scholars Striving 4 Success removed children from New York City public schools, rather than working to improve the school system itself. Why do you think they opted for that approach? What are other methods that the program could have employed to help a greater number of children?

3. Kendra writes that her parents had to be overachievers just to accomplish what white, middle-class Americans might deem "normal." What were the social and institutional barriers that made the path to success more difficult for BIPOC individuals when they were growing up? And what barriers continue to impact achievement to this day?

4. In many ways, Kendra's pleather trench coat was like an armor for her. Did you have a signature clothing item in high school? What did you hope it would say about you, and what did you hope it might hide?

5. A few of Kendra's BIPOC classmates seem to buy into respectability politics in order to fit in at Taft. How does this strategy for integrating into the school's social scene fall short? What might the lack of engagement of Taft's other BIPOC alumni illuminate about its lasting effects?

6. With different dining tables, hangout spots, and friend groups, campus segregation at Taft is evident. What steps do you think the white students could have taken to break down these barriers? How could other schools or workplaces implement a similar strategy?

7. Kendra and Yara bond over a number of TV shows and movies. What pop-cultural touchstones have stuck with you since high school, or even longer? How did they resonate with you at the time and why do you think you remember them to this day?

8. Kendra recognizes many of the privileges that give her a leg up in the college application process. In what ways does higher education in the United States work to reinforce existing inequality, not only with race, but with other marginalized groups? Who does the admissions process prioritize?

9. Emma Hunter wrote her article about campus diversity over a decade ago, yet Kendra recounts numerous similar incidents at Taft in the years since. How might Taft, and other white

institutions, have better addressed bigotry and intolerance within its student body to ensure they weren't perpetuated?

10. Kendra notes that teachers at The Hartmann School created curriculums that didn't center whiteness. Thinking back on your own educational experience, how did your teachers and classes center dominant perspectives and stories? What historical moments or cultural narratives did you leave the American educational system with a skewed perspective about? Is there anything you wish you learned sooner?

VISIT **GCPClubCar.com** to sign up for the **GCP Club Car** newsletter, featuring exclusive promotions, info on other **Club Car** titles, and more.

@grandcentralpub   @grandcentralpub   @grandcentralpub

ABOUT THE AUTHOR

Kendra James is an executive producer at Crooked Media and was a founding editor at Shondaland.com, where she wrote and edited work for two years. She has been heard and seen on NPR and podcasts, including *Bitch Sesh*, *Lovett or Leave It*, *Yo! Is This Racist?*, *This Is Love*, *Star Trek: The Pod Directive*, and more. Her writing has been published widely in *Elle*, *Marie Claire*, *Town & Country*, *Women's Health Magazine*, *Lenny*, *The Verge*, *Harpers*, *Catapult*, and *The Toast*, among others.